The **Guardian**
INTERNET GUIDE

For Helen McClellan

The Guardian
INTERNETGUIDE

Jim McClellan

First published in Great Britain in 2000 by
The Guardian
119 Farringdon Road
London EC1R 3ER

A catalogue record form this book is available from the British Library.

ISBN 1-84115-4385

Designed and typeset by Blackjacks, London.

CONTENTS

• •

Acknowledgements

I would never have managed to finish this book without the advice, support and patience of my editor, Mathew Clayton. Cheers, Matt. It was much appreciated. My agent Cat Ledger sorted out things as efficiently as ever for me. Thanks also to Jonathan Baker of Blackjacks, who not only did a brilliant job with the design, as usual, but was also on hand to offer some useful technical advice.

In places I've reworked some of the journalistic pieces I've done over the years. Thanks to the various editors who've helped me out over the years, in particular Matthew Collin, John Godfrey, Sheryl Garratt and Charles Gant. Thanks also to Vic Keegan, Neil McIntosh and Jack Schofield at The Guardian Online for their continued support. This year, I also owe a debt of gratitude to the BBC Imagineering department, who gave me a chance to look at the net from a different angle. Cheers in particular to Rowena Goldman, Fiona McKenzie and Abi Spurling. Thanks also to Apple and Gateway 2000 for the loan of equipment.

As usual, friends and family were kind enough to put up with me whilst I finished this book off. Thanks in particular to my mum Helen and my brothers Jon and Rob, Phill, Graham, Jonathan and Lydia, John and Karine, Peter Sutherby, and Pat and Geoff. Big shouts also to Graham and Moira, Nicki and Russell, George and Janet and Sheryl and Mark. Finally, thanks once again to my kids, Lee and Cameron, who put up with me spending way too much time in the attic and, most of all, as usual, to Kim.

INTRODUCTION

• •

The aim of this book is to help you make use of the net. The idea is to get you online and reaping the benefit as quickly and easily as possible. At the same time, I suspect that you'll want to know a little bit more about the net than just the straight 'how to' advice. Most net guides effect what you might call a 'dummy-ing' down of their readers. You agree to identify yourself as an 'Idiot' and then are led very slowly, step by step, through the confusing world of the net and the software you need to use it.

I agree with the need for clear and simple instructions on how to do things but I don't think people are dummies just because they don't know how to work a web browser. And I don't think that you need to switch off the bulk of your brain when you sit down to read a net manual. Some cultural/historical information can make it easier to grasp certain aspects of the net. My hope is that, by the end of this book, as well as knowing how to use certain programs, you'll have accumulated a measure of what might be called net literacy, or perhaps 'net savvy' – that is, a more general knowledge of the online world which ought to help your dealings there run more smoothly.

Unlike many other net manuals, this one won't be mindlessly gung-ho about the net. I am pretty enthusiastic about the online world. But

< 13 >

there are plenty of things connected with the net that I don't find that convincing as yet (WAP phones, for example) and plenty of activities I don't personally devote that much time to (online chat, for example). It may be that the stuff that I don't like will be the stuff that particularly draws you in. That is one of the good points about the net. Whatever some techno-gurus might suggest, getting online is not like signing up for some monolithic crusade. You don't have to buy into the whole program. You can pick and choose.

This book is aimed primarily at absolute beginners. My aim is to help you progress – or should that be regress – from upstanding healthy examples of Homo Erectus to stoop-shouldered, screen-eyed, mouse-clutching versions of that lesser known but quickly growing species – Homo Connectus. That said, I hope there will be useful information in here even for those who are comfortably navigating the web.

Section 1 – *Before You Get Connected* gives you some general advice about getting your bearings online. It also takes apart some of the things people have said about the net over the years. If you're in a hurry to get online, you could skip the latter and save it for later.

Section 2 – *Getting Connected* gives advice on the hardware and software you need, along with tips on getting an internet connection and connecting for the first time.

If you already have a computer, modem and net connection, go straight to **Section 3 – *Getting to Grips with the Net***, which offers detailed advice on how to get the most of out the main net activities:

< 14 >

The World Wide Web

The web is usually the thing people immediately 'get' when they go online. The multimedia part of the net, the web is made up of sites (or pages) put up by everyone from multinational media corporations to charities, pressure groups and, yes, ordinary people like you. On the web, you can read online magazines that feature text and graphics, or you can watch videos, download music, buy books and CDs, book flights and holidays, even play games. You can move between sites by clicking on hypertext links, wandering far from the pages you originally accessed. This section will tell you how to find your way round the web and how to work with your browser (the software program you use to move around the web) so that your time online is more productive.

Searching the web

One of the hardest things online is finding your way to the information you're interested in. That's why you need search sites – online resources that keep track of what's out there and point you in the right direction, usually. This section will tell you how to use search engines, online directories and other search sites. There are also a few tips about using the web as a general research tool.

Downloading files and software

The net is packed with interesting files and useful bits of software. Using your web browser (or FTP software – FTP is a bit of compuspeak which stands for File Transfer Protocol), you can find files and software you're interested in and download them on to your computer. You can also upload files and software. This section will give you the basics on downloading and offer some general advice on keeping track of material you get from the net.

< 15 >

Multimedia and plug-ins

You will encounter various types of multimedia on the web – video clips, sound files, animations and interactive games. Your browser will be able to handle much of what you find, but if it can't you may need to augment it with specific plug-ins or add-on programs. This section tells you which plug-ins you'll need and where to find them.

Email

Email is one of the things people immediately latch on to when they first get online. The attractions of being able to communicate with friends around the world for the cost of a local telephone call are pretty obvious. This section tells you how to send and receive email, looks at web-based mail and concludes with some advice on how to get the best out of email without it ruining your life.

Online communities

The net is great for one-to-one communication. But it really comes into its own with group conversations, bringing together people who share common interests and want to discuss them further. It's great for building a sense of community. Via online discussion groups, you can share your thoughts with a like-minded group and see what they have to say in response.

Many of these groups – for example, mailing lists and Usenet news-groups – are asynchronous bulletin boards. In plain English, that means that you post your thoughts, someone else reads them and posts a response and over time you build up a kind of conversation (or 'thread', as the online jargon has it). Thanks to online chat, you can also indulge in real time text conversations with groups of people. It's true that people

< 16 >

often talk dirty, creating private chat rooms where they can indulge in collaborative one-handed typing. But they also talk about much else, swapping news and ideas.

This section will tell you how to find the discussion groups that suit you and how to make the most of them. Some online communities – Usenet newsgroups and IRC chat rooms – can get rather raucous and anarchic. So you'll also find a few survival tips here.

Simplifying things a little, the two most popular activities on the net are communicating with other people and getting information. Consequently, I've split this section up into two strands that reflect these two activities. If you're interesting in information, start with the web, move on to searching, then look at downloading. If you're interested in people, start with email, then move on to online communities. That said, things on the net are never that clear cut. So feel free to read this section in any order you like.

In this section I've concentrated on giving detailed advice about the latest versions of the two most popular browsers – Netscape Navigator (which is part of the Communicator package of net tools) and Microsoft's Internet Explorer. If you sign up with one of the major internet service providers, you'll probably get one of these (or be offered a choice if you're lucky). If you're using something older or newer, don't worry. Browsers don't change that much and you should still be able to follow the advice.

You can use your browser to handle email, to chat and participate in discussion groups and to download files, so I've also concentrated on these in the relevant chapters. However, I've also included pointers to alternative standalone programs you could use instead. So don't feel you have to use the browser for everything. This section goes into things in a fair amount of detail. The idea is to help you to minimise hassles when

< 17 >

you're just getting started. The later sections are less detailed – the assumption being that you will be more comfortable with the net.

Section 4 – Taking the Web to the Next Level deals with the different kinds of media content you can now find online – in particular music, video and animation. It also covers net shopping, faster connections to the net and advice on putting up your own web page.

Section 5 – The Essential Clicks features a list of around two hundred recommended web sites – some are useful, some are amusing, some are a waste of time (but in a good way). If you're wondering where to go on the web, this should give you some ideas. You'll also find an introduction to the various Guardian web sites here.

Section 6 – Looking After Yourself Online offers advice on protecting yourself and your kids online. It covers privacy, censorship, junk email, legal issues and features some general survival tips.

Finally, at the back of the book you'll find information about UK internet service providers. Throughout the book you will see various captions boxed-off from the main text, featuring useful bits of information – look out for:

Read about it online
The net is often the best place to find out about the net, especially the latest developments. So every now and then, I'll include details of sites on the net where you can find more information on a particular topic.

< 18 >

Jargon file

Brave new worlds require brave new words. The net and its related technologies come with all manner of slanguage, jargon and puzzling technical terminology. Some of it is amusing, some of it is irritating. Check
these boxes to find out what it all means.

Tips

These feature bits of advice I've found useful, tricks of the trade, rules of
thumb and all that.

Perhaps we should kick off with a sort of all-purpose tip, which is: if you
feel a little nervous about getting online, don't worry. Self-induced techno-
phobia is often the biggest problem people face when dealing with
computers. It's true that connecting to the net is still harder than it should
be but it's nowhere near as hard as it used to be. If you know how to use a
PC running Windows or an Apple Mac, you will crack the net, no problem.

As proof, I cite myself. I've never studied computers or computer
science. I've got a vague idea how they work, but no deep technical
knowledge. In fact, I got interested in computer culture and the net via
literature. In 1986, I read *Neuromancer*, the novel in which SF writer
William Gibson first developed his vision of cyberspace, and became
interested in computer networks. I read more about the net, made some
geeky friends and shoulder-surfed a bit in the early nineties, eventually
getting online properly at the start of 1994.

This may not be what you want to hear from the author of a net
guide on which you've spent good money. But the point is, if I managed
to figure out the net, so can you. I did it in part by flicking through the
odd manual, although there weren't that many when I started and most
read as if they were compiled by malfunctioning artificial intelligence

< 19 >

programs. Mostly though, I just tried things out, messed about with software, clicked buttons and pulled down menus to see what would happen.

With some net pursuits, you do need to learn some technical text commands (some chat programs for example), but most online software is pretty intuitive. Tinkering is the way to learn. People who aren't familiar with computers are often worried that they will 'break' them if they press the wrong button. Once again, it's true that computers are still not as robust and reliable as they should be, but they're not that feeble. And there are always support lines and guarantees to fall back on. So get stuck in and you'll soon be hooked.

Once you find your telephone bills going through the roof and your social life in ruins, if you're looking for someone to blame, feel free to drop me a line – **jim.mcclellan@guardian.co.uk**. Though I've done my best, there are bound to be a few errors in the book you're about to read – if only because things are constantly changing on the net. Companies merge or go out of business. New bits of software, new ideas or new sites appear out of nowhere and take the net by storm. At a more basic level, web sites just go offline or change addresses.

So if you find something that's wrong – an address that doesn't seem to work, for example – just drop me a line and I'll do my best to point you in the right direction. Mistakes aside, if you just feel like telling me what you think of the book, it would be great to hear from you. Lots of people did just that after reading the first two editions of this book and their thoughts and ideas were a great help when it came to doing this update. Thanks to everyone who wrote in.

If you do drop me a line, I'll do my best to reply, but the mail does pile up. I do read everything I receive. But I don't always manage to reply to all the emails I get. So if I don't get back to you, please accept my apologies here. ▲

< 20 >

1 BEFORE YOU GET CONNECTED

● ●

Get your online bearings

Some net guides and manuals start with lengthy histories of the development of the internet and even detailed technical descriptions of how it all works. This can be pretty interesting. Really. And it can help you use the net in a more productive way. However, I'm not sure it's the best idea in the world to force beginners to bone up on the history of US Cold War research institutions and the intricacies of packet-switching before they've even had a chance to look around online.

To get started online, to orient yourself on the net, you only need to know a few basics. You don't need a detailed knowledge of the net, but it helps to have some sort of mental picture of it. One way of thinking of the internet is as a network of networks. This gets across the fact that the net isn't one coherent, unified entity, it's a multiplicity. It's always good to remember this when people try to boil the net's variety down into one thing, and tell you that, for example, the net is naturally libertarian in its political outlook.

At a very basic level, a computer network is a collection of computers – say in an office – connected in such a way that they can communicate

< 21 >

Jargon file - Packet-Switching

When messages are sent via a network, they are broken up into individual packets that are then sent separately. Besides parts of the original message these packets contain details of the place they came from, and the address they're going to, amongst other things. ▲

with each other and share information. The net takes this to a global scale. It's a kind of global network that has emerged as more and more local and national networks hook up with each other. To connect to and communicate with each other, computers rely on shared standard languages, or, to use the technical term, protocols.

When you're online, you'll encounter different sorts of protocol. For example, there's FTP, aka File Transfer Protocol, which allows you to upload or download files to and from the net. The World Wide Web, the

Read about it online - Net Histories

Once you're online, if you do feel like reading more about the net and how it has developed over the last three decades, a great place to start is 'A Brief History of the Future' (published by Weidenfeld and Nicholson), by The Observer's net columnist John Naughton. Start with his web site at **http://www.briefhistory.com**. If you want to delve further into recent online history, try Wendy Grossman's 'Net Wars' (published by New York University Press). You can read the book online at **http://www.nyupress.nyu.edu/netwars.html**. ▲

< 22 >

> ### Jargon file - Top Down, Bottom Up
>
> Two related terms you hear a lot online. The former refers to
> authoritarian/hierarchical structures in which order (and other things)
> are imposed by the people at the top. The latter refers to more open
> grass-roots structures in which order (and other things) emerge from
> the actions of ordinary users and trickle up. ▲

multimedia part of the net, relies on something called HTTP – Hyper
Text Transfer Protocol. The new mobile phones that let you access data
services via the net use WAP – as in Wireless Application Protocol. And
the basic protocol which enables the net to work by letting computers
round the world communicate with each other is TCP/IP – aka
Transmission Control Protocol/Internet Protocol. All these letters may
look like the leftovers from a game of Scrabble, but after a while you will
get used to them and will use them without thinking.

Another way to think about the net is as a many-to-many network.
This is shorthand for the fact that, when online, everyone can send as
well as receive messages. In contrast, broadcast TV is often characterised
as a one-to-many network – meaning one node or station sends messages
and all the rest of us can do is consume those messages. Some businesses
are attempting to bring the top-down, one-to-many model of TV to the
net (the theory being that this will bring ordinary users online). But never
forget – the net lets you send messages, publish your own ideas, and
upload your own videos.

< 23 >

Net addresses

So how do you and your information know where you are and where you're going on this wonderfully various many-to-many network of networks? Thankfully, the net, like the real world, has a system of addresses. All computers connected to the internet have a unique IP (as in Internet Protocol) address. This is a collection of four sets of numbers, separated by full stops/periods (e.g. 123.45.56.891). Incidentally, there are plans to extend and expand this system, in order to cope with the increased demand for net addresses.

Obviously large groups of numbers are not the easiest things to remember (or type). So, as well as the IP addresses there is also something called the Domain Name System which translates all those numbers into words. Along with an IP address, each computer connected to the net has its own unique domain name. A few years ago, many people found these online addresses as forbidding as IP numbers. But now newspapers can run features about the latest dot.com kids without worrying that their readers won't get the point. Collectively, we seem to be getting our heads round online domain names. If you still find them a bit confusing, don't worry. They're pretty easy to figure out.

Take the address for the Guardian's web site – **http://www.guardian.co.uk**.

The *first* part – **http://** – refers to the protocol used to access this address, in this case Hyper Text Transfer Protocol.

The *second* part – **www** – indicates which part of the net we're talking about – in this case, the World Wide Web.

< 24 >

The *third* part – **.guardian** – is the name of the institution or people running the site/the computer it's stored on.

The *fourth* part of the address – **.co** – is known as a 'top level domain'. It tells you what sort of institution is behind the site. So **.co** indicates that it's a commercial/business site.

Various other identifiers could appear here:

.ac	indicates a college, university or other sort of academic establishment
.edu	also indicates academic establishments, used mainly in the States
.gov	a government-run site
.mil	a site run by the military
.org	used by non-profit organisations
.com	the non-country specific version of .co, this is used by companies that want to look like global businesses
.net	used mainly by internet service providers

There are plans to add a variety of new top-level domains in the near future – things like **.firm** and **.store** – but at the time of writing, these haven't been finalised.

Finally the *fifth* part of the address – **.uk** – tells you in which country the site is located. These are generally pretty easy to figure out – **.jp** is Japan, **.de** is Germany, as in Deutschland, and so on. Sites that use the **.com** can get away without indicating which country they're in. To put it another way, they can present themselves as global businesses,

< 25 >

which may be one reason why **.com** addresses are preferred by go-ahead online entrepreneurs.

The addresses for email work in the same way, with the name/nickname of the person (or department) you want to contact appearing before the basic domain name, as in **jim.mcclellan@guardian.co.uk**.

Once you get used to it, the domain name system is pretty easy to use. And that's what most people do – just get on with things without giving it a second thought. However, domain names and the things people do with them are a source of endless fascination, or irritation, for some net users. The result is a kind of net name subculture, which encompasses entrepreneurs, blaggers, politicians and artists.

Early on, some people took advantage of the mainstream business world's failure to get the net and, in a practice known as cybersquatting, bought up famous domain names e.g. **www.bootsthechemist.co.uk**. Their hope was that the company in question would cough up serious money

---

Read about it online – .tv nation

Addresses that end with **.com** still seem to be the most desirable of internet locations. However some countries are also in a position to sell punters the online equivalent of a des res. For example, over the last few years, the Polynesian island Tuvalu has been selling the rights to use its **.tv** domain to businesses around the world. Other desirable domains include **.to** – short for Tonga, which means you can have addresses like **http://www.ready.to/rock**. For an interesting story from the webzine Salon about these 'domain names from paradise', go to **http://www.salon.com/tech/feature/1999/05/17/tonga/index.html**. ▲

< 26 >

Read about it online - sex.com

Some domains are desirable for obvious reasons and people will do anything to get hold of them – for a fascinating story about the ownership of the lucrative name sex.com, go to Wired News at **http://www.wired.com/news/news/business/story/19140.html**. ▲

to get its name back. Some did, apparently. But if you try that kind of thing now, you'll probably end up in court. More than likely, if you're tangling with a big name – be it a corporation or a person, you'll also end up on the losing side.

Of course, a case involving some cheeky net user buying up a pre-existing well-known brand name in the hope of making a few fast bucks isn't going to tax the great legal minds of the nation. Other domain disputes are more problematic. What happens if you share the same name as a celebrity? Why should said celeb assume they have a divine right to the dot.com version of their name, especially if you got there first?

Celebrity cybersquatting is now well known enough to make the front pages of the papers. Diana George, the primary school teacher who was first to register **leoblair.com** and **leoblair.co.uk**, mere minutes after the announcement of the birth of the new Blair baby, got plenty of press. The qualities also spilled a fair amount of ink over Mark Hogarth, who bought up hundreds of domain names relating to famous authors. Jeannette Winterson took him to the World Intellectual Property Organisation Arbitration and Mediation Centre and won back various net addresses relating to her name.

< 27 >

Read about it online – Cybersquatting

A good place to keep up with the latest news about cybersquatting is the special page devoted to the subject at the satirical net news and culture webzine The Register. You'll find it at **http://www.theregister. co.uk/content/29/11947.html**. If you want to find out how much that domain name you've registered might be worth, try the domain name brokers ShoutLoud, who run an online valuation service at **http://www.shoutloud.com**. ▲

Some net users have advanced conspiracy theories about the CIA connections of one of the organisations that makes a fat profit from running the domain name system (Network Solutions Inc.). Everyone from artists to gamey entrepreneurs have attempted to set up alternative domain name systems. The US and the European Community have also engaged in a long political wrangle about how best to administer and extend the domain name system in the future. Once you get online, you'll be able to read a lot more about all this. In fact, a keen interest in net addresses is probably one of the key signs that you're well on the way to becoming a screen-obsessed Homo Connectus.

One key sign is when you start using Network Solutions' WHOIS database to find out who has registered certain domain names **http://www.networksolutions.com/cgi-bin/whois/whois**. This might not sound like much fun, but it has become a useful investigative tool for journalists and others. While 'The Phantom Menace' was being made, *Star Wars* fans kept watch on the domain names George Lucas was registering and were able to conclude from this that the film,

< 28 >

Read about it online – Domain Names

To find out more about domain names on the net – how to register them, how to sell them, who runs them and much else – try Internet Goldrush – **http://www.igoldrush.com**. A non-profit corporation called ICANN (as in the Internet Corporation for Assigned Names and Numbers) has been set up to deal with the technical management of the domain name system. Many net activists are worried that it will overstep its brief and allow governments a way of exerting some control over the net – for more on this, go to ICANN Watch **http://www.icannwatch.org**. ▲

which was shrouded in secrecy at the time, was going to feature something called a pod race. (Lucas Films had apparently registered **http://www.podracer.com**).

Mapping the net

Addresses only go so far when it comes to finding your way around online. It's also helpful to construct a kind of mental map of the net. By this, I don't just mean something as practical and accurate as an A-Z – although there's some fascinating work being done on producing

Read about it online – Mapping

If you want to have a look at some recent efforts to provide visual maps of cyberspace, go to **http://www.cybergeography.org/**. ▲

< 29 >

workable maps for the net. It's more a question of conceptual images or the metaphors you use when you think and talk about the net.

If you use a standard computer with a graphic interface (i.e. a screen full of little cartoon icons) and a mouse, you'll be used to what computer types call the desktop metaphor. This means all the images of folders, files and trash cans you see on your screen. By making your PC seem familiar, these symbols help you to interact with your computer. Much net software continues the desktop metaphor, even when it doesn't seem that good a fit – for example, though awash in travel imagery, the Navigator browser lets you 'bookmark' your favourite web sites.

However, some net theorists have argued that at a higher level we use a few general metaphors when using the internet and that these metaphors make this strange new technology seem more accessible. Hence, we think of the net as being like a huge global library, or a community meeting place, or a souped-up shopping mall. We think of it as a new frontier, or even as a kind of prototype interactive TV delivering something approaching video (or rather thirty-second video clips) on demand.

Jargon file - Interactive TV

Much hyped in the early nineties before the net came along. This was supposed to be a TV set you could use to order pizza and videos and generally control when you saw certain TV shows. Some people used to say that the net killed off interactive TV. They were wrong. It remains the holy grail for certain big tech companies such as Sky Digital and Microsoft. ▲

< 30 >

You could argue that the first example of a net metaphor is to think of it as a space in the first place, to think that, to rework Gertrude Stein, there is a 'there' there. Actually, the sense that cyberspace is a separate, different 'place' may be on the way out. It may have been produced by the way people accessed the net at first – via personal computers and monitor screens they often thought of as windows onto a new world. And it certainly helped many people get used to this new technology.

But as the novelty of the net fades, it may start to seem less appropriate. That sense of cyberspace as somewhere you visit via your screen may disappear as more of us access the net via mobile devices like phones and handheld electronic personal organisers like the Palm Pilot. It could be replaced by a sense that the net is entwined tightly with the real world, that as we move through real space, we are also travelling through computer networks.

That awful cliché of the early nineties – the information superhighway – was obviously a kind of net metaphor (the net as digital motorway). It was used by the American Vice President of the time, Al Gore, when he needed to sell the American public the more intangible (not to say dry) idea of a National Information Infrastructure. The contagious spread of I-way imagery was much bemoaned, often by the same people who liked the idea of 'cyberspace'. But both these images were performing the same kind of function. They were familiar images that helped us get a handle on the immaterial realm that crackles into life over the wires.

Metaphors, like the net as library or community, help us first grasp the online world, then get things done. Some critics argue that we need to choose our net metaphors carefully, because they will determine what sort of net we end up building. You can see what they mean. As

< 31 >

Read about it online - Cyberspace Isn't a Place

American critic Jonathan G.S. Koppell has argued that the cyberspace metaphor has been instrumental in creating a misguided sense that the net was a separate realm where government shouldn't intervene. You can read his piece on the subject on The Atlantic Review's site at **http://www.theatlantic.com/cgi-bin/o/issues/2000/08/koppell.htm**. Certainly some people got carried away by the cyberspace idea – like US net pundit John Perry Barlow, who wrote the rather daft 'Declaration of the Independence of Cyberspace'. Read it at **http://www.eff.org/pub/Misc/Publications/John_Perry_Barlow/barlow_0296.declaration**. ▲

mentioned above, many big media companies have invested heavily in the mainstream-friendly idea that the net might be 'like television' and have pushed development in that area (e.g. in sending real-time video over the net). Whilst it's true that some areas of the net are a bit like television, overall the net as television metaphor offers a drastically diminished, rather passive idea of what the online world is and might be in the future.

Perhaps the best thing here is to be flexible. No single metaphor tells the whole story about the net. And all of them can apply at the same time. You can shift between them, depending on what seems useful at the time.

Try before you buy

After getting a little over-conceptual, perhaps we should end by coming back down to earth. If you haven't actually been online before, do try the

< 32 >

net before you spend any real money. You need to get an idea of what it's really like. You may find that the net isn't really for you. Probably not. But there are no guarantees. So be sensible and try before you buy.

The easiest option is to go round to a friend who's already online and blag a few hours on his or her computer. People often suggest you persuade a wired-up buddy to give you a guided tour. I've done a few of these site-seeing sessions and people always start looking slightly glazed midway through – usually somewhere between the online bookstore amazon.co.uk and Need to Know, the UK zine/mail-out that serves up a weekly shot of hip geek tech news, wind-ups and gossip.

It may be my choice of sites. Then again, the net is not something you watch other people doing. The point is that you find your own way around. You connect to the information and people you choose. So if you do head round to your net-literate friend, get them to show you round for a while, but then ask to be left alone for a couple of hours so you get on with things.

If the computers at work are hooked up to the net, try it out there. Remember, though, that your boss is paying and is more than likely using a piece of software (sometimes called spyware) to check on what the employees do online. So check first that it's alright.

There are other places where you could go for a test run in cyberspace. The local library may have a few PCs hooked up to the net. Alternatively, try your local cybercafe. Most towns and cities now have one. They were very popular when the net first came to public attention. Then, as more and more people got online at home and in the office, it looked like they might go out of business. Thanks to web-based email accounts that you can access from anywhere in the world (see page 185 for more on this), they're now backpacker hangouts, places where

< 33 >

Jargon file - Cybercafe

A cafe complete with a few terminals where you can buy coffee and access the net for an hour or so. ▲

travellers can stay in touch with home. As a result they've become, if anything, more popular than ever.

Cybercafes can be a little confusing if you've never been online, but there should be help on hand to get you started (alternatively, you could take this book along and cut to the later sections). The better places usually have reasonably quick connections and the latest software. If you're not sure where your local is, there are plenty of online lists of UK cybercafes (admittedly, if you're not connected, they're not going to be that much use). For more info, try Internet Magazine's list **http://www. internet-magazine.com/resource/cybercafes/index.html**. Alternatively look for the Internet Cafes section on the UK Yahoo **http://www.yahoo.co.uk**.

Read about it online - easyEverything

The company behind easyJet has launched a new chain of cheap cybercafes. Called easyEverything, these charge £1 for an hour online and are open twenty four hours a day. The first easyEverything opened just round the corner from Victoria BR station in London – perfect for all those foreign backpackers. For more information, try **http://www.easyeverything.com**. ▲

< 34 >

Net myths deconstructed

People have said a lot of vaguely contentious, mildly dubious or just plain daft things about the net over the last few years. A lot of these things have appeared in the media. So even if you haven't been online, you may have been exposed to them. Once you get online, you realise pretty quickly that most of these claims don't really stand up. It can be hard to believe that the net will soon bring about an era of world peace and plenty for all whilst simultaneously waiting fifteen minutes for a web page to load. Ditto the idea that the net will bring social and moral collapse.

However, if you're not online, the silliness of some ideas may not be so immediately apparent. So before we go any further, it might be helpful to clear your head of some of the dafter things that have been said. Think of this chapter as a quick debriefing session, a Pass Notes for cyber babble.

Disposing of the bulk of cyber-hype is relatively easy. You can cut through whole swathes of it in one go. For example, over the last decade, various techno-prophets and computer industry hucksters have suggested that the net will usher in a new utopian age in which everyone gets along, the poor of the world get rich (or empowered, or something), our kids get smarter and everyone gets happier. Conversely techno-critics have suggested that the net will bring about the collapse of society and turn us all into screen-obsessed zombies who never leave our homes.

These days, it's hard to believe people really came out with this stuff. They don't so much anymore, though some politicians still seem to think that hooking schools up to the net will automatically transform our education system for the good. The problem with this kind of thinking is that it imagines that technology has a kind of magical power

< 35 >

Read about it online – Net Surveys

If you want to read the latest surveys of the net population and what they get up to, go to the site maintained by the Irish net consultancy Nua **http://www.nua.ie/surveys/**, which features details of, and links to, most recent net surveys. ▲

to effect change on its own – good or bad. Obviously, technology can bring change. But it does so because people choose to use it in certain ways. The net is no different. It's primarily a tool. The really interesting thing about it is it's a multi-purpose tool, one whose uses we are all still discovering.

OK – that's the bulk of cyber-hype dealt with. Let's pick off a few more misguided net myths one by one.

▶ *Everyone talks about the net being a worldwide phenomenon but really it's just an American thing*

Yes, there are lots of Americans online. But I'm sure the rest of us outnumber them. And some Scandinavian countries may boast a higher overall percentage of national population online. But there are lots of Americans online and they have set the tone (libertarian and anti-government) for net culture. More generally, claims for the net's global reach are overstated. Most of the Southern hemisphere still isn't connected. That said, things are definitely changing. There are more and more UK, European and Asian sites online (and luckily for us Brits, foreign sites often feel they have to do a version in English, because there are so many Americans online).

< 36 >

Jargon file - Chat Room

An online space where you can chat (i.e. exchange text messages in real time) with a group of other people. ▲

▶ *The net is a sort of digital locker room, a toy for the boys*

There are still more men online than women – a recent survey found that 52% of British men questioned had used the net, as against 39% of women. However, things are changing – the online service AOL has claimed that over 50 per cent of its users are women. Unfortunately, many men do behave exceedingly badly online, especially the troglodytes in some chat rooms. But there are ways to deal with them – see page 222. More generally, there really is nothing inherently male about the net. The theory that it is 'a guy thing' often seems like something dreamt up by boys who don't want to share.

▶ *The net is a youth thing. If you're over forty you won't get it*

Many older people don't have any experience of computers. So it's no

Read about it online - Silver Surfers

There are lots of American web sites aimed at older users – try Third Age **http://www.thirdage.com**. For something similar in the UK, have a look at I Don't Feel 50 **http://www.idf50.com**. Alternatively, check out Hairnet **http://test.hairnet.org**, the UK's first internet training scheme for the over-50s. ▲

< 37 >

surprise that they feel vaguely net phobic. But think of the benefits of getting online: staying in touch with family and friends, shopping from home, accessing useful information (e.g. on health, holidays and finance). Older people can get as much out of these as the young. And many have the time and the money for the net. Indeed the smarter dot com companies now deliberately target so-called 'silver surfers'. So if you are an older reader, do have a go.

▶ *The net is packed with geeks and nerds. So it can be of little use to ordinary, well-adjusted people like me*

When it first hit the headlines at the start of the nineties, the net was a rather geeky place. No surprise there, really. Geeks were one of the largest groups on the net, primarily because they helped build it. But that was then. The net has gone mainstream in the last ten years. There's plenty to interest people who don't spend their lives pondering continuity errors in Star Trek.

▶ *Most of the information on the net is rubbish – just not worth bothering with*

There's an awful lot of witless stupidity on the net. But before you use that as a reason to stay offline, wander into your nearest bookshop. What do you see? Jeffrey Archer novels and shelves of *Men are from Mars, Women are from Venus* claptrap. Milton, Blake, Joyce and Jane Austen don't usually take up the bulk of the display space. The net is just like TV, radio and print. There is a lot of rubbish but there's good stuff too, if you look.

▶ *The net lets you find out what ordinary people really think*

There are indeed web sites where ordinary folk talk about their hopes, fears and favourite breakfast cereals. However, journalists can take all

< 38 >

this too seriously. Show them a couple of sites enthusing about an upcoming film and they immediately write about the massive grassroots buzz surrounding the new hot movie. Those sites might be bona fide. But they might be fakes put together by clever marketing types. The truth is, the net is part of the media now. It's still an open form of media that ordinary people can use, which is great. But it can also be manipulated by all the usual suspects. Just remember this when you go online.

▶ *Log on to the net and you will immediately be assaulted by pornographic images*

There is a lot of porn online – some of it foul stuff. Generally it doesn't leap out at you when you log on. You're more in danger of being 'assaulted' by the images peering down from the top shelf in your local newsagent. You usually have to go looking for porn online (though not always – for more on this, go to page 319). A hormonal teenager would have no problem finding it. Of course, in pre-net days, hormonal teens generally found ways to get hold of pornographic images. Still the net does make it easy – the barriers that exist in the real world – the top shelf, shop assistants willing to enforce the over-eighteen rule – aren't there yet. However, there are plenty of things parents can do to protect their children and further frustrate their teenage sons. There's more on this on page 323.

▶ *Log on to the net and you will immediately be assaulted by perverts and paedophiles*

Paedophiles do use the net, just as they use telephones and the mail. They go online to swap pornographic imagery and there is also evidence that some hang out in chat rooms popular with teenagers and children. However, paedophiles are not online in anything like the numbers some

< 39 >

alarmists claim. Parents should ignore the panic mongers but take sensible precautions – as they would with the real world. This whole area is covered in more depth on page 319.

▶ *The government should do something to protect our children from the horrors of the net*

Where material online is clearly illegal, as with child porn, action is already being taken by UK internet service providers who choose to block access to newsgroups that circulate it. Most people can agree on the need to do something about child porn, but other areas (hardcore porn for the over-eighteens, political 'hate speech') remain more contentious. Protecting children without ruining all the good things about the net remains a difficult problem. It won't be solved by rushing in some new kind of law. A better way forward might be to let individual users control what their computers can access via special software, but this certainly isn't the problem-free solution some claim. Again, there's more on this on page 325.

Read about it online – Illegal Material

Under pressure from the police and the government, the UK net industry has made attempts to deal with the problems posed by child pornography. If users find child porn (or other illegal material online), they are encouraged to report it to The Internet Watch Foundation, who will then attempt to take some sort of action. Read more about what they're up to at **http://www.iwf.org.uk/**. ▲

< 40 >

▶ *If you give out your credit card details online, hackers will get hold of them and use your account to subsidise their crack habits*

Online security still isn't quite what it could be, but worries about using credit cards online often have more to do with technological novelty than with a sensible appreciation of the risks involved. You don't usually worry about giving out your credit card number over the telephone, but do you know where the card number you handed over will be stored? Hackers tell stories of swapping stolen card numbers, but they often get them by breaking into poorly protected computers at companies who collected them in normal ways (via mail and the telephone).

▶ *Everything is cheaper on the net*

Cheerleaders for internet shopping often point out that online entrepreneurs don't have to deal with the same overheads as real world businesses. It's much cheaper to set up shop online than in the local high street. Consequently, they can, in theory, pass their savings on to consumers in the form of cheaper prices. In practice, they have other kinds of overheads to consider – huge advertising bills, for example. And whilst many net shops start out offering great discounts, the ones that want to survive often have to return to pricing the bulk of their products more realistically. That said, it is possible to find bargains online, if you shop around. There's more advice on this on page 267.

▶ *If you connect your PC to the net, it will soon be awash with strange computer viruses*

Viruses aren't like virtual Exocets – they don't deliberately seek out your PC as soon as you get online. If you get a piece of email entitled "!!! This is a Virus – Your Machine is already infected !!!", it's a wind-up. The only

< 41 >

thing in danger of being infected is your mind – with groundless worries. However, always virus-check software you download from the net. And be careful with email that arrives with attached Microsoft Word documents. These can carry viruses. And if you open them, you will get infected. That was how the 'Melissa' and 'Lovebug' viruses spread. The solution is to be suspicious of Word attachments, especially those that arrive unexpectedly and contain slightly stilted messages and subject lines. If you weren't expecting something, always check with the person who apparently sent it before you open it. There's more on this on page 342.

▶ *On the net no one knows you're a dog*

The punch line from a famous cartoon showing two dogs in front of a computer. The net does let you communicate in relative anonymity. In an online chat room, people know as much about you as you choose to tell them. Hence, one of the great male online pursuits – going to a chat room and pretending to be a woman. All harmless fun – usually – though online anonymity can be abused and some of the most enduring spaces on the net are those where people give their real names and take responsibility for their words. That said, the net is not as anonymous as it might seem. Everywhere you go in cyberspace, you leave trails that can be followed fairly easily. There's more on this on page 329.

▶ *The net is a functioning anarchy – no one's in charge and that's why it works so well*

One of the great net clichés, and true, up to a point. A Cold War invention, the net was conceived as a decentralised communications network. The idea was that without an obvious centre through which all messages passed, it would be less vulnerable to enemy attack. OK, so there is no

< 42 >

central command. And the committee of boffins – the Internet Engineering Task Force **http://www.ietf.org** – that sets the technical standards that keep the net running is a very open and democratic structure. However, there is a central organisation in charge of administering the system of net addresses. And whilst the government doesn't control the net, if you keep posting reports on your web pages about what MI5/MI6 are really up to, you may receive an unwelcome dawn wake-up call.

▶ *The net lets ordinary people take on and beat the powers that be –*
   everyone from big business to big government
The net does let ordinary people have their say. You can set up your own web page and there's every chance that it will be just as good as the efforts of some big media corporation. Whether it will attract the same amount of traffic is another matter. The web is an increasingly centralised affair. To a certain extent, it's our fault. We choose to visit the big sites with the big advertising campaigns. According to some surveys, in 1999 we spent one fifth of our online time at the ten most popular

---

Read about it online - Net Ratings

When it comes to measuring online traffic, Media Metrix has just about established itself as the leading player. Visit their site at **http://www. mediametrix.com**, and you can see which sites are currently drawing the most traffic, both in Europe and America. Putting together online ratings seems more of an art than a science. For a good account of some of the problems faced, try Scott Rosenberg's piece on the subject at Salon **http://www.salon.com/21st/rose/1999/02/05straight.html**. ▲

< 43 >

sites. However, there are signs that the decentralised net is making a return, via so-called peer to peer networks, which let ordinary users share files and information. The best known is Napster, which lets people swap MP3 music files. Plenty of new services are trying something similar. There's more about this on page 234.

▶ *If you don't get online now, right now, you'll be left behind, you'll be toast, roadkill on the superhighway*

A variation on standard computer industry ad hype – that if you don't buy a PC now, you'll never catch up. Taking cyber-hypesters at their word, net critics often ask about those who will be left behind because they can't afford the net, suggesting that a two-tier society of information-haves and information-have-nots will be created. Cyber-hypesters generally reply that no one will really be left behind, that there won't be information-have-nots, just information-have-laters. They suggest that we should be grateful to the info-have-nows because they're testing bug-ridden products that will eventually be sold much more cheaply to the mainstream when they actually work. This is pretty glib. Access to the net for the poor remains a problem. As for the claims that you have to get online or risk being info-highway roadkill, or something, there are lots of good practical reasons for getting online. Worrying that you'll be 'left behind', that you won't be hip and up to the minute if you don't, is not one of them. ▲

< 44 >

2 GETTING CONNECTED

So you're ready to get online. You want that information-at-your-finger-tips cyber-blast and you want it now. In the past, your next step involved getting your hands on a personal computer and a modem, connecting that to a telephone line and setting up an account with an Internet Service Provider. Now you have other options. In theory, you don't have to struggle with a personal computer of some sort. There are other devices you can use to access the net. You can also choose between different types of connections. And there's a bewildering array of deals on offer from different ISPs, each tailored to different kinds of user.

In the past, getting online could be rather fraught, mainly because the technology involved was so unreliable and hard to use. Now both hardware and software have improved. PCs come with everything you need to get online. The software supplied by ISPs is now designed to make the process of connecting for the first time as easy as possible. However, getting connected is not exactly hassle-free, if only because you now have a whole series of different choices to puzzle over. Call it the curse of modern consumer capitalism. But don't worry. In the next section we'll offer some pointers and advice which should help you get the right deal for you. ▲

< 45 >

Hardware

In theory, you don't have to rely on the personal computer when it comes to accessing the net. You can also use personal digital assistants (aka PDAs), pocket PCs, WAP mobile phones, TVs fitted with special set-top boxes, games consoles, even so-called internet appliances designed for the sole purpose of getting you online. However, I think the standard personal computer is still your best bet. Entry-level machines now treat the net as a standard consumer option they need to take into account. Both PCs running Windows and Apple Macs now come with everything you need to get online, from internal modems to pre-installed connection software. The price of both has also dropped over the last few years. They're still not cheap. But the days of needing to spend over £1000 to get started online have gone. In comparison, the alternatives don't quite measure up – not yet anyway. But in case you're tempted, here's a quick run down of what's on offer.

Accessing the net via a wireless device

You may just have heard about the mobile internet. The idea has received a certain amount of press over the last year or so. The media and the computer industry need to hype something connected with the net. For most of 1999 and the first part of 2000, it was e commerce and net shopping. Once that particular bubble burst, mobile internet became the big new thing that was about to radically change life as we know it. Techno-pundits have since filled many column inches with suggestions that in the future most people will go online via some kind of portable device with a wireless connection to the net. To back this up, they have brandished dubious surveys and pointed to the fact that

< 46 >

Jargon file – E Commerce

A catch-all term for business of all kinds that's done online. For a while, some techno-types got completely hooked on the 'e' prefix. They went on about e shopping, e life and e government. As a result, cynical geeks began to refer to them as 'e-tards', which seems about right. ▲

people like their mobile phones and PDAs much more than they like their PCs.

True enough, though the reason people like their phones and PDAs so much is because they are simple, user-friendly devices that do one or two things well. As they add more functions and become more complex, they may become as glitch prone and irritating as PCs. In fact, some wireless internet devices are there already. Take WAP phones. These are mobile phones that use Wireless Application Protocol to connect to the internet. While you're out and about, you can, in theory, use your WAP phone to access all sorts of information – everything from your email to sports scores and news headlines.

It sounds great. And I'm sure it will be, in a few years time. But at the moment, WAP phones just don't deliver. They offer slow connection speeds. They're hard to use – the keypads are very fiddly and the tiny screens are hard to read. They're unreliable – you often lose your connection in the middle of trying to do something. And despite all the hype (the worst example being BT Cellnet's ludicrous 'Silver Surfer' TV ads), many WAP phones don't really let you access the net. Instead you're locked into a particular company's WAP portal, and the service provided by the companies that have paid money to be there.

< 47 >

If you do get out on to the net, it won't be the multimedia web you read about in the papers and see on TV. WAP phones can't access pages written in HTML – the language used to create web pages. Instead, they let you view specially created pages written using WML – aka Wireless Markup Language. There are more and more of these around – the Guardian has its own WAP pages where you can access news stories. But these services are like a throwback to the old early nineties text-based net. They're worse, in fact, since their screens can't really show more than a couple of sentences in one go.

Consequently, there's already been a WAP backlash as early adopters realised that the new gadgets didn't even come close to living up to the hype. That doesn't mean that wireless internet devices won't turn out to be good things in the long run. WAP may not survive, though. There are competing protocols and technologies that seem better. But in five years time, there will be lots of useful wireless internet devices. Some people may only access the net through these devices.

But at the moment, you really don't want a WAP phone (or a PDA or pocket PC for that matter) as your sole way of getting online. At the

Read about it online - WAP Backlash

For a good round-up of the current state of play regarding WAP, try 'Shall We Scrap WAP', by The Guardian's computer correspondent Jack Schofield. You'll find it on The Guardian site at **http://www.guardian.co.uk/Archive/Article/0,4273,4056871,00.html**. For more on WAP and its implications, try **http://www.shirky.com**, an excellent site put up by US net writer Clay Shirky. ▲

< 48 >

moment, they're a supplementary technology, something you get as well as a PC – if you have the money. They can be great for people who need to access email and other bits on information while they're out. In other words, they're good for business people who are on the road a lot. Once you get online, you might be tempted. If so, there's more information on page 282 about WAP phones and WAP services. But for the moment, if you're just starting out, you don't need the hassle. Believe me.

Accessing the net via your TV

Set top boxes that let you access the net via your TV have been hyped as perfect for non-computer types and are being promoted energetically by big media companies. I'll admit that these are getting better. But I'm still not completely sold on the idea of checking out web pages and doing my email via the TV. The problem isn't just that TV monitors still aren't best suited to delivering legible text (and there's still an awful lot of text online). It's more that accessing the web via the TV set raises the wrong sort of expectations.

The web isn't really like TV yet – for most of us online, video is still scratchy and very small screen. And watching TV and wandering round the net are two very different experiences. To use some fairly hideous online slang, the net is a lean-forward thing and TV is a lean-back thing. In other words, TV is more passive and the net is more active. With the latter, you need to be up close to the screen, figuring out what to do and where to go next. And it's not easy writing email perched on the couch pecking away at a cross between a TV remote control and a miniature keyboard.

It's worth keeping tabs on set top boxes though, especially as super fast 'broadband' connections to the net become more available.

< 49 >

Read about it online – Web TV

One of the better known companies, when it comes to accessing the web via TVs and set-top boxes, is the American outfit Web TV (owned by Microsoft). Interestingly, their web page stresses interactive TV services more than net access. Find out more at **http://www.webtv.net**. ▲

Broadband will make it possible to deliver material over the net that looks OK on TV screens – for example, video on demand. After being talked about for a while, broadband connections and services are now being offered to ordinary UK net users. There's more on this on page 251.

As fast connections become more widespread, the TV will probably will merge with the computer in some way and you will use this new piece of kit to access some part of the net. Too many people with a lot of money want it to happen. But whether it will be the net as we know it today is unclear. It will probably be some sort of extension of the services currently

Jargon file – Broadband

This has become the term of choice to describe high speed access to the net, though geeks will tell you that really it refers to a method of data transmission in which several discrete channels pass down a single wire, as in cable TV. Incidentally, people who use the word 'broadband' will also never talk about a wire or a connection if there's any possibility they can use the word 'pipe' instead. Perhaps it makes everything sound more substantial. ▲

< 50 >

being tested by BSkyB on Open, its interactive TV network (find out more at the web site **http://www.open-here.co.uk**.

Perhaps you've read about this. If your TV is already hooked up to a Sky Digital Satellite set top box, you should now be able to access the Open network and sort out your bank account via the small screen (if you have an account with the right bank). You can also try out various interactive services. For example, you can change camera angles and call up statistics during football matches. During the same match, you can send email to a friend – presumably to wind them up if their team is losing. You can order pizza online. If you see a music video online that you like, you can buy the CD immediately, via one of the big name retailers Open has signed up.

If you've already signed up with Sky Digital, you might as well have a look at Open. The service is free. However, what's on offer isn't the net. It's what's known as a walled garden. It offers a televisual version of the old online services, where you didn't go out on to the net but just stayed on their little network.

OnDigital are offering genuine net access – for more information, try their web site at **http://www.ondigital.co.uk**. You need to be an OnDigital subscriber to use the service, obviously. Once you've signed up, you get an OnNet box to put on top of your OnDigital box. The service offers a standard 56k connection, secure shopping and free upgrades. Again, if you're already signed up with them, you might as well give it a look. Should you choose something like this as your sole means of accessing the net? Personally I'm not convinced. But if you don't have a computer and you know you want to check out the TV channels OnDigital is offering, it's probably worth a look. But remember. Though the TV ads make a big deal about how you won't have to buy a computer or modem

< 51 >

to get online, you will have to pay subscription fees and call charges. These can add up. And I have a feeling that if you find you enjoy the online world, you may end up moving onto some kind of personal computer connected to the net.

That's not to say that connected TVs won't become more popular over the next decade. Indeed, in the future. Our homes will be filled with all sorts of information appliances that are all connected to the net in some way. We'll use each one to do something different. We'll do some things via our smart TVs. We'll do others via more PC-like device. But that's a way off yet.

One last word about set top boxes. The big cable and satellite companies don't have this area all to themselves. There's a theory that games consoles will, over the next few years, become the set top box of choice, the way interactive entertainment finds its way into the average living room. That's presumably why Microsoft has moved into the market, with its proposed X-Box games console. That's due out in 2001, apparently. However, the Sega Dreamcast already lets you access the net

Read about it online – Online Gaming

Sure, Sega's Dreamcast lets you send email. But you get the feeling that most people who buy it will be interested in multi-player online gaming in mind. American Dreamcast owners (and PC users who sign up) can play against each other via Sega.Net – check **http://www.sega.net** for a look at what they do. Online multi-player gaming is available via Sega's Dreamarena site – for a preview of what's on offer, go to **http://www.dreamcast-europe.com**. ▲

< 52 >

via your TV. In fact, Sega made net access a key part of the early marketing for the console. Sony's new Playstation 2 has also been designed with net access in mind, though it doesn't come with a modem as standard.

The word is that the company doesn't want to make too big a deal of the Playstation 2's net capabilities now. They will focus more on it in a few years, when fast broadband connections become more widespread. That makes sense. At the moment, you should buy a games console like the Dreamcast to play games. If you then want to try out the net with it, fine. But be prepared for a rather underwhelming experience. Also don't expect the flexibility and choice, in terms of software and internet access, that you get with other devices. Again, if you're really interested in the net, at the moment you should stick with a device that's more focused around what it has to offer. But if you want to find out more, try Sega's Dreamcast Europe site **http://www.dreamcast-europe.com** or Sony's Playstation home page **http://www.playstation-europe.com**.

Accessing the net via an internet appliance

According to some critics, the future of mass-market net access won't be some kind of set-top box/TV combo but a specially designed information appliance – a cheap gizmo designed specifically to let people use the net and nothing else. The first examples of this idea are beginning to appear in the States. What's on offer is essentially a kind of web terminal or network computer – a very stripped down machine that usually doesn't come with a big hard drive or other applications. All you can use it for is to access the net. So you get a monitor with internal modem installed and basic connection and browsing software pre-loaded, along with a wireless keyboard.

< 53 >

The whole combo is designed to be easy to use and self-upgrading. It's also, in some cases, free. The companies behind them hope to make their money from internet access. To get the machines, you sign up to get net access from them for a long period of time (sometimes as long as three years). One example of this kind of thing is NadaPC's iCEBOX, which hit the US market in October 2000 **http://www.freemac.com/home.html**. This is the latest incarnation of the 'Free PC' idea, which was popular about two years ago in the States. There, companies gave away very basic PCs and looked to make their money from charging for net access and collecting and selling data from users about what they did online.

Other companies charge for their internet appliances, though they're still a lot cheaper than the standard PC. For example, at the time of writing, Compaq's iPaq internet appliance was priced at around $200 – that's if you sign up with its companion net service (provided by the Microsoft Network). If you don't, it costs around $600. Find out more on the Compaq site **http://www.compaq.com**. Another variation is to give away the appliance, but charge users for membership of a 'network' as well as monthly net access. That seems to be what's on offer from the American company Netpliance, via their iOpener machine. Find out more at **http://www.netpliance.com**.

The computer – Mac or PC?

I hope I've convinced you that a personal computer is still the best bet for getting online. Next we probably need to address the Mac versus PC thing. When it comes to buying a home computer to access the net, you have a choice between an Apple Macintosh or an IBM-compatible PC running Microsoft Windows. (Of course, you could go for one of the other machines – Acorns, Amigas and the rest, which are fine, but less

< 54 >

Read about it online – Mac News

The net may be dominated by PC clones but there are plenty of sites that specialise in news about Apple Macs and iMacs in particular. For general news try MacCentral **http://www.maccentral.com**. For some hard core Mac gossip, try Mac Addict **http://www.macaddict.com**. For specific iMac news and views and loads of links to similar sites, try the iMac Channel **http://lowendmac.com/imac/index.shtml**. ▲

well-supplied when it comes to net software.) Though some people pursue it with religious intensity (mainly Mac owners – most PC owners don't love their machines enough), the Mac/PC debate is one of the more boring things about computer culture.

Actually the choice is pretty simple. If you want to be able to swap files and other bits and pieces with friends and work colleagues, you should buy the same sort of computer as them, which will usually mean a computer running Windows (Microsoft has 90 per cent of the PC market). If you want something easy to use, some sort of Apple Mac is still usually the best bet, despite the advances made by Microsoft. The Mac is also still the choice of many creative professionals – artists, journalists, designers and publishers. If that's what you do (or hope to do in the future), the Mac is probably what you want.

Perhaps the real difference between what we might call Macolytes and PC clones is that the latter accept that they're buying a fallible piece of machinery. They expect it to go wrong. People who buy Macs know they're buying more than a machine. They are buying into a kind of cult based around a piece of technology that once promised to change the

< 55 >

world, a cult obsessed with the superiority of its icons and interface.
Macolytes had a big boost a couple of years ago with the arrival of the
iMac, which has re-established Apple's reputation for consumer-friendly
design (and did a lot for its bank balance in the process). They've since
followed it up with a selection of very nice-looking machines – the iBook
and the G4 – that's the one with the transparent cube.

Having used an iMac whilst working on this book, I can confirm
that they are very nice-looking computers. They're affordable. They're
easy to set up. They have everything you need to connect to the net.
They come with pre-installed connection packages for several of the big
ISPs – some free, some subscription-based. They also make connecting
relatively easy (something that previous Macs didn't always do, for all
their much-vaunted user-friendliness). However, new PCs do all this as
well. OK, you can't pick one that matches your curtains, though whatever PC you do buy, it will have a floppy drive, something iMacs seem
too cool for.

< 56 >

The truth is, it's as easy to set up a new PC as it is an iMac. It's also easy to find an ISP that's happy dealing with PCs. That didn't used to be the case with Macs. You did have to hunt around a bit. One of the first ad campaigns for The iMac's described it as 'the internet for the rest of us', which is a great line. Unfortunately, on the net, the rest of us are using PCs. The net remains a very PC-centric place. At the moment the bulk of new net software comes out first for the PC. Of course, that may not be an issue. It's easy to get all the Mac software you need to access the net. Missing out on a few supposedly cutting edge programs that don't work that well may not cause you to lose much sleep. In the end, the decision is yours.

Modems

Here's the bad news. A computer isn't the only piece of hardware you need to get online. You also need a modem, which will convert the digital information your computer works with into audio signals that can then be sent down a standard telephone line. (The name's a compression of the technical term Modulator Demodulator, by the way). Here's the good news. Virtually all new PCs and Macs now come with internal modems as standard.

However, if your computer doesn't already have something suitable installed, you can buy an external modem. You connect this to your

---

Read about it online – Modem Help

There's lots of useful advice online about modems. Try 56k.com **http://www.56k.com** or Modem Help at **http://www.modemhelp.com**. ▲

< 57 >

computer via one of the serial ports at the back of your machine and it sits on your desk, next to your phone. External modems usually need to be plugged into the mains (unless they're USB devices set up to run off the power source your computer uses). Generally, they're easier to replace if they go wrong or you buy something newer and faster. You can also watch their status lights flashing on and off and kid yourself you know exactly what's going on. Of course, you can always buy an internal modem and open up your machine and install it yourself. They don't require an extra power source, which may be an issue if you're short of sockets at home. They also save on cable spaghetti.

If your computer doesn't already have a modem pre-installed, you can spend anything up to £200 on a top-of-the-range item, which these days is a multi-purpose beast which doubles as a speaker phone and does your voice mail and faxes. However, the first thing you should think about when buying a modem isn't that snazzy voice mail feature but the speed at which it can send information, measured in bps (or bits per second). The higher the speed, the faster data gets sent back and forth between you and whatever you're accessing online. So in this case, speed is good.

If you're using an old modem, the absolute minimum speed you should put up with is 28.8 Kbps (which means data gets sent at 28,800

Tips - Modem Speed

Is it that important? Yes, but . . . Sometimes things are just slow online and it's nothing to do with your connection. Whatever you get, you'll wish you had something faster. ▲

< 58 >

Tips - Serial Ports

If you do decide to use an ancient machine to get online (e.g. pre-95), you'll need to make sure it can cope with modern modems. Look in the manual and check that the serial port you are going to hook your modem up to (usually COM2) has something called a 16550 UART. Alternatively, if you've got a PC, go to the DOS prompt and run msd.exe, which should tell you what you need to know. If you don't have a 16550 UART, you'll need to upgrade your serial port – not something you want to get into if you're not that comfortable with computers. ▲

bits per second). Nowadays 56.6 Kbps modems are standard. For various technical reasons, they receive data at 56.6 Kbps but send it back at 36.6 Kbps. In addition, only in ideal conditions will they receive data at 56.6 Kbps. Most of the time they'll chug along at something between 40 and 50 Kbps. If you decide to go for a faster connection than that offered by the standard telephone line, you will need a different sort of modem. There's more on this on page 251.

How much power do you need?

If you're buying a new computer, you don't really need to worry about power. Even the cheapest model will more than likely come with everything you need to access the net in all its multimedia glory. Prices and specs change month by month in the computer business. But as this book was going to press, even entry level PCs (priced between £600-800) had at least: a speedy Pentium III processor, 64 Mb of RAM, a 10 – 15 Gigabyte

< 59 >

hard disk, 48-speed CD ROM drive (or a DVD drive), 8 Mb 3D video card, 15 – 17 inch monitor, sound card, speakers and 56.6k fax modem, plus software. For around £650, you could get an iMac with a 350MHz Power PC G3 processor, 7GB hard disk, 56K modem, 64Mb RAM and the colour scheme of your choice. Some of the more consumer oriented companies are beginning to offer iMac-like PCs – for example Gateway now sells something called the Astro, which clearly mimics the blobject aesthetic of the iMac. Whether you choose to go for an iMac or a PC, the entry-level versions are more than adequate if you're just getting started online.

If you're planning to use an old computer, power will be an issue. So long as you don't expect the multimedia animations and video feeds, so long as you're happy with reading and writing text and don't want pretty pictures, you can actually get by online with a very low tech, low spec computer – an old 486 DX PC that runs Windows 3.x and has 8 Mb of RAM and a couple of hundred Mb of hard disk space or an old Mac from the mid-nineties. But I really wouldn't advise it. Struggling along with this will be very, very tiresome. And you'll only be getting half the

Read about it online - Blobjects

Apparently, 'blobject' is the term of choice among designers for products that go for curvey, organic lines, like the iMac. I first came across the term in an excellent piece about blobjects and modern design by the US science fiction writer Bruce Sterling which first ran in the magazine Artbyte. You can find it online at **http://www.artbyteonline.com/shared/articles/blobjects/blobject.html**. ▲

< 60 >

net. You might as well use a WAP phone. If you want to see a bit more of what's on offer online, the minimum requirements are:

RAM You can just about get by with 16Mb but you're better off with 32Mb (64Mb if possible). It will make the latest web browsers run a lot quicker.

Hard Disk Browsers and other bits of software are getting ever more bloated and once online you might find yourself amassing a sizeable collection of software and downloaded files. Realistically you'll need at least a 1Gigabyte hard disk – though something bigger would be preferable. Most new machines come with much more.

Multimedia If you want to listen to music or watch video clips online, you need a decent soundcard and speakers, a video card with a megabyte or two of video RAM and graphics accelerators. Most new computers now carry this kind of thing as standard. If you think you might want to telephone people via the net, you might find a microphone useful.

Processor Speed This isn't as much of an issue as some make out, but a reasonable Pentium won't hurt. Even if you buy second-hand these days, you're likely to get something like that.

Monitors Size is up to you, though there's something slightly domineering about some of the huge computer monitors now appearing on the market. More important, if you're going to use a creaky old PC, check that your monitor has at least 256 colours. If you're buying new, don't worry about this.

< 61 >

Operating Systems Though you can, in theory, get by with a computer that runs an old operating system (i.e. Windows 3.x), everything becomes that bit more fiddly. You have to get separate bits of software for different tasks. Windows 95/98 and NT have the programs you need to get online already built into them. The same goes for Macs from System 7.5 on.

CD ROM Drive This has been a standard on new PCs for donkeys years. In fact many new PCs now have DVD ROM drives. On the off chance that you are running an ancient computer which doesn't have a CD ROM drive, you should be aware that getting software on floppy discs is going to be a real problem.

Modem As mentioned above, you can get by with a 28.8K modem but something that runs at 56.6K will make your life online a lot easier. 14.4K modems are much too slow for the web these days.

Laptops

If you move around a lot and need to take your PC with you, you could go for a laptop. It's pretty easy to find something that fits most of the above requirements (though you might have to take a drop on processor speed if you're on a budget). You'll need a PCMCIA modem, which is about the size of a credit card and slots into the back of your machine. These cost more than standard PC modems.

The same goes for laptops in general. Mobility costs. To complement the iMac, Apple launched the iBook, which looks just as swish and has some useful net features. For example, you can set up its AirPort feature, which works in a similar way to a cordless telephone

< 62 >

Read about it online – Bluetooth

The iBook's Airport gives you a glimpse of a wire-free future that will be ushered in properly by Bluetooth, a set of standards for wireless communications. Bluetooth devices can communicate with each other over distances of at least 10 metres. Which means that you can be downstairs working on your laptop and print off a document on your printer upstairs. Soon everything we have will be Bluetooth compliant, say techno-gurus, and our devices will communicate with each other. You know the routine – your fridge will contact your mobile phone to tell you you're out of milk. Beyond the smart fridge hype, Bluetooth is interesting. Find out more at **http://www.bluetooth.com**. For a guide to Bluetooth basics, try Mark Tran's introduction on the Guardian site at **http://www.guardian.co.uk/Archive/Article/ 0,4273,4026255,00.html**. ▲

and lets you dial in to the net without having to be sat near your telephone socket.

Future proofing

When it comes to buying new computers, computer magazines sometimes tell you to look at something mid-range, which tends to mean shelling out anything from £1000 to £1,500, plus VAT. Apparently you should do this to ensure a bit of future proofing. Put simply, this means spending money to ensure that, in the eyes of the industry at least, your shiny new PC doesn't become a worthless piece of junk the day after you buy it. In the computer business, obsolescence doesn't

< 63 >

have to be deliberately planned. It's the way of the world. Chip speeds increase and the cost of memory falls almost month by month. Matching this, software developers continually increase the size of their products to take advantage of these gains, resulting in what cynics refer to as 'bloatware'. So whilst everything seems to be changing, everything also seems to be standing still. What all this apparently means for the ordinary punter is that you need to buy mid-range if you want your machine to have enough power to handle the new software programs that come out the year after you buy it – hence future proofing.

Actually many people make do with the software bundled with the computer when they bought it. They don't always go out the next year and buy the new version of Microsoft Office or whatever. That said, it

Read about it online – Moore's Law

Why does your PC feel like a worthless piece of junk a year after you bought it? Blame Moore's Law, the principle first laid down in 1965 by Gordon Moore, co-founder of the chip company Intel, who suggested that the number of transistors you can pack on to a single chip will double every eighteen months. Actually he didn't quite say that, but that's what people decided he said, and he went along with them. Moore's Law is the reason that computers that cost the same get faster and faster each year. Tech journalists often claim that Moore's Law no longer applies or is about to, in the jargon, 'hit a wall'. For the record, Gordon Moore thinks it's good 'til 2012. Read his thoughts on Intel's site **http://developer.intel.com/pressroom/archive/speeches/gem93097.htm**. ▲

< 64 >

is nice to feel that the machine you bought a few months ago hasn't already been dismissed as an antique by the industry. If you do have the money to 'future proof', the thing is go for first is extra RAM – you can never have enough of that stuff. Then go for a big hard disk. Processor speed isn't that important unless you're going to play lots of computer games – in which case, the faster the better. If you don't want to buy a completely new computer, you can upgrade your existing model. If you're reasonably handy, you can do this yourself. Inserting extra chunks of RAM into a PC is actually pretty easy. However, if you are a computer innocent, the idea of fiddling with computer innards will undoubtedly seem a little daunting. You can get people to upgrade for you, though by the time you've paid for them and the extra components, you might find you could have bought a new machine for the same money.

Buying a computer

Be sensible – do a bit of research before you buy. Read the consumer computer magazines. Scope out the prices and specifications on different brands and models. Think a bit about what you want. Once you've done this, you can either go to a shop or buy direct from one of the big manufacturers. This is a matter of taste. Some people like to play around with something before they pay. I've always bought direct and had no problems. More and more, you can specify exactly what you want.

As mentioned above, the new machines from some computer manufacturers (e.g. Dell, Gateway) now come with the software needed to connect to the net via their own free ISPs. This is undoubtedly very convenient. But it's not hard to find the software you need to connect to one of the free ISPs (especially if you use a PC). Discs are given away by

< 65 >

Tips - Buying a Computer

Before you buy, think about what else you plan to do with your computer. If all you're going to do, aside from going online, is word processing, you don't need a screamingly fast processor and gigabytes of disk space. On the other hand, if you want to play computer games (especially the latest generation of 3D efforts), then a faster machine with a lot of memory and special graphics cards is a big help. ▲

banks, high street stores and newspapers. So, on its own, this shouldn't be a reason to buy from one of these companies.

You may see all sorts of brilliant deals advertised in the computer magazines. But before you bite, think a bit about the companies behind them. You want reliability from your PC. You want to be able to take it back to the manufacturers if problems occur (or at least give them a call). Some of the companies offering those great prices look like they might not be around that long.

Should you buy a second-hand computer? Obviously this will save you a lot of money, though it can be a minefield for beginners, worse

Tips - Guarantees

Wherever you buy your computer, it's worth spending money on extending guarantees or service warranties. Computers remain unreliable machines. It shouldn't be that way. They should be as reliable and robust as the average TV set. But they still aren't there yet so it's a good idea to cover yourself. ▲

< 66 >

than second-hand car dealing. If you are going to buy an old machine, take along a computer-literate friend so you don't get conned. That said, this could be worth investigating. The computer world is full of speed junkies who sell off perfectly good machines so they can get the latest, fastest thing. So you may find a real bargain.

Your connection

You have your computer and modem. The next thing you need is a connection to the net. The best bet for the beginner is the telephone line. It's simple and just about everyone's got one. All you need to do is plug in your modem jack and you can get started.

Once you get keen on the net, you may want to move on to something faster – either an ISDN line or one of the so-called broadband connections that are beginning to reach the UK market. You'll find more about these on page 251. But for the moment, if you're just starting out, use your telephone line while you get your bearings. As well as being expensive, some broadband deals tie you down for a year. And it may turn out that you don't like the net that much or that the things that you like (for example, email) won't really be that much better with a fast connection.

Before you get started, remember to disable call waiting if you have it. Otherwise it may break into your net calls and cut you off. You may

Jargon file - ISDN

The letters stand for Integrated Services Digital Network. ISDN lines offer fast connections to the net – up to 128 Kbps, with some jigging about – and can carry voice calls at the same time. ▲

< 67 >

Tips - Family and Friends

Look at the latest pricing offers from BT, if you get your telephone service from them. It's probably a good idea to put the number of your internet service provider on your Family and Friends list or make it your Best Friend number. You will save a bit of money. Not much, admittedly, but every bit helps. ▲

also experience problems if you've set your telephone up to withhold Caller Line Identification (CLI), information that is forwarded with calls made from BT residential lines (it helps the 1471 function work). You can remove this on a call-by-call basis, though it is a bit fiddly. Basically, you need to get your net dial-up software to add 1470 at the start of your net account number. Whilst we're on the subject of BT services, Call Minder can be useful. This takes voice messages while your line is engaged, then calls you afterwards to tell you that you have voicemail. If you become a heavy net user, you can get an extra line, which will let you keep track of how much you are spending on the net. ▲

Internet Service Providers

Your computer is hooked up to your modem, which is plugged into your phone line. Next you need to dial up someone who can provide you with a connection to the internet, as in an internet service provider, or ISP. The ISP business has changed an awful lot over the last few years. If you want to find out how, keep reading. If you just want to get online, skip this section and head to page 74.

< 68 >

When the net first began to become a mainstream thing, back in the mid-nineties, if you wanted to get online, you had to choose between the internet service providers (ISPs) like Demon **http://www.demon.net** and the online services like AOL **http://www.aol.co.uk**. ISPs were cheap but not very user-friendly. They charged a flat monthly fee for a connection to the net and the software you needed to get about. Online services were more attuned to ordinary users, but were costly and corporate. They charged you by the minute for access to the net and to their own private networks of services – databases of information, online editions of well-known magazines and newspapers, cinema listings, travel information, shopping, user forums, live chat rooms, online celebrity chats and much else. You paid your telephone bills with both models.

In truth the distinction was never that clear cut. The online services moved quickly to the flat rate pricing offered by the ISPs. Some of the companies that described themselves as ISPs offered the same sorts of things as the online services. However, in the autumn of 1998, the old choice between online services and ISPs was made obsolete by the arrival of Freeserve **http://www.freeserve.net** and the rise of the free ISPs. Dixon's Freeserve wasn't the first ISP to attempt to make a go of not charging users for net access and relying instead on taking a cut of the telephone calls they generated. The X-Stream Network was the real pioneer here. But Freeserve took it to the masses. Now the choice was between an ISP where you paid some kind of monthly charge and an ISP where all you paid was your telephone bill.

Within a year, Freeserve became the UK's largest ISP – knocking AOL off the top spot. It went on to become the first British internet company to be successfully floated on the stock market. In retrospect, their initial success is easy to understand. By removing the price barrier of monthly

< 69 >

subscription fees, Freeserve made trying the net out a virtually risk-free option for mainstream punters who had computers but hadn't yet made the leap online. As a result, a whole series of companies not previously known as net companies followed them into the free ISP business – high street stores, newspapers, banks, football clubs, computer manufacturers and games companies.

It's fair to say that the free ISP boom helped make the net a mainstream thing in the UK. But as the market got increasingly crowded, companies had to work harder to attract and hold on to their users. Some offered users shares in their company in return for time spent online. Some offered loyalty points. Some even offered money. However, it soon became clear to most industry analysts that the real way to compete against the free ISPs was to start offering deals on telephone call charges – in other words, to start moving to the kind of telecoms pricing model you find in the US, where people play a flat monthly rate for unlimited local calls. The big subscription ISPs and AOL began to experiment with pricing packages that cut the cost of calls, usually in the evenings and at weekends.

But the first company to really bite the bullet and move things towards unmetered access was Screaming.net, a free ISP set up in 1999 by the electronics retail chain Tempo and the Surrey-based telecommunications provider LocalTel. Screaming.net's big idea was to offer free telephone calls at off peak times (i.e. the evenings and the weekends). Though it did try to roll its service out gradually, it experienced serious problems when it first got started, with the service very slow during the 'free' periods. But, after user protests and lots of bad press, things did get sorted out. And it became clear that so-called unmetered access (in which the user pays a flat monthly fee that covers net access and unlimited calls, either twenty four

< 70 >

hours a day or at evenings and weekends) was going to be the next big thing in the ISP business.

The net magazines have been campaigning for unmetered access for a while now, claiming that it's what most serious net users want. They do have a point. If you're not constantly worrying about your telephone bills, you can start to really look round the net. You can browse net shops at your leisure, hang out in online communities, play games and much more. That's the hope of many UK net businesses who think their operations will only really take off when unmetered access reaches the mainstream. The government seems to think the same way too.

So if everyone wants it too happen, why has unmetered access so far proved to be such a shambles? Because it has, ever since Alta Vista UK announced back in Spring 2000 that it was planning to launch an unmetered service in the summer. Unsuprisingly, it made front-page news. Net users rushed to sign up for the service. Keen not to lose ground, lots of other ISPs rushed to announce their own unmetered services. But pretty soon it became clear that the Alta Vista UK offer was proving complicated to implement (the company changed its partner ISP in June). And before the end of summer, the company had to admit that it had never even begun to set up its service.

Alta Vista received a hammering in the press – justifiably – with some people claiming the whole thing was a marketing stunt designed to help them raise their UK profile. Other ISPs did manage to actually get their unmetered services up and running. But despite attempts to roll the services out gradually, users reported difficulties in connecting and very slow download speeds when they did get online. In the autumn of 2000, ISPs like Virgin, LineOne, WorldOnline and Breathe announced that they were either putting their unmetered services on hold or canceling them.

< 71 >

Read about it online – CUT

The Campaign for Unmetered Telecommunications (as CUT) has led to fight for flat rate pricing of local telephone calls here in the UK. Its web site is a good place to go to keep up with developments in the area **http://www.unmetered.org.uk**. ▲

So why aren't things working? Clearly the ISPs weren't ready for the levels of traffic they attracted. This isn't just a matter of large numbers of people wanting to log on. It's become clear that people use unmetered services less efficiently than standard ISPs. They're hang around and waste time (which is kind of the point, really). They also are more likely to try out high bandwidth activities like online gaming and streaming video. And some users try to stay logged on permanently. Line One said that 40% of traffic on its original unmetered service was created by 10% of the users who attempted to stay logged on 24 hours a day.

However, the real problem, according to the ISPs who've experienced difficulties, is the way the telecoms market works in the UK. At the moment, the ISPs are trying to charge their users a flat rate but have to pay the telecoms companies who supply them by the minute. In particular, BT continues to control the "local loop", the last link from the general telephone network to a phone or modem and for a long while, it seemed to be doing its best to continue to charge for access to this on a metered basis. As a result, Oftel, the telephone regulator, stepped in and told BT to offer the ISPs a flat rate pricing system known as Flat Rate Internet Access Call Origination (aka FRIACO).

< 72 >

Critics suggest that BT is unwilling to lose the increased revenues that come from all those net access calls. Countering this, BT points to the fact that it has introduced its own unmetered service, SurfTime. At the time of writing it's priced at £5.99 a month for unmetered access evenings and weekends or £19.99 a month for twenty-four hours a day. However, to get this you have to use one of the ISPs who have signed up with BT. Many of the best known ISPs haven't, as yet, because they claim the service is overpriced, confusing (users are billed by BT and not the ISP) and a thinly disguised attempt by BT to keep some kind of control over the internet access business.

At the time of writing it seemed that FRIACO was likely to be introduced in November 2000. Certainly AOL seemed to think so. In September the company announced its own unmetered scheme. It costs £15 per month and, at the start, the plan was to restrict it to existing AOL users. When FRIACO arrives properly, unmetered access will become economically viable for ISPs. At the time of writing, it isn't, which is why ISPs are trying to subsidise their services, either by advertising, voice calls or schemes in which users have to spend a certain amount of money shopping online every month.

In a way, the confusion of the current situation is not unlike the early days of net access. Back then, consumers had to put up with badly designed software and bad general service. Then the free ISP boom forced ISPs to get their acts together. Software became a lot easier to use and access improved. Now consumers have to contend instead with a confusing array of different pricing models. And net access has returned to being as frustratingly busy and slow as it often was in the mid-nineties.

Many analysts have suggested that the ongoing chaos is hurting the image of the net, turning off the kind of mainstream consumers net

< 73 >

Read about it online - ISPA

UK ISPs have their own trade organisation, the Internet Service Providers Association (aka ISPA UK) which was set up to counter misrepresentation of the net and lay down a code of practice for ISPs in Britain. For a peek at their idea of acceptable ISP behaviour (with respect to user privacy and the like), go to **http://www.ispa.org.uk**. ▲

businesses need to survive. They have a point. However, as someone once said, things can only get better. When FRIACO is implemented properly, things should get sorted out and we should move to a situation in which there's a standard flat rate price for unmetered net access, much as, back in the mid-nineties, most ISPs charged around £10 a month for their services. It may take a while – a year to eighteen months at least. But it will happen. And when it does, the net should really take off in the UK.

Choosing an ISP – the quick way

If you're just starting out and you want to get online fast, you really don't have to waste too much time picking exactly the right ISP. Instead, get your hands on a disc from one of the better known free ISPs and just do it, as it were. It's not that hard these days. Connection packages have been designed to make things easy. Generally they walk you through the whole process of getting online for the first time. Once you're connected, have a look around and don't worry too much about your telephone bills. Instead, concentrate on figuring out what you like about the net. Once you figure that out, you'll be in a better position to pick the right long term ISP.

< 74 >

So how do you get your hands on discs from the free ISPs? First, if you've bought a new computer, you may already have something. Many come with software from some of the bigger ISPs pre-installed. Alternatively, give the ISPs a call. You'll find a list of telephone numbers for some of the better known operations on page 349. Alternatively, buy one of the big net magazines – Future Publishing's .net and Emap's Internet are probably the two best known. Often they come with discs from some of the big ISPs. They also feature extensive lists of all the ISPs currently operating in the UK, (plus contact details). You may be surprised by how many there are.

You can also pick up discs for the free ISPs on your local High Street. Freeserve discs are given away at branches of Dixons. You can get Tesco's discs at Tesco supermarkets and WH Smith discs from WH Smith, obviously. Woolworths usually have the Netscape Online discs. Once you're online, you can also download connection packages from free ISP web sites, which makes it easy to switch around, if your first choice ISP isn't performing that well. Once you've got the software you need, go to page 89 where you'll find some tips on connecting for the first time. Then once you've been online for a while, come back to the following section.

Choosing an ISP - the painstaking way

Some people love researching and pondering their product choices. And there is plenty to ponder when picking an ISP. It's rather like sorting out a mobile phone. There are lots of different offers to sort through. If you prefer to get everything straight before you commit yourself (and your money), here's some advice.

< 75 >

Check the reviews

When it comes to choosing an access account, it can help to ask around among friends who are online and find out which ISP they use and what they think of them. Then again, perhaps that's not such a good idea. Moaning about your ISP is default behaviour among net users. Perhaps you'd be better off trying one of the net magazines. Both *Internet Magazine* and *.net* run regular looks at ISP performance. *Internet Magazine* is particularly useful here. It regularly rates all the major ISPs, using a series of tests that check how easy it is to connect and how fast those connections are. Results are given for last month's performance. But there's also a chart showing performance over the last half year, which is useful. New ISPs can often start well, then slip down the charts as they become overwhelmed with traffic.

Comparing ISPs

There are a few basics that all ISPs now provide. They all let you connect via a local call. All of them give you the software you need though their interpretation of that usually means a web browser and nothing else. More often than not, you're offered Microsoft's Internet Explorer, though some ISPs do give you a choice between Explorer and Netscape Navigator. Beyond that, the things on offer do vary a little.

For most people, the most important thing to think about when you're trying to pick an ISP is cost – there's some detailed advice on that in the following section. In the mean time, here's a few of the other things you should think about.

Email Most ISPs give you your own email account, usually a POP3 mail account – though a few try to get you to make do with a free web email

< 76 >

Jargon file - POP3

POP3, as in POP3 mail, stands for Post Office Protocol, version 3.
This is the protocol that is used when it comes to receiving email.
SMTP (aka Simple Mail Transfer Protocol) is used to send email. POP3
is pretty much the standard and helps you pick up your mail while
you're travelling. ▲

service. Most, but not all, will also give you unlimited email addresses on
the same account. This can be useful for families, since it means each
family member can have their own personal address.

Newsgroups Some of the newer ISPs don't bother with the newsgroups,
figuring perhaps that they belong to the old geeky net. They may be
right. On the other hand, newsgroups may turn out to be your thing.
Whilst you can access them via the web, it's not as convenient as doing
it via an ISP's news server. Also, check on which newsgroups an ISP
carries and whether they'll get certain groups if you ask.

Jargon file - Client/Server

Two bits of technical jargon for the price of one: you can't have one
without the other. Servers are central computers on which data is
stored. Clients are the software programs that access data stored on a
server. In a more general sense, client often means any bit of software
that accesses information via a network. ▲

< 77 >

Software As mentioned above, most ISPs will supply a web browser on their installation disc. You can use this to do pretty much everything online. However, you may want the choice of using separate programs to do your mail and download files. Old school net users reckon that ISPs should supply you with an email program, a newsreader and an FTP client for downloading files. If this is an issue, call and find out what an ISP can do beyond the basic browser.

Content Most ISPs offer their users some sort of 'content', usually via a homepage which features news, community areas where you can chat and post messages, shopping services, search engines and much else. Generally you don't have to sign up with a service to access their home page. You don't need to use Freeserve as your ISP to visit their homepage, for example. There are exceptions. You do need to sign up to AOL to access its chat rooms and information services. Whilst there is a lot of content available for free on the net, if an ISP has access to a specific information resource you want, it's as good a reason as any to sign up – provided their basic net access provision is up to scratch.

Support Telephone support used to be one of the big differences between the free ISPs and those that charged subscriptions. The latter generally charged support calls at local rates. Free ISPs used to charge around £1 a minute. Now that the differences between free ISPs and subscription-based ISPs are less clear cut, the whole area of support charges has become similarly blurred. Some ISPs charge between 50 and 25 pence per minute. Some offer free support calls while you're getting started. A few offer free support all the time. It is possible to get too hung up on the need for technical support. Many free ISPs have made

< 78 >

Tips – Give Your ISP a Call

One way of figuring out whether your ISP is likely to provide a decent service is to give them a call. How long does it take to get your queries answered? How helpful are they? Do you get stuck on hold? And if you do order software, how long does it take to arrive? If your call meets with an unhelpful response and the software is slow to turn up, it's as good an indication as any that their net access service may not be quite up to scratch. ▲

connecting so easy that you often don't need much help. That said, it may be an issue for you. In addition, find out when the telephone support lines are open. If you're going to be using the net in the middle of the night, a nine-to-five support line isn't going to be much use.

Mac Support PC users are the dominant population online and many ISPs are generally much happier dealing with them rather than Mac users. However, some ISPs make a point of being Mac friendly. At least it narrows down the field if you're a Mac user. Good places to start are Direct Connection, Tesco.net or Virgin. But look around. You may find some useful tips on good ISPs in the various Mac magazines.

Connections When you start out, you're probably going to be connecting via a standard telephone line and a modem. Eventually you may want to upgrade to something quicker – an ISDN line for example. If this might be the case then it is worth checking that your ISP can cope.

< 79 >

Tips - Old 56K Modems

If you're using an older computer or one you bought second hand, you may just encounter some problems with older 56K modems. When these were first introduced back in 1998 there were two competing standards – x2 and K56flex. The dispute was resolved, a standard was agreed (called V.90) and now all 56K modems work the same way. But back then, not all the ISPs supported both types of 56K modem. If you have an older machine with a 56K modem, find out what sort it is, then check with your ISP that everything will be OK. More than likely it will be. ▲

Track Record You could also look into the background and history of the ISP you're thinking of using. Don't immediately assume that a well-known high street name will be any better at providing net access than someone you've never heard of. It all depends on who that famous name is working with.

Access You don't want to sign up to an ISP then discover that you can't actually get online because the lines are always engaged at peak time. It can be just as bad to get online and find that things move incredibly slowly because the ISP is over-subscribed and can't cope with the traffic. You could call and make some enquiries. Ask about their subscriber to modem ratio. People say you should be looking for something around 15 to 1. Some ISPs start out well, then word spreads, then they fall back. So ask whether they're prepared for this. Ask if they can they add more bandwidth quickly. If you're a business user, you'll need to be able to rely on your net service. So find out if they can guarantee access – obviously something you'll have to pay for.

< 80 >

Jargon file - Bandwidth

This is a term for network capacity, as in the amount of data that can be sent over a net connection. It's the scarce resource of the digital age – there's never enough of it. Incidentally geeks use this in a more metaphorical way too – stupid people are referred to as 'low bandwidth'. ▲

Web Space Virtually all ISPs offer you space online where you can put up your own web pages. The amount of space varies – anything up to 50 Mb. Most assume that if you do get into this, you'll treat it as a bit of fun. If you get serious, you may find yourself having to pay the ISP for hosting your pages. This is perhaps looking a little far ahead but if you do put up a page and it becomes 'too popular', your ISP can cut it off. You might want to check their policy on this.

User Names and Domain Names Some ISPs let you pick your own user name. Some don't. If that's the case, find out the kind of thing you're likely to be stuck with. If you're planning to use your net connection for business purposes, some ISPs will help you with registering the appropriate domain name (i.e. something like daves-hot-pies.co.uk), though it may cost you quite a bit. It may be useful to find out what's on offer.

Extra Services In a bid to position themselves as family-friendly, some ISPs offer free filterware packages that will stop your kids accessing 'unsuitable' sites. There's more on this on page 319. In an attempt to attract business people, other ISPs offer things like unified

< 81 >

message services – i.e. a telephone number you can use to pick up voicemail, email and pager messages. If you're a business person who's on the road a lot, a service that forwards your email to a web mail account might be useful. Many ISPs now offer this. Some subscription-based ISPs offer free virus-checking programs and extras like Real Audio feeds, so you can add music to your web site.

Spam and Advertising Some ISPs take action to try to stop it before it gets to your mailbox. Others will offer advice and, in some cases, spam-filtering software. Spam can be very irritating, so find out what an ISP does to stop it. Of course, some ISPs cover their costs by pumping ads at their users while they surf. This bothers some users. Others just filter it out. Personally, I find it more irritating when an ISP customises a browser so that it features the company's logo all over the borders. This is less common than it used to be, but you still see it every now and then.

Old PCs If you have a PC running Windows 3.x or a pre system 7.5 Mac, you will also need a TCP/IP stack to get online. A TCP/IP stack is several bits of software in one – TCP/IP software, packet driver software and sockets software – each of which is needed in order to send and

---

Jargon file – Spam

Net slang for unsolicited email sent in bulk to thousands of users at once, i.e. electronic junk mail. It's also a verb – you can spam someone as well as receive spam. The name comes from the Monty Python sketch and is supposed to refer to the way it keeps on coming. ▲

< 82 >

Jargon file - TCP/IP

As mentioned before, TCP stands for Transmission Control Protocol.
IP stands for Internet Protocol. Both protocols (think of them as networking
languages) allow your computer to communicate with the internet. ▲

receive data across the net. Many ISPs now live in a post-Windows 95 world and so may not be able to help you here. So call and find out if they can send you what you need.

Cutting the cost of getting online

Basically, when it comes to price, there are three kinds of internet access deals on offer. There's the free ISP deal, in which you don't pay for net access but you do pay your telephone bills. There's the old style subscription ISP deal, in which you pay something for a net access and then pay your telephone bills too. Then there's the new style subscription ISP deal, which offers unmetered access – that is, you pay a flat monthly fee that covers both net access and your telephone bills.

Ideally, you want to get fast reliable access for the lowest possible price. This doesn't necessarily mean the cheapest unmetered deal currently on offer. There's always a trade off to be made. Often the companies offering the lowest price draw huge levels of traffic, can't cope and hence provide slow access. In addition, an unmetered deal may not be right for you if you don't use the net that much. If you only go online for a few minutes every day – doing email and the occasional search, and if you only ever connect at the evenings or at weekends, you may be better off sticking with a standard free ISP and paying your telephone bills.

< 83 >

One word of warning though. It is easy to get carried away online and lose track of time. Some of the old style online services used to gamble on this happening. They offered cheap deals for people who thought they would only use the net a small amount each month. However, if you went over the allotted hours, you ended up paying a higher rate for the extra time. Those kind of deals aren't around much these days. But your telephone bill can still add up. So, if you're dubious about the merits of unmetered access, keep a diary of your time online for a few weeks. Then do some sums.

My suspicion is that, once you get online, you'll find yourself hanging out there more and more. Lots of things on the net – from chatting and shopping to downloading media files and free software programs – take time. And it's nice to be a bit more relaxed while you're online. If you're always worried about the telephone bill, you end up furiously downloading web pages and reading them offline. It's nicer to just concentrate on the page you're looking at rather than the money it's costing you.

Ultimately, I think most net users will want some form of unmetered access. If you're out at work all day and you mainly use the net in the evenings and weekends, you won't need a full unmetered deal. Instead, look at an ISP that offers free off-peak calls for a flat monthly/annual fee. Perhaps the best known of these is BT's SurfTime **http://www.bt.com/ surftime**, which, at the time of writing charged £5.99 a month for unlimited off peak access. But you have to connect via an ISP that's participating in the scheme. There are plenty of other ISPs offering their own off-peak packages (for example, Demon, Freeserve and Claranet). If you aren't going to confine your net use to evenings and weekends, you'll need to look at full unmetered access.

< 84 >

As outlined previously, unmetered internet access is going through what you might call a transitional phase. Things are changing very quickly. So the first thing you need to do is get some up-to-date information. Buy the net magazines to see what they have to say about current unmetered deals. Better still, get online and go to Net4Nowt **http://www. net4nowt.com**, which has details of all the current unmetered deals along with user reviews. Alternatively *.net* magazine runs a special forum **http://www.netmag.co.uk/forums/forum_isps.htm** where readers can compare notes on their unmetered experiences.

There are all sorts of deals out there. Some ISPs offer completely free access – but you have to look at ads while you surf. Others charge a joining fee but nothing beyond that. Others charge an annual fee instead of a monthly rate. Others charge a monthly fee but drop it if you make a set amount of standard calls using a special dialler that you put into your telephone socket. This re-directs your calls so that your ISP, or the telecom company it has a deal with, can bill you instead of BT. With some ISPs, you have to spend a certain amount at their net shop to get your free calls.

Tips – Join the Queue

Some of the more sensible ISPs (e.g. Freeserve and AOL) are restricting access to their unmetered access deals. It means that once you get online with them, you're probably going to be able to rely on the service. So join the queue. If you want unmetered access in the meantime, experiment with another service. Just avoid anything that involves some kind of long-term commitment. ▲

< 85 >

All these conditions have been brought in to find ways of making unmetered access pay. ISPs have also brought in all sorts of other rules in an attempt to control traffic levels and improve their general service. Some ISPs will only let existing subscribers sign up to their unmetered services at first. Most ISPs also reserve the right to throw you off the service if you abuse it. Fair enough, you might think. But abuse is defined in rather interesting ways on some services. For example, many ISPs have complained that their unmetered services are being hamstrung by small groups of users who stay online virtually 24 hours a day. They've warned these hard core users and, in some cases, kicked them off the service. You might think the whole point of unmetered access is that you can connect for as long as you want. But clearly not.

Some unmetered services outlaw what you might think of as standard net activities – like instant messaging and online gaming. Others won't let attempt video conferencing or listen to online radio stations. This is all about reducing high intensity activities in order to save on bandwidth and provide a better service. However, some of the prohibited activities may be amongst your favourite things to do online. So check the rules before you sign up. Most unmetered services will also stop your connection if you've been online continuously for a certain period of time – anything from 2 to 6 hours. You can usually connect again straight away. But if you're in the middle of downloading some software, this could be rather irritating. Once again, read the fine print before you sign up. If you do, you may also discover that your chosen ISP won't deal with you unless you have a BT line (many won't) and that they also won't take your business if you're using an ISDN line.

If you get really serious about the net, you may want to move on to an unmetered broadband deal like ADSL or cable. These are more expen-

< 86 >

Tips - Don't Tie Yourself Down

Flexibility is crucial where ISPs are concerned. If you can't connect easily at peak times and if when you do, things move very slowly, you should be able to change to someone who can do better. Easier said than done, if you're committed to a year-long deal. So always balance flexibility against cost. If someone requires you to sign up for a year, see if they can provide you with some reciprocal commitment regarding levels of service. ▲

sive than standard unmetered deals, and at the moment are aimed more at business users. But prices are coming down. There's more on this on page 253.

Family users

Cost may not be the most important thing for you. If you're more worried about getting the right service for your family, it may be worth looking at ISPs that sell themselves as family friendly. Many of these services supply filtering software. Some, like AOL, have their own controls that parents can set up to protect their children from some of the dodgier things online. Often their conferences and chat rooms are moderated, which means, in theory, that there's someone around to deal with the pests that pop up occasionally in the online world.

Personally, I think some of these companies rather over-sell their family credentials. There's often not much difference between their service and that provided by standard ISPs. That said, you don't always have to choose between your family and your bank balance. AOL recently

< 87 >

Read about it online - AOL Critics

This certainly isn't a reason not to choose AOL, but you should be aware that AOL users are still the subject of significant prejudice and occasional abuse online. The hardcore geek elite assume that all AOL users are incompetent and accuse the company of delivering a bad service and of being anti-net and pro-censorship and on a mission to take over the world. If you want to know why some older members of the online population thinks that 'AOL sucks', try **http://www.aolwatch.org/**. ▲

announced its own unmetered deal – unlimited access costs around £15 per month. At the time of writing, it's limited to be people who are already AOL subscribers. That may change, so it's worth keeping tabs on.

One final thing with regard to access providers like AOL. They also sell themselves as female friendly too. AOL, in particular, claims that women make up over 50% of its users. Obviously, the thing about the net is you can seek out communities you want to hang out in. But AOL's non-geeky, non-male image may also appeal.

Business users

If you're using the net for your business, whether you run it from home or from a small office, whilst you want value for money, you also probably want reliability and technical support. You want to know you're going to be able to get online when you want. If you're running a site, you're going to want that to be accessible at all times. You may also want help adding new features to it. If you're on the road, you may need services like email forwarding.

< 88 >

In that case, talk to a range of ISPs, explain what you're after and see if they can meet your needs. Be up front about what you want to do online and what you expect. They may be able to guarantee access for a certain price. They may also have special unmetered deals tailored to small businesses and home offices. Some of the old-style online services used to sell themselves as business-friendly operations. Compuserve used to target professionals and it still remains popular with some business people. It does offer some useful business-oriented content and conferences. The likes of Compuserve also claimed that because they really were global ISPs, they would let you access the net and your email as you travelled round the world. This is becoming less of an issue, thanks to web mail and cybercafes. But it's still worth investigating services like Compuserve.

Next step

You now have several discs from various free ISPs. Alternatively you may have gone to the trouble of setting up an unmetered access deal and you have your chosen ISP's connection disc in your hand. The next step is to actually get online. Don't worry. You may have heard that connecting to the net is a deeply fraught experience. It used to be. It isn't any more. ▲

Connecting for the first time

Talk to anyone who started out on the net back in the mid-nineties and you will undoubtedly hear a few first-time-connection horror stories. An early subscriber to Demon, the UK's first ISP, apparently commented that setting up an account and connecting was 'a bit like giving birth – so difficult that afterwards, you can never quite remember how you did it'.

< 89 >

(This comes from 'net.wars', Wendy Grossman's enjoyable book about net culture).

Back then, if you'd actually bought into all that techno-hype about how you had to get online right now or risk being left behind, experiencing difficulties connecting for the first time was deeply depressing, even vaguely humiliating. It was as if you'd bought a car but then couldn't figure out how to get the key into the ignition. There you were, ready and willing to get with the program. All around you, people seemed to be moving effortlessly forward into the smart new digital future. But you just couldn't hack it.

The worst thing about all this was, nine times out of ten, it wasn't your fault. In the early days, internet service providers seemed to set out to make the whole process as difficult as possible. Their connection software often refused to connect to anything but still made a mess of your hard disk in the process. Their 'easy to follow' guides always seemed to be written by someone fluent in C++ but with only a passing acquaintance with English. When you did get through to their telephone support line, you discovered that it was manned by the CEO's idiot kid brother.

More generally, ISPs were so keen to talk up the net, they failed to tell first-timers that it still wasn't 100 per cent reliable, that sometimes you could do everything right and still not get online. The good news is that things are a lot easier now. Many ISPs have learnt from their mistakes and now go out of their way to help out nervous newcomers. Of course attempting anything for the first time is always a little disconcerting. But don't worry. This will be easy. The thing to remember about all those connection horror stories is that eventually people sorted out the problems and got online.

< 90 >

Installing your modem

If you buy a new computer, it will more than likely come with a pre-installed modem. If you do need to install your own external modem, it should be a problem-free process. Hook your modem up to your computer, turn it on, then turn on your machine. Often your computer will detect your new modem and then ask you to insert the special installation disc it came with.

If that doesn't happen, if you're running Windows 95/98, it's pretty easy to set the installation process going yourself. Click the *Start* button, then select *Settings*, then *Control Panel*, then double-click on the *Modems* icon. You'll then be walked through the installation process and prompted to insert the disk. Then it's just a question of specifying the modem you're using from a list of possibles. Once that's done, if you need to, you can always click on the *Properties* button to change the settings. The only thing you really need to worry about here is connection speed. Always pick a speed well above that officially listed for your modem, preferably double.

The connection

Competition between ISPs is now so fierce that any company whose installation software isn't easy to use is asking for trouble. Most ISPs now provide introductory packages that walk you through the installation and configuration process and make the first connection for you, setting up your account automatically. All you have to do is put one of their discs in your computer and follow the instructions. They all work slightly differently, but they're all roughly the same, if you see what I mean.

Typically, once the disc has started, you may first have to enter some information about your system – whether you're using Windows 95 or

< 91 >

98 or some version of the Mac OS. Then you click on a **Register** button and the disc will use your computer's internet connection package to dial up the ISP. You'll usually go to a registration form. To fill it out, just click in the relevant boxes. At this point, you'll pick a password and confirm it. As usual, with passwords, don't pick something obvious. Go for a combination of words and letters. You'll also be given the chance to choose your email name – i.e. the name that will go at the start of your mail address at the ISP (as in **jim@anotherisp.net**). You'll probably also have to specify your modem's connection speed.

Look out for something about the ISP sending you email in the future about all their wonderful projects. It's up to you, but generally I prefer not to get too much of this kind of stuff. So make sure the relevant box is ticked or unticked as necessary. Once the form is sent, you usually get a message confirming the details you entered. Often you get something telling you that your nickname/email name has already gone and you have to come up with something else. From here you can click on your browser and you're ready to go.

Alternatively, sometimes, once the set up process is done, you'll be disconnected. You can then connect properly by starting your browser. That will also start up the connection file created on your disc by the ISP. Once your connection software is running, you'll hear the modem open the telephone line and tap out a number. If your ISP isn't engaged, you'll hear chirruping fax-like noises as your modem establishes a connection. Onscreen, you'll see a dialog box that tells you what's happening – when your computer is dialing, when it's verifying your password. Once you're connected, a dialog box will appear telling you you're online. This usually has a **Disconnnect** button you can use to log off. It also keeps tabs on how long you spend online,

< 92 >

Tips – Connecting With a Free Trial Disc

If you're using a free trial disc from a subscription ISP or online service like AOL, things work in roughly the same way. Each trial disc usually has a number on it, which you have to enter at some point. You also have to give your credit card details – part of the security procedures to make sure that you don't keep trying to log on for free with trial discs. You shouldn't be charged, unless you decide to sign up at the end of the trial period. However, some companies have had problems here. So check your next credit-card bill just to make sure there haven't been any mix-ups. ▲

which can be very useful. As you'll discover, it's easy to lose track of time online. Your browser will then load its homepage. It will usually be something put up by your ISP. Congratulations. You're online. Now it's just a matter of deciding what you want to do.

You don't have to click on your browser to connect to the net. These days, most ISP installation packages create a little icon that sits on your desktop. Click on this and it will start the whole connection process and launch your browser. You could also manually start up the connection file yourself. For example, with Windows 95/98, open the *Dial-Up Networking* folder (You'll find it in the *My Computer* folder on your desktop). In here you'll see the connection file your ISP's installation software created. Click/double-click on this and you'll connect to the net.

< 93 >

Connecting with pre-installed ISP software

As mentioned before, iMacs come with several ISP connection packages. To use one, start up the ***Internet Setup Assistant*** (you'll find it in the ***Assistants*** folder – alternatively, select the ***Apple*** menu, then ***Internet Access***, then ***Internet Setup Assistant***). This walks you through setting up an account, prompting you for details of the modem and telephone connection. Then it asks whether you want to register with an ISP. If you indicate that you do, you're asked to pick your country, then you're offered a choice of various ISPs. You're given some information (about charges or the lack of them) to help you make your choice. Once you're satisfied with your choice, the Internet Setup Assistant will dial up the ISP and start your browser. Then you'll go to the ISPs registration page. You then fill out the form and choose your password. Then, usually, Internet Setup Assistant will kick back in and remind you of the details you entered. You may then be disconnected. If you are, you can then get back online and browsing by double-clicking on your browser icon or on the ***Browse the Internet*** icon.

New PCs tend to come with free trial accounts for both AOL and Microsoft's own ISP, MSN. You can also use the ***Internet Connection Wizard*** to sort out an account. On some new PCs, you sometimes see an icon on the desktop for this. If you don't you can start the ICW by clicking the ***Start*** button, then ***Programs***, then ***Accessories***, then ***Communications***. Select the ***Internet Connection Wizard***. You call up a screen that offers you various choices. Choose to sign up for a new internet account. The program will then dial up a page that has information about various ISPs, some free, some subscription-based. If any takes your fancy, you can set up an account with one of them.

< 94 >

Connecting with an older computer

If you are using an older computer, there's much more potential for hassle. To connect to the net, you need something called a TCP/IP stack. As mentioned before, if your computer runs Windows 95/98, Windows NT or Macintosh System 7.5 (and anything after that), then you already have something suitable. Your ISP's introductory package will work with the TCP/IP stack already on your machine. When you install it, it will create a connection file that it will then use each time you call up your ISP. However, if you're running Windows 3.x, you will need to install a TCP/IP stack. Your ISP should have sent you what you need – probably a version of Trumpet Winsock. If you have an older Macintosh, you'll need MacTCP/MacPPP. Talk to your ISP about this.

Manually configuring your connection

If you are running Windows 3.x and using something like Trumpet Winsock, you will have to manually configure your TCP/IP stack. Usually, you can kick the process of by selecting the *File* menu, then *Setup*. You'll then have to enter various bits of information – a list follows shortly. If you're running a more modern computer, you may still have to manually configure your own TCP/IP stack. Alternatively, you may want to change the details on an account you've already installed.

Windows 95/98 features an **Internet Setup Wizard** that makes the whole process easy. Set it going by clicking the *Start* button, then selecting *Programs*, then *Accessories*, then *Internet Tools*, then *Internet Setup Wizard*. The choose the *'set up an internet connection manually'* option. Alternatively, click/double-click on the *My Computer* icon, then *Dial-Up Networking*. Click/double-click on *Make a New Connection*, then follow the directions. By the end, you will have created a connection

< 95 >

file for your ISP. When you want to connect, just click/double-click on that icon. The Mac Internet Setup Assistant will also walk you through the process of making a new connection or re-configuring an existing one.

In both cases, you will need some technical information, addresses and telephone numbers. Your ISP should send you what you need. Alternatively, look for Readme text file on the disc they send. This should have the information you need. As you go along, you may need to enter some of the following:

Domain Name This is your ISP's domain name – something like **yourserviceprovider.net**

Domain Name Server/IP Address Four numbers separated by full stops. This is the computer version of the domain name

Dial Up Telephone Number The number you use to connect to your ISP

Username and Password The name and password you chose or were assigned when you subscribed

Email Address Your own personal email address – as in **yourname@ yourserviceprovider.net**

Email Account Username and Password Relevant if you have a POP3 mail account – and you probably will

Mail Server This is the address of the computer that handles mail at your ISP – something like **mail.yourserviceprovider.net**

< 96 >

News Server The address of the computer at your ISP that handles Usenet newsgroups – usually something like **news.yourserviceprovider.net**.

This shouldn't be too confusing, but if you do have problems or if the basic information your ISP sent you seems unclear, then call them. It's in their interest to get you online as quickly as possible.

Troubleshooting

ISPs now make connecting pretty easy. But despite everyone's best intentions, things don't always go smoothly. Here's a few problems you might encounter.

▶ *The dial-up number your ISP gave you is engaged*

This is more likely to happen if you're calling during peak time – in the early evening, between seven o'clock and ten o'clock. If they encounter a busy line, many connection software packages will automatically try again a few times. If this doesn't work, wait a while and then have another go. If you find it happening a lot, you may want to call your ISP to ask what's going on.

▶ *You connect but it all seems incredibly slow*

Welcome to the net. Unfortunately, that's sometimes the way things are online. That's why people sometimes refer to it as the World Wide Wait. You can try connecting at different times of the day, though if you've signed up to an off-peak unmetered access deal, you may not want to do that. Sometimes problems are caused because your provider just has too many subscribers online and hasn't upgraded bandwidth to cope. An efficient ISP should be able to keep things running smoothly as they grow.

< 97 >

If things seem persistently slow, call your ISP and ask if they've been experiencing problems.

> ▶ *The modem makes all the right noises and you seem to connect fine but when you try to start up your web browser, you can't get anywhere*

It may be that you haven't actually established a proper IP connection. Your connection software will usually tell you if that is the case. If you're really keen, you can check the connection with a program called Ping. Your ISP may give you this as part of the start-up kit. Some versions of Windows 95/98 come with Ping included. You can access it via the *Start* button. Select *Run* then use the *Browse* button to look for the Ping program. Start Ping up and type in a domain name (e.g. **http://www.guardian.co.uk**). If you have established a proper connection, this should be converted into an IP address, i.e. a group of four numbers separated by full stops. If that doesn't happen, you have a problem. It could be that your software isn't configured properly. Alternatively, your ISP might be having trouble. Either way, look at your TCP/IP software and check the various addresses and names against the information sent by your ISP. Try connecting again. If you still have problems, call your ISP.

> ▶ *Your modem dials up without any apparent hitch, you seem to get through fine, but then nothing happens*

This could be because your ISP's computers are down. This doesn't happen as often as it used to but is still not completely unknown. You could try telephoning customer support to find out what's going on but other frustrated users will probably be trying to do the same thing, so you might not get through.

< 98 >

Managing multiple ISP accounts

At the height of the free ISP boom, analysts suggested that in the future people would have several free net accounts and would switch between them. You can see why they thought that. Old-style free ISPs don't tie people up with long agreements, so if they don't perform well, users are free to try someone else. That said, the analysts in question forgot the role inertia plays with many people online. Most people can't be bothered. Service has to get pretty bad before they change accounts. Of course, with the arrival of unmetered access, things have changed again. Once you've set up an unmetered deal, you need to stick with it to reap the benefit. If you start using another ISP account, you're going to start paying your telephone bill on a per-minute basis again.

However, if you don't commit yourself to an unmetered account, if you want to set up several free ISP accounts, so you've got an alternative if your main choice is particularly slow one evening, it's easily done. As mentioned before, you can download connection software from the web sites of most of the big free ISPs. Although you can download lots of ISP connection packages, only one can be your default – i.e. the one that starts up automatically when you launch your browser. If you don't want to use your default, locate the connection you want to use in *Dial-Up Networking*, and start it from there. If you're using *Internet Explorer*, it's also very easy to change the default connection. Select the *Tools* menu, then *Internet Options*, then click on the *Connections* tab. In the *Dial-up settings* box you'll see all the net accounts you've installed. Click on the one you want as the default, then click the *Set Default* button.

One thing to watch out for. Some ISPs reconfigure your browser so that it uses a proxy server – a computer which stores copies of popular web

< 99 >

pages and hence helps speed up access times. This will cause problems when you try to access via other net accounts. But it can easily be fixed.

▶ In **Internet Explorer**, select the **Tools** menu, then **Internet Options**, then click the **Connections** tab. Click on the relevant account in the **Dial-up settings** box, then click on **Settings**. In the dialog box that comes up, remove the tick in the box next to the line **Use a proxy server**.

▶ In **Navigator**, select the **Edit** menu, then **Preferences**, then click on the **Proxies** section in the **Category** box on the left (you'll find it in the **Advanced** section). Put a tick in the box next to **Direct connection to the internet**.

Finally, if you do run several ISP accounts, email can be confusing, unless you use a single free web mail address (more on this on page 185).

Next step
Right – you're online and ready to go. Where you go next is up to you. If you fancy browsing the web, go to the next section. If email sounds like it might be your thing, head to page 167. ▲

< 100 >

3 GETTING TO GRIPS WITH THE NET

Before you start, a quick word about the way this section is organised. I've started with the basics of the web, because that's the most popular part of the net. Email comes a close second, so you could start there instead. Following on from the basics of web browsing, you'll find information on searching the web, then on downloading files and accessing multimedia. The email section is followed by advice on online communities, which means everything from mailing lists and newsgroups to chat rooms and instant messages. So there are two distinct strands here – one concerning getting information from the net and one concerning using the net to communicate with people. It might make sense to pick one and follow it all the way through to the end. Then again, the distinction isn't that clear cut. In other words, feel free to read these sections in whatever order you like. ▲

The World Wide Web

Many people seem to think the web is the net, end of story. And it's true that the services you find elsewhere online – chat rooms, newsgroups,

< 101 >

mailing lists – are now available on the web (albeit in a slightly different form). But strictly speaking, the web is just one part of the net, the bit where you can not only read text, but look at pictures, watch video, listen to music and navigate 3D graphic worlds. It's also the bit that comes with an easy-to-use graphical user interface a.k.a. GUI. Instead of typing complicated commands, you use the mouse to just point and click to wherever you want to go. The writer David Hudson **http://www. rewired.com/** has described the web as a cross 'between a slick magazine and very slow television', which catches its hybrid nature and its ability to be both exciting and frustrating at the same time. For many e commerce types, the web is simply 'where the action is'. Certainly, it's the most commercialised part of the net. However, it isn't just a global shopping mall. It still has a human dimension. It still lets ordinary individuals tell the world exactly what they're thinking.

Like a lot of things online, the web began in the academic world and is, believe it or not, a British invention. It was developed by British physicist Tim Berners-Lee at CERN (the European Particle Physics Laboratory in Geneva). To help researchers share resources more efficiently, he extended an old idea – hypertext. In a hypertext document, certain words or phrases are marked as links. Click on these and you go to another document with a connection to the first – an essay on a related subject or a table of statistics. Hypertext links let you move between documents, following up specific ideas or trains of thought. Berners-Lee adapted this for computer networks. So a document stored on one computer (or server) could be linked via a network to another on a different computer. He first came up with the idea in 1989. Over the next two years or so, he developed HTML (HyperText Markup Language) which could be used to format and link text documents on a network and wrote the first

< 102 >

Read about it online – Tim Berners-Lee

Tim Berners-Lee is the director of the World Wide Web Consortium, which oversees the web's development and tries to make sure it retains common standards. His home page **http://www.w3.org/People/Berners-Lee/** is a good place to catch up on new web developments. ▲

web browser/editor, the first web server and most of the communications software. Berners-Lee made his various innovations available online in 1991. Things really took off when the first graphic web browser appeared in 1993. Called Mosaic, it was developed at the National Centre for Supercomputing Applications at the University of Illinois (by, among others, Marc Andreessen – who went on to co-found Netscape).

The World Wide Web and Mosaic caught on for several reasons. They were user-friendly, looked OK and, most importantly, were available for free. If Berners-Lee and the Mosaic programmers had set out to make money, other companies would probably have created 'new improved' versions of HTML that weren't compatible and everyone would have got bogged down in a battle over standards. By giving their

Jargon file – Standard

A format that is approved and accepted by the computer industry as a whole. Standards serve ordinary users because they mean that products – hardware and software – produced by different companies will work with each other. ▲

< 103 >

ideas away, they helped establish a standard everyone could then use. Faced with the highly commercial web of today, it's easy to forget it started in what some people refer to as the internet gift economy. But those roots are important and still exert an influence.

The web also caught on because HTML is relatively easy to use. After a couple of days of study, people could create their own web pages. When the web started, many people did just that, not for profit but for fun or to get something off their chest. Personal homepages became a sort of digital folk art. Some were pretty awful. But others were clever, thoughtful and passionate. Whilst big companies struggled to 'get' the web, many ordinary users just got on with it. The rudimentary nature of the technology meant that someone in a bedroom could create a site that beat the big money efforts of well known companies.

The conventional wisdom is that, as the web has gone multimedia, it's become harder for ordinary users to compete with big companies. However, it's still possible for someone with a good idea to succeed on the web. Some well-chosen words can still beat flashy graphics. Perhaps the attitudes of web users (and the journalists who review web pages) are

Jargon file - Web Pages, Web Sites & Homepages

Let's get these straight before we go any further. A web page is a document, usually formatted in HTML. A web site is a collection of pages put up by an individual, institution or business. A homepage can be (a) the first page your browser shows when it starts; or (b) the first page of a web site. But most non-geeky types now think of a homepage as a personal web site put up by an ordinary net user. ▲

< 104 >

Read about it online - Mahir Mania

Personal homepages can still have an impact. Take the case of Mahir Cagri, a Turkish man whose dodgy English and insistent exclamation marks ('I Kiss You!!!!!') made his page a massive web fad in 1999. His site was actually tweaked by a hacker to make it more comic. Despite this, Mahir became a global celeb (briefly). Since then he's appeared in dotcom ads. Find out more at Salon **http://www.salon. com/directory/topics/mahir/index.html**. ▲

the real problem. As the web has become more slick, there has been a creeping tendency to see personal homepages as the preserve of cranks. This isn't fair. Have a look round a few personal homepages. Try some of the big web community sites like Yahoo Geocities **http://geocities. yahoo.com/home/**, Tripod UK **http://www.tripod.co.uk/** or Fortune City **http://www.fortunecity.com**. Sure, big commercial sites are exciting and useful, but in your rush to get the latest sports news or buy the latest Zadie Smith novel online, don't forget about the other side of the web.

Software

To access the web, you need a web browser. Over the years, browsers have become both multimedia devices capable of handling sound, video and 3D graphics and multi-purpose net tools you can use to do your email, download software from FTP sites, read newsgroups and more. There are two big players in the browser business – Microsoft and Netscape. Netscape's browser has always been called Navigator – except that, somewhat confusingly, it's now part of Communicator, a 'suite of

< 105 >

net tools'. Microsoft's browser is Internet Explorer. You can get this in the basic browser version or with all sorts of extra programs. Which browser should you use? It's up to you. They're both good programs, though factors beyond simple usability may influence your choice. If you despise Bill Gates and all his works, you'll want to go with Netscape. Alternatively, even if you don't like Internet Explorer, you may want to stick with it because it works in the same way as all the other Microsoft software you have. Really, you should just make your decision, pick a browser, then forget about it and get on with the interesting stuff – i.e. wandering around the web.

In the past, picking a browser was part of the 'Browser Wars' between Netscape and Microsoft. This is an old story now, but in the late nineties, it was a live issue. Simplifying things somewhat, Netscape was the first company to see the commercial potential of the web and the first version of Navigator took over online when it was released for free in 1994. It took Microsoft a while to 'get' the net (i.e. realise that as computers became ever more connected, the browser might turn into an 'Operating System for the net', capable of supplanting the ubiquitous

---

Read about it online – Anti-Microsoft Sites

The web is heaving with them – some silly, some very serious. In the latter category is the page on Microsoft and anti-trust issues maintained by the Consumer Project on Technology **http://www.cptech.org/ms/**. Not everyone online hates Microsoft. The Ayn Rand-ite magazine Capitalism has organised a pro-Bill campaign at **http://www.moraldefense.com/microsoft/**. ▲

< 106 >

Windows). When they did, it took them a while to catch up with Netscape. But by 1999, journalists concluded that they had won the war, because more people used Internet Explorer than Navigator.

In the meantime, however, the American courts have ruled that Microsoft unfairly used its dominance in the operating system market to win the browser war. Mircrosoft is appealing, but, as they tend to do in the world of high tech, things have moved on, and in a way, the courts are arguing over old news. Microsoft is beginning to focus on a post-PC world with its .NET initiative **http://www.microsoft.com/net**, a plan to make the net the basis of a new operating system that works across different devices. For analysis of this strategy, try design guru Jakob Nielsen's page **http://www.useit.com/alertbox/20000625.html** or C Net's round-up **http://news.cnet.com/news/0-1003-201-2130272-0.html**.

In addition, Microsoft's main opponent isn't really Netscape any more. In 1998, AOL bought the latter, which meant geeks could no longer see the company as the plucky little guy fighting the evil Microsoft hordes (not that it had ever really been possible to see things that way, but that's another story). Over the next few years, both AOL and Microsoft will compete to become the dominant force in the online world. According to some the skirmishing is already starting. Microsoft recently released MSN Explorer **http://explorer.msn.com/home.htm**, a mainstream friendly package of net tools (browser, email, instant messaging, media player and more, all in one program) clearly designed as competition for AOL's latest package of software (AOL 6.0 if you're counting). Wired did a good piece on the new browser war – you can find it at **http://www.wired.com/news/technology/0,1282,39732,00.html**.

Did the old browser war benefit ordinary punters? Well, both big browsers are available for free. But though both companies kept adding

< 107 >

Read about it online - Web Stalker

The digital art world got in the browser wars, via the Web Stalker, an alternative browser produced by I/O/D. To download it (and read some interesting thoughts on the browser wars), go to **http://bak.spc.org/iod/**. There are plenty of other artists' browsers you can mess around with now – try Shredder **http://www.potatoland.org/shredder** or Netomat **http://www.netomat.net/**. ▲

new features that 'differentiated' their product, both browsers ended up essentially the same. And because they rushed them out too quickly, neither was as reliable as it ought to be. That said, things are getting better, perhaps because the war isn't such a live conflict. Microsoft is still on Internet Explorer version 5.X, the same as when I updated this book last year. They've tweaked it and corrected bugs. But it's still version 5.X, and it seems to work fine for most users.

Netscape seemed to get stuck on version 4.X of its Communicator/ Navigator package. Navigator 5.X has never quite happened. In 1998, Netscape allied itself to the Open Source movement and released the source code for Navigator 5.0 to programmers around the world, so that they could adapt it and release their own version. The AOL deal seemed to put the kibosh on this and instead, Netscape has come up with something called Netscape 6, which was officially released just as this book was going to press. This extends Navigator and integrates new tools like instant messaging (more on this on page 225). Netscape has said that Netscape 6 is not a replacement for Navigator, which continues to be available. And some early reviewers have suggested that the new browser is better suited

< 108 >

to more experienced surfers who will know how to take advantage of its various features. If you want to find out more, there's a quick review on page 277 in Section 4. However, the advice in this book will still refer to IE5 and Navigator 4.X, since these are the versions your ISP will probably supply you with. If you're starting out, use the browser your ISP sent you at first. If you really don't like it, go online (either to **http://www. microsoft.com** or **http://www.netscape.com** then look around for the download sections) and get the other one. (There's advice on how to do this on page 151) Alternatively, look for the cover discs given away with the specialist net magazines. When you go to download Communicator or Internet Explorer, you'll be offered various options. If you only want to use your browser for the web, go for the browser-only option. Otherwise, get the full versions, which come with all sorts of useful programs.

In general, the Mac versions of the browsers are roughly the same as their Windows counterparts. Some menus have different names and some things that feature at toolbar buttons in the Windows browsers are accessed by little tabs at the side of the screen in the Mac equivalents. For the most part, Netscape does a better job than Microsoft when it comes

Tips – Alternative Browsers

You can opt out of the browser war. Try Opera, an increasingly popular Norwegian browser **http://www.opera.com**. Alternatively, Neoplanet **http://www.neoplanet.com** claims to offer all the functionality of its competitors, but says it looks a lot better. Mac users should try iCab **http://www.icab.de** or OmniWeb **http://www.omnigroup.com/ products/omniweb/** if you've got Mac OS X. ▲

< 109 >

to making its Mac and Windows browsers roughly the same. If there are differences that are confusing, I'll try to point them out as we go along. Incidentally, both browsers have menu links that take you directly to web pages where you can get new versions/upgrades. It's useful to check in here every now and then, especially if you use Internet Explorer – there are always lots of bug fixes and security updates on the Microsoft page.

▶ In *Internet Explorer*, get online and select the *Tools* menu then *Windows Update*. You'll go to a page where you can download various Windows-related upgrades and extras.
▶ In *Navigator*, get online and select the *Help* menu, then *Software Updates*. You'll go to a page where you're walked through the upgrade process

Surfing the web for the first time

You don't need to configure your browser before you can get moving – if all you want to do is look at the web. You will need to enter some information if you're planning to use it for email and Usenet newsgroups, but otherwise you can get going without any hassle. So, get online, then start your browser (i.e. click/double-click on its icon on your desktop). When it loads, you'll most likely see either a Microsoft start page (if you're using Explorer) or the Netscape homepage (if you're using Navigator). Alternatively, your ISP may have configured your browser so that you go to their site. (You can change your browser homepage – more on this later.)

Whatever page loads first, you should see text, graphics, pictures and little icons. To the right there will be a scroll bar that lets you move up and down the page. You'll see words either highlighted or underlined – these are hypertext links. As you move your cursor over the highlighted

< 110 >

words, the arrow will change to a pointing finger, indicating a click-able link. If you click on this, you will move to another document or web page – either on the same computer or on another one on the other side of the world. On many corporate web sites, you'll also see colourful banner ads – usually featuring eye-catching animations. Click on these and you'll go to the site they're advertising.

You may also encounter frames, image maps and forms. Frames are different sections within a browser window. You might have a basic document in the main part of the window, with an index to the web site as a whole framed off on the left. Clicking on a link in the index in the left frame will cause a new page to open in the large main frame. Image maps are large graphic images, different portions of which are links to other documents. As you move the cursor over the image, you'll see the pointing finger appear, indicating the links. Forms are like forms in real life. Just click in the dialog box, type in the information, then look for a *Send* button to click. You often have to refine the information you send via drop-down menus. Just click on the arrow pointing down to bring up a menu, select the relevant category, click then move on to the next question.

OK – let's surf. Move the cursor over a link and click on it. If you haven't picked an email link, another page will load. Find a link on that and

Read about it online – Surfing

It is one those bits of net slang everyone loves to hate. If you can't stand the term, blame Jean Armour Polly, who is officially accepted as the person who first came up with it back in 1992. Find out more at **http://www.netmom.com/about/surfingmezz.shtml**. ▲

< 111 >

click on it. You'll go to another page. Find a link and click that and another page will come up. You're surfing. Not that hard really, and, as you can now see, the term is a little grandiose for such a sedentary activity. Incidentally, the conventional wisdom is that, while people surfed a lot in the past, now they just go direct to the sites they want. I'm not sure if that's true. Sometimes it's still interesting to just ramble around and see what turns up.

The buttons on the main toolbar are the easiest to use for basic navigation. If a page starts to appear that you don't like, click the *Stop* button. That stops the page from loading. Click the *Back* button and you'll return to your previous page. Click the *Forward* button and, surprise, surprise, you'll go forward to the page you just left. If you've followed a long set of links and just want to get back to your home/start page, click the *Home* button. As you go back through pages you've visited, you'll see that the links you clicked have changed colour. It's a simple way of helping you keep track.

How about going to a site you select for yourself? Let's try the Guardian's site. For this, you'll need the Guardian's URL (it stands for Uniform Resource Locator) or web address – **http://www.guardian.co.uk**. As I explained earlier, web addresses are the sum of a few standard parts. First is the protocol **http**, it stands for HyperText Transfer Protocol and is used to send web pages across a network. Next comes the domain name of the computer that hosts the site **www.guardian.co.uk**. In this case, the computer is a web server – hence the **www** bit. The Guardian URL ends there, but URLs can specify a specific document (e.g. **document.html**) and the directories in which it's stored. Click in the location bar at the top of your browser, just underneath the main tool bar, then delete the address that's there. Type in the Guardian URL, then hit *Enter/Return* or click on the little *Go* button at the right end of the location bar. Alternatively:

< 112 >

▶ In *Internet Explorer*, select the *File* menu, then *Open*, then write the URL in the text box and click *OK*.

▶ In *Navigator*, select the *File* menu, then *Open Page*, then write the URL in the text box. Check that the line *Open location or file in* has a tick next to the *Navigator* box. Then click *Open*.

▶ In *Internet Explorer* for the *Mac*, select the *File* menu, then *Open Location*, then write the URL in the text box and click *OK*. Alternatively, just write the URL in the location bar and click the *Go* button.

Mouse menus

Using the left mouse button to click on a link will bring up that link (or download a file or an image). Right-click on something on a web page – a link, an image, the page background even – and a "mouse menu" will appear offering you various options (saving the page, or 'creating a shortcut' – more on these later). Mac users don't have a second mouse button, so they can't right-click. However, with newer Macs (and the newer browsers), you can call up mouse menus with a sort of delayed action click. Click on a link, but hold down the mouse button. Don't let it click. A mouse menu should appear. Choose the option you want all the while holding down the button. Then release the button, letting it click. Here's a simple navigational trick that mouse menus make easy. At some point on the web you will find yourself waiting for a page to load. You can open up a new browser window and check out another web page while you wait. In fact you can open several, though if you open too many you may end up slowing everything down. Using two or more browser windows at once can be useful if you're looking at a page of useful links. You can keep that page open and explore the links in new windows.

< 113 >

▶ In **Internet Explorer**, right-click on the link you're interested in, then select **Open in a New Window**. Alternatively, select the **File** menu, then **New**, then **Window**.

▶ In **Navigator**, select the **File** menu, then **New**, then **Navigator Window**. Alternatively, right-click on the link you're interested in, then select **Open in a New Window**.

More complex navigation

The **Back/Forward** buttons are useful enough if you're reading and moving between a few pages. If you build up a longer trail, then want to get back to an early page, you'll need something else.

▶ In **Internet Explorer**, look at the **Back/Forward** toolbar buttons. There's a little inverted triangle to the side of each. Move your cursor over it and it turns into a button. Click on it and a list of sites appears. Click on the one you want.

▶ In **Navigator**, you can pull the same trick with the **Back/Forward** buttons. You can also select the **Go** menu and at the bottom, you'll see a list of sites previously visited. Select the one you want.

With both browsers, you can also pull down a list of the URLs you entered in the location bar by clicking on the pull-down menu at the right end of the box. The above methods don't always work. Say you're on a site and you follow a set of links through it to a page you want, then use the **Back** button to come back to the front page, then follow a new set of links to a different document on the same site. The new trail of links will be recorded over the previous set, so that when you use the **Go** menu or the **Back/Forward** menus, you'll only see that latest trail. For a

< 114 >

proper list of all the pages you've visited, you need to use the *History* file, a list of sites you've visited in this particular session (and over previous days). To access this:

▶ In **Internet Explorer**, click the *History* button on the toolbar (or the *History* tab if you're using the Mac version) and the history list will open in a separate frame (sometimes called a browser bar) on the left of your main browser window. Look for the site, click on it and it will come up in the main window. To remove the browser bar, click the *History* button again.

▶ In **Navigator**, select the *Communicator* menu, then *Tools*, then *History*. A separate window will open showing the sites you visited. Click on the one you want and it will open in the main window.

You can use the *History* file while you're online. But you can also go offline and use it to view sites you've previously visited – a basic form of what's known as offline browsing. If your web use is confined to reading certain sites, the *History* file will definitely save you some money. Visit the sites you're interested in, make sure they've downloaded completely, then log off and read them offline via the *History* file.

▶ In **Internet Explorer**, select the *File* menu then *Work Offline*. Then click the *History* button. You'll then be able to move around as you wish within the history file, which is laid out by date and sites visited on each day.

▶ In **Navigator**, first set it up for work offline. Select the *Edit* menu, then *Preferences*, then *Offline*, then check the box next to *Offline Work Mode*. Then access the *History* file as normal.

< 115 >

You can specify how long you want your browser to keep details of pages in the History file.

▶ In **Explorer**, select the **Tools** menu, then **Internet Options**. Look for a section on **History** on the **General** dialog box, where you'll be able to change the number in the box next to the line **Days to keep pages in history**, then click **OK**.

▶ In **Navigator**, select the **Edit** menu then **Preferences**. In the **Navigator** dialog box, in the **History** section, change the number in the box next to **Pages in history expire after X days**, then click **OK**.

▶ In the **Mac** version of **Explorer**, select the **Edit** menu, then **Preferences**. An **Internet Explorer Preferences** dialog box will appear. In the category box on the left, select **Advanced** in the **Web Browser** section. Then change the figure in the **History** section as required.

The History file is an interface for documents stored in a file known as the cache. If you extend your history file, but don't also allow more disk space for your browser's cache, you won't be able to access some of the earlier entries (there's more on the cache below). If you feel weighed down by the past, in both browsers there's a **Clear History** button in the

Tips – Searching History

Internet Explorer 5 will now let you search the History file to find a particular page you've visited in the past. Click the **History** toolbar button then click the **Search** button at the top of the browser bar. You can also use the **View** button to change the way your History list is ordered. ▲

< 116 >

section where you specify the size of the history file. Navigator now has a button here that also lets you clear the location bar history.

Getting to your favourite sites faster

Browsers let you keep a list of your favourite sites, so you can access them a bit quicker.

▶ In *Internet Explorer*, if you're on the page you want to mark, select the *Favourites* menu, then *Add to Favourites* or just right-click in an empty part of the page, then select *Add to Favourites* from the mouse menu. An *Add Favourite* dialog box will come up. Ignore all the stuff about subscribing to the site for the moment and tick the option to just add the page to your *Favourites* list, then *OK*. To use your *Favourites* list, click the *Favourites* button on the toolbar. It will open in a browser bar on the left of the main window. Click on the site you want to go to and (if you're online) it will load in the right-hand window. To remove the browser bar, click the *Favourites* button again. If you don't like the browser bar, you can use the *Favourites* menu to view your list.

▶ In *Navigator*, click the *Bookmark* button (which is to the left of the location bar), then select *Add Bookmark* or right-click on an empty space on the page and select *Add Bookmark* from the mouse menu. To access your bookmarks, click the *Bookmark* button and a list will come up. Click on the site you want to go to.

Both Navigator and Internet Explorer will let you bookmark sites without having to access them. Say you see a link on a page that looks good but you're too busy to get it now. Right-click on the link and *Add*

< 117 >

Read about it online – Online Bookmarks

Some sites now let you store your bookmarks online, so that they're accessible whatever machine you happen to be using. Try Backflip **http://www.backflip.com**, Blink **http://www.blink.com** and HotLinks **http://www.hotlinks.com**. The last two set out to aggregate users' bookmarks, learn what's popular and then build better web directories as a result. The former lets you construct your own mini-directory using your bookmarks. ▲

Bookmark/Add to Favourites. It's pretty easy to build up a big file of Bookmarks/Favourites after a while. So start filing them in specific folders as soon as possible.

▶ In *Internet Explorer*, select the *Favourites* menu, then *Organise Favourites*.

▶ In *Navigator*, click the *Bookmarks* button then select *Edit Bookmarks*. Once you've put your bookmarks in folders, Navigator will let you put a particularly useful folder on your Personal toolbar. Just right-click on it then select *Set as toolbar folder*.

If you build up a big Favourites/Bookmarks file, it can be time-consuming finding your way to the entry for the site you want. You can get round this by creating an Internet Shortcut. This is an icon on your desktop. Click on it and your browser will launch and load that site. The quickest way to create a Shortcut is first to access your chosen site. Then resize the browser window so you can see your desktop.

< 118 >

▶ In *Internet Explorer*, click on the *Internet Explorer document* icon by the location bar and then drag and drop the icon on to your desktop.

▶ In *Navigator* click on the *Page Proxy* icon by the location bar and then drag and drop it on to your desktop.

Shortcuts are useful, though they can clutter up your desktop. Instead you can put buttons on the toolbar for sites you access regularly.

▶ In *Internet Explorer*, look for the word *Links* on the toolbar to the right of the location box. There's a little ridge by the word. Click on this, hold down the button and slide it to the left to reveal the *Links* bar (and hide the address box). Alternatively, move it down and the whole *Links* bar will be displayed below the location bar. You'll see various buttons that will take you quickly to various Microsoft sites (e.g. Best of the Web, Product News). Then go to your chosen site and drag and drop the *Internet Explorer document* icon on to the *Links* bar. A button will be created. Click on that in future and you'll go directly to that site.

▶ In *Navigator*, check that your *Personal Toolbar* is visible (via the *View* menu). This is a toolbar of quick links to Netscape pages listing new or cool sites. To add buttons for sites of your choice, access the site, then drag and drop the *Page Proxy* icon on to the *Personal Toolbar*.

▶ In the *Mac* version of *Internet Explorer*, you should have something called a *Favourites* toolbar. If you can't see it, call it up via the *View* menu. Then, when you are on a page you like, take the page icon to te left of the address box and drag and drop it on to the *Favourites* bar. A shortcut button will be created

< 119 >

Troubleshooting

Sometimes you won't be able to get to a particular site. Your browser will usually tell you what the problem is and flash up some sort of error message. Here are a few problems you may encounter.

▶ *Your browser says it is unable to locate the server or that the server doesn't have a DNS entry*

Check that you entered the URL correctly. Remember that URLs are case sensitive. If that's all fine, try again. If you get the same error message, it may be that the server at the site is down or that the site has closed down.

▶ *A message comes up saying that the "Connection was refused by Host"*

Don't take it personally. The site you're trying to access is probably very busy. Try again and if you get the same message, leave it until a different time of the day.

▶ *You seem to get through to the site but a page comes up saying File Not Found*

The site may have been reorganised and the page you're looking for moved. You can usually find the document you want by working back through the site URL. For example, if you can't get anywhere with **http://www.hipsite.com/index/television/simpsons.html**, it may be that the document **simpsons.html** is now in a different directory. Click in the location bar, delete **/index/television/simpsons.html**, leave **http://www.hipsite.com** intact and hit the **Enter/ Return** key. This will take you to the front page of **hipsite.com**. From there, look links to take you to the document you want.

< 120 >

▶ *You get an error message saying that the Document contains no data*
Most URLs end with a web document – in the example above, the document is **simpsons.html**. With URLs that don't end with an **.html** or **.htm** document, the browser will look for a default document – something like **index.html** – which it can display. If there isn't one, it can get confused and show the above error message. Go to the site's front page (by taking the directory path out of the URL, as above) and look for a link to the page you want.

▶ *You get into the site you want but things move very slowly and the page seems to seize up*
Again, a problem caused by excess traffic on a site. Sometimes all you can do is wait – and keep track of progress by checking the **Status** bar in the bottom left of the browser, which tells you roughly how much of the page has loaded. Sometimes you can get somewhere by hitting the **Stop** button, then the **Reload** button (in Navigator) or the **Refresh** button (in Internet Explorer). Your browser will try to get the page again and this time you might be able to get through.

▶ *You're on a page, you click a link and nothing happens or the wrong page comes up*
Broken links are less common nowadays, but they're still around. The average web site usually offers several different routes to its various sections. So look around on the front page for an alternative link to the page you want.

Customising your browser

Your browser is set to do certain things by default – for example, load

< 121 >

your ISP's site as the homepage. You can personalise your browser and speed up your web surfing by making a few changes. First, try altering your browser's homepage. Many ISPs hope you won't do this. Their business models are built on you always starting your surfing at their site (where you'll be exposed to the advertising they've sold).

▶ In **Internet Explorer**, select the **Tools** menu, then **Internet Options**. In the **General** dialog box, in the **Home** page section, enter the URL you want in the **Address** box. The **Use Blank** button means your browser will show a blank page as its home page, which will make it load quicker.

▶ In **Navigator**, select the **Edit** menu, then **Preferences**. In the **Navigator** dialog box, you can choose a blank page or, in the **Home** page section, enter your chosen URL in the Location box. You can also use your bookmarks as a homepage. They're stored in a page called **bookmark.htm**. You should find it in the Defaults folder in the **Communicator** program files.

Tips - Portals

Big media/technology companies like AOL and Microsoft want you to use their portals as your homepage. The idea behind portals is that they can 'supply all your net needs on one page'. In a way, they do – they offer free email, search engines, online shopping, homepage areas, news, weather and much more. Unfortunately, they all look and feel exactly the same. They can be useful, so long as you don't hang around, but get out on to the web proper. ▲

< 122 >

You can speed up your surfing by blocking the visual or multimedia elements of a web page, though this may make the pages rather dull.

▶ In **Internet Explorer**, select the **Tools** menu, then **Internet Options**, then **Advanced**. In the **Multimedia** section, remove the ticks in the boxes next to **Show picture**, **Play animations**, **Play videos** and **Play sounds**.

▶ In **Navigator**, select the **Edit** menu, then **Preferences**, then **Advanced**, then remove the tick next to **Automatically load images**.

▶ In the **Mac** version of **Internet Explorer**, select the **Edit** menu, then **Preferences**. Then look for the **Web Content** page in the **Web Browser** section.

When pages come up, you'll see a small icon where the image should be and possibly a caption describing the image. If you want to see a particular image, click on it and it will load. Alternatively, in Navigator, select the **View** menu, then **Show Images** and all the pictures on a particular page will load.

You can also remove some of the toolbars so that you can see more of the web page you're accessing. To try out the various toolbar options, in Internet Explorer and Navigator, select the **View** menu. Try out various permutations here to see what you're comfortable with (i.e. which buttons and menus you actually need when you're wandering round the web). Navigator can even be set to show text-only toolbar buttons – select the **Edit** menu, then **Preferences**, then **Appearance**, then under **Show toolbar as**, tick **Text only**.

Actually, there's nothing to stop you removing all the toolbars.

< 123 >

▶ In **Internet Explorer**, select the **View** Menu, then **Full Screen**. You'll still see a small toolbar of buttons. You can remove these by right-clicking on the toolbar and selecting **Auto-hide** from the mouse menu. The toolbar will disappear, but it will return if you move the cursor to the top of the screen. To return to the standard set of toolbars, click on the **Maximise** icon in the top right hand corner of the screen.

▶ In **Navigator**, just click on the little raised tags at the left end of each toolbar. Then click them again to make them reappear.

▶ In **Internet Explorer** for the **Mac**, there's no **Full Screen** option via the **View** menu, though you can use it to remove all the toolbars for a less cluttered view.

If you do hide all the toolbars, you can use keyboard commands to navigate. People who are comfortable with the keyboard often find this quicker and easier than using the mouse. Here's a quick list of useful keyboard commands (or shortcuts):

Internet Explorer

Alt + Left Arrow or Backspace	Move back one page
Alt + Right Arrow	Move forward one page
Ctrl + Tab	Move forward within frames
Shift + Ctrl + Tab	Move back within frames
Alt + A + A	Add the current page to your favourites list
Esc	Stop loading a page
Ctrl + O	Open a new location or file
Ctrl + N	Open a new browser window
Ctrl + R	Refresh the current page

< 124 >

Ctrl + S	Save the current page
Ctrl + P	Print the current page
Ctrl + F	Find something on the current page
Ctrl + I	Open your Favourites list
Ctrl + E	Open the Search Assistant
Ctrl + H	Open History

Netscape Navigator

Alt + Left Arrow	Move back one page
Alt + Right Arrow	Move forward one page
Ctrl + A	Highlights the text on a page
Ctrl + C	Copies highlighted text to the clipboard
Ctrl + I	Pulls up the Page Information
Ctrl + O	Open a new location or file
Esc	Stop loading a page
Ctrl + N	Open a new browser window
Ctrl + R	Reload the current page
Ctrl + S	Save the current page
Ctrl + P	Print the current page
Ctrl + F	Find something on the current page
Ctrl + B	Open your Bookmarks file
Ctrl + H	Open History

The cache and saving documents and images from the Web

Every page you visit is saved by your browser in a file known as a cache (Internet Explorer calls the cache its 'Temporary Internet Files'.) The idea is to speed up your browsing and do a little towards saving the net's

< 125 >

limited resources. Whenever you visit a site, your browser will first check in its cache to see if it already has the relevant page. And when you click the *Back/Forward* button, rather than getting the page all over again, your browser retrieves it from the cache. You can improve your browsing speed by changing some of the cache settings.

▶ In *Internet Explorer*, select the *Tools* menu, then *Internet Options*, then the *General* tab. In the *Temporary Internet Files* section, click the *Settings* button. You can then specify how much disk space you want the cache to use. The bigger you make the cache, the more it can store to call on during revisits. However, you don't want to overload your hard disk, so don't go mad. In the *Check for newer versions of stored pages* section, make sure that *Every time you start Internet Explorer* is selected. This means your browser will check the page if you haven't yet visited it in the current session online, but if you have, it will get the stored version from the cache.

▶ In *Navigator*, select the *Edit* menu, then *Preferences*, then *Cache* (it's in the *Advanced* section) to call up the relevant dialog box. With Navigator you have to type in the amount of space for both the *Memory Cache* and *Disk Cache*. This is obviously a little trickier, since you need to know how much space you have to play around with. It's probably not a good idea to go for less than the default. With the line *Document in cache is compared to document on the network*, make sure that *Once per session* is ticked.

▶ In the *Mac* version of *Internet Explorer*, select the *Edit* menu, then *Preferences*. Then click on *Advanced* in the *Web Browser* section.

< 126 >

Once you've specified the size of the cache, your browser will fill it up, then as you add new pages it will dump the old files. This process can slow down your browsing. You may see everything slow down onscreen and hear your computer rattling away as it gets rid of old files. To avoid this and to free up disk space:

▶ In **Internet Explorer**, click the **Empty Folder** button in the **Temporary Internet Files** section.
▶ In **Navigator**, click both the **Clear Memory Cache** and **Clear Disk Cache** buttons in the **Cache** dialog box.
▶ In the **Mac** version of **Internet Explorer**, in the **Advanced** section, click the **Empty Now** button.

Both browsers (in their Windows version, at least) make it easy to access and read the pages saved in the cache.

▶ In **Internet Explorer**, select the **Tools** menu, then **Internet Options**, then **General**, then click the **Settings** button, then the **View Files** button.
▶ In **Navigator**, select the **File** menu, then **Open Page**, then click the **Choose File** button to look for the **Cache** (it's in the **Users** sub-directory of the **Netscape** folder).

However, the best way to check back on pages you've previously visited is the History file. Of course, you need to remember when you visited them. So if you find a page you know you'll want to refer back to, why not go ahead and save it anyway.

< 127 >

▶ In **Internet Explorer**, select the **File** menu then **Save As**. You can choose to save the page as a complete web page (or 'web archive'). If you choose the former, when you open it again (with an application that can handle HTML, like your browser), it will retain the formatting it had on the web. If you choose text, all you get is the text and some basic formatting.

▶ In **Navigator**, select the **File** menu then **Save As**. You can then choose to save the page as either HTML or text. If you want to save a page complete with the images, you need to select the **File** menu, then **Edit**. Then select the **File** menu, then **Save As**.

If you're saving a page with frames, click in the frame you're interested in before you start. You can save the images from web pages by right-clicking on the image, then choosing **Save Image As** (in Navigator) or **Save Picture As** (in Internet Explorer) from the mouse menu. Some web pages feature sound and video files and you can save these. However, since you'll often need special plug-in programs to play these, it's best to use those to save multimedia files. There's more on this on page 160.

Rather than save web pages that seem particularly useful, you can always print them out for future reference.

▶ In **Internet Explorer**, select the **File** menu, then **Print**. On the **Print** dialog box, in the **Print range** section, make sure **All** is ticked. If you want to see whether the page is going to look something like it does on screen or if you want to pick out certain pages to print, select the **File** menu, then **Print Preview**. Then select the **File** menu then **Print**, then specify the pages you want. If you want to print an individual frame, right-click in the frame, then select **Print** from the mouse menu.

< 128 >

▶ In **Navigator**, the easiest thing to do is use the **Print** button on the toolbar. If you only want to print a few pages from a big web document, select the **File** menu then **Print Preview**. You can then find out the page numbers you want. Then select the **File** menu, then **Print**, then specify the pages you want.

Finally, if you get very keen on speeding up your browsing, it might be worth investigating Web proxy servers. These are local servers that keep copies of the most popular sites. You can set your browser to get those copies rather than going out on to the net proper. Some ISPs have their own web proxies, so ask about it. To set your browser up to use a proxy:

▶ In **Internet Explorer**, select the **Tools** menu, then **Internet Options**, then **Connection**, then click the box next to **Access the Internet using a proxy server**, then enter the details your ISP will give you in the relevant text boxes.
▶ In **Navigator**, select the **Edit** menu, then **Preferences**, then **Advanced**, then **Proxies**. Mark the box next to **Manual proxy**

Read about it online - Browsing Tips

The specialist net magazines, .net and Internet are a good source for browser tips and tricks. .net does a page about Internet Explorer 5 **http://www.netmag.co.uk/ie5/default.htm**, where you can find out more about IE5's hidden depths. For more Navigator information, try Netscape's own page **http://home.netscape.com/browsers/using/** or the Unofficial Netscape FAQ **http://www.ufaq.org**. ▲

< 129 >

configuration then click the *View* button, then enter the details of the proxy – your ISP should supply these.

▶ In the *Mac* version of *Internet Explorer*, select the *Edit* Menu, then *Preferences*. In the *Network* section, look for *Proxies*. Put a tick next to *Web proxies* then enter the address your ISP has given you. ▲

Searching the Web

Neo-Luddite critics often moan that the net is so disorganised, that even when there is useful information online it's impossible to find it. If all the search sites disappeared overnight, they might have a point. As it is, modern net search tools now make it relatively easy to find information. Like a lot of things online, they could be better. But if you take the time to learn how to use them, they work well enough.

In theory, there are two distinct types of search site – search engines and directories. Both let you search through databases of links to different web sites. They differ in the search methods they offer and how they assemble their databases of links. Search engines rely on autonomous software programs (aka bots, spiders or crawlers). These roam the web collecting details about different pages – the URL, the title, the keywords chosen by the creator of the page as a summary of its content, known as meta tags, and usually these days, the whole text of a page. A database is created from the bot's findings. Users then search this and turn up links to different sites, grouped in order of relevance. Directories offer collections of links, arranged into different categories and themes. The directories employ people to do their searches and assemble their lists of sites. But some also use bots. They also accept

< 130 >

submissions sent in by site webmasters. You can use a search engine to search a directory's links. But you can also drill down through different directories looking for the sites you want. Aside from general directories, there are lots of specialist sites that index links in a particular field.

Actually, the distinction between search engines and directories is so blurred nowadays as to be pretty useless. It's better to refer to them all as search sites. There are still a few 'pure' search engines out there, but most come with a directory of some sort as well. These days, the big search sites feature all sorts of other services from free email to chat rooms. The people behind companies like Yahoo don't even like to use the word 'search' any more; they refer to themselves as a 'media company'. Indeed, the leading search sites are amongst the biggest of the portals. The best known are:

AltaVista	http://www.altavista.com
Direct Hit	http://www.directhit.com
Excite	http://www.excite.com
FAST Search	http://www.alltheweb.com
Go	http://www.go.com
Google	http://www.google.com
Hotbot	http://hotbot.lycos.com/
Look Smart	http://www.looksmart.com
Lycos	http://www.lycos.com
Northern Light	http://www.northernlight.com
Yahoo	http://www.yahoo.com

Yahoo, Excite, Lycos, Look Smart and Alta Vista all have UK-based sites up and running too. Just substitute **.co.uk** for **.com** in the URL. If you want

< 131 >

to try a homegrown search site, visit UK Max **http://ukmax.com**. Most of the sites mentioned are fine, though my favourite is Google. In part, this is because it's concentrating on searching rather then selling itself as a media company. As a result, the pages are pleasantly uncluttered by ads – not something you can say about other search sites. The real reason, though, is that Google seems to deliver more relevant results than the rest.

As you'll discover shortly, most search sites serve up too many results that have nothing to do with your original query. This is, in part, caused by unscrupulous web designers who try to mislead search engines and get their sites higher up the lists of results by misusing the meta tags on a web page. Meta tags describe the content of a page and are used as a reference point by search engines. In a practice known as spamdexing, some designers deliberately assign inaccurate meta tags to their pages, hoping to draw more traffic. In a way, Google is a reaction to all this. It ranks its search results according to how many other sites link to each entry. It also takes into account the ranking of those sites doing the linking. The idea is that if a lot of highly ranked sites link to a particular site in a particular field, it's more likely to be relevant in some way to the original query. This may sound a bit complex, but it seems to work.

Read about it online - Paid Searches

With GoTo **http://www.goto.com**, companies pay to be ranked higher in the search results. If this sounds a bit dubious, at least GoTo are up front about this. Many well-known search engines commonly sell 'keywords' to advertisers, so if you search for a particular topic, a relevant ad will appear on the results page. ▲

< 132 >

Tips - Be a Web Voyeur

If you're having trouble with your own searches, why not amuse yourself for a while with Metaspy **http://www.metaspy.com/**. It lets you sneak a peek at the searches other people are doing on Metacrawler **http://www.metacrawler.com** by flashing up the keywords currently being searched for. It's strangely compelling. ▲

The other big problem with search engines, aside from irrelevant results, is that they don't cover most of the web. According to a survey published in 1999 by the NEC Research Institute at Princeton, the best site – Northern Light – only covered around 16% of the web. You can still read the report at **http://wwwmetrics.com/**. To make sure you search more of the web, try the MetaSearch sites. These let you combine results from several of the major engines. Merely covering more sites doesn't necessarily guarantee better end results, but sites like MetaCrawler **http://www.metacrawler.com/**, Dogpile **http://www.dogpile.com**, and Search.com **http://www.search.com** are worth a look.

Using a search engine

Search engines look pretty easy to use. Just enter your subject in the text box, click the button and in a matter of moments you'll be linked to exactly what you're looking for. That's the theory. The reality is a page that tells you that the search engine has found several hundred thousand pages that contain the terms you entered. If you follow the links to these pages, you'll discover that many have little or no connection to the subject you're interested in. The problem is that if you don't enter your search terms

< 133 >

properly, most search engines will do a general search on all the words in your query. They will turn up pages that feature them all, pages that feature some and pages that feature only one. As you can imagine, that's a lot of pages. So if you want to get useful results, first learn to use a search engine properly. Whichever one you pick, read the Help file so you know how to refine your search properly. That way the engine in question at least has a fighting chance of turning up something appropriate.

As an example of what to do, let's try Google (**http://www.google. com**). To enter a query, just type some relevant terms into the text box and click on the *Google Search* button. Unlike some search engines, Google only returns those pages that include all of your search terms. In addition, Google also gives a higher ranking to those pages in which your query terms appear near each other. So, to plan a holiday in France, you should type *holiday france* in the text box. To restrict a search further, just add more terms. For example, *cats pets homes* will yield more relevant results than just *cats*. One thing that may trip you up – Google ignores common words, which it refers to as stop words. It disregards words like 'the', 'where' and 'how', as well as some single digit numbers and single letters. They say that these terms usually don't help when

Read about it online – Natural Language Queries

Some web sites now let you enter natural language queries in their text boxes – as in "Where can I find a website about fishing?" Ask Jeeves **http://www.ask.co.uk** is the leader in this field, though standard search sites like Alta Vista **http://www.altavista.com** now allow for something similar. ▲

< 134 >

Read about it online - Search Tips

One of the best sites I've found for advice about searching is About.com's Web Search page **http://websearch.about.com/**. This has news and reviews, plus links to all sorts of useful resources. ▲

searching and can slow things down. You can make sure stop words are included, by using the '+' sign. Make sure you include a space before the '+' sign. So to search for 'Star Wars, Episode I', you'd have to enter *Star Wars Episode +1* in the text box.

You can use the minus sign to exclude certain terms from your search. Just put '-' in front of the term you want to exclude. A search for *bass –music* will return pages about sea bass rather musicians. Again make sure you include a space before the minus sign. You can search for specific phrases or names on Google by adding quotation marks. Words enclosed in double quotation marks, as in "Martin Amis", will appear together in the results that are turned up. If the phrase includes a Google stop word, you'll need to use the '+' sign to make sure it gets included. Google treats hyphens, slashes, periods/full stops, equals signs, and apostrophes as 'phrase connectors'. As you might expect, these connect words – so if you enter *mother-in-law*, it's treated as a phrase even though the words aren't in quotation marks. To use Google to search for pages containing either word A or word B, you'll need to use a capitalized 'OR' between terms. So to search for a holiday in either London or Paris, you'd have to type *holiday london OR paris*. As you'll see from that example, searches on Google are not case sensitive. Everything you enter in the text box is treated as lower case.

< 135 >

You can restrict a search on Google to its own directory **directory. google.com**. If you search for *Saturn* within the *Science > Astronomy* section of the directory, you'll only get links to pages about the planet. You won't get links to pages about Saturn cars or the old Sega Saturn game console. You can further restrict some searches on Google via certain 'operators'. For example, if you want to search a specific domain or site, use the 'site' operator. So to search the Guardian site for information about privacy, enter *privacy site:www.guardian.co.uk* in the text box. Unlike lots of search sites, Google doesn't let you do 'wildcard' searches. On some other search sites, if you tack the asterisk on to the end of a word, they will search for other similarly spelled words that contain up to five additional letters. So a search using the term *breed** will look for breed, breeders and breeding. In contrast Google searches for the words exactly as you enter them in the search box. Incidentally, you can refine your searches further (e.g. you can ask for results only in certain languages) at Google via the *Advanced Search* link. The other search engines work in roughly the same way, though each has it own quirks. So you really do need to read those help pages before you start.

When you've sorted out your search terms, click the *Google Search* button. After a while, Google will take you to a results screen which will

Read about it online - Tracking the Engines

To find out which search engine is currently deemed to be the best, try Search Engine Watch **http://www.searchenginewatch.com/**, which regularly ranks the big names and has lots of search tips and a good explanation of how search engines work. ▲

< 136 >

probably tell you that it has found thousands of pages that fit your search. It ranks the pages found in terms of relevance and shows you links to the top ten. You should see the title of the page, plus the address, then an excerpt from the web page, which shows how your search terms are used in context on that page. The search terms should be in bold, so you can tell quickly whether the result is a page you want to visit. At the end of the text, you should also see a link to *Similar Pages*. Click this and you'll turn up pages related to this particular result.

Browsers and searching

Navigator and Internet Explorer both have *Search* toolbar buttons which provide quick links to search sites.

▶ In *Internet Explorer*, click the *Search* button (or the *Search* tab in the *Mac* version) and a browser bar with a search box inside it will open. Use the box and your search results will appear in the browser bar. Click on the links shown and the site comes up in the main window (while the search results remain in the browser bar). If you want to see the search engines you're using (and remove one or two), click the *Customise* button.

▶ In *Navigator* click the *Search* button and you go to the *Netcenter* search page where you'll find links to all the big sites.

Both browsers will also let you do a quick search via the location bar.

▶ In *Internet Explorer*, enter the terms you want to search then hit *Return*. Internet Explorer will use its *AutoSearch* function and list the results in a browser bar on the left. It may also load a page in the

< 137 >

main window, if you searched for a particular word and that word is also a **.com** address. For example, enter the word 'soccer' and hit Return. AutoSearch will find various football-related sites and list them in the browser bar. But it will also load **http://www.soccer.com**.

▶ In **Navigator**, enter the terms you want then hit **Return**. You will then go to a search results page at **Netcenter**.

Mac Users – aside from the **Search** buttons, if you have a newer Mac, you can also use its built-in search tool Sherlock.

▶ In **Internet Explorer**, you can start it up via the **Apple** menu.

Both browsers now have a nifty little **What's Related** function, which uses technology from a program called Alexa **http://www.alexa.com** to call up lists of sites that previous users thought were similar to the site you're accessing now. It can point you in interesting directions.

▶ In **Internet Explorer**, select the **Tools** menu, then **Show Related Links**.
▶ In **Navigator**, click the **What's Related** button on the right of the location bar.
▶ In the **Mac** version of **Internet Explorer**, you can access **What's Related** via the **Tools** menu.

In a similar vein, sites that feature collaborative filters can sometimes take you towards interesting pages. Collaborative filters work by pooling recommendations from individual users then cross-referencing them. If you like records A, B and C and another person likes records B, C and

< 138 >

D, there's a chance that you may like record D and that the other person might go for record A. Collaborative filters are used a lot on shopping sites to recommend new purchases. For example, Music Buddha **http://www.mubu.com** lets you listen to sound clips and rate them, then the site recommends music you might want to try (and buy). At Movie Critic **http://www.moviecritic.com**, you sign up, then rate various films and then other films will be recommended to you. At Jester, a collaborative joke filter **http://shadow.ieor.berkeley.edu/humor/**, you rate 15 sample jokes, then Jester starts sending you new gags it thinks will make you laugh. For some thoughts on whether this tells us something about the nature of jokes, try 'The Humor Quotient' at Feed **http://www.feedmag. com/essay/es231_master.html**.

Using an online directory

If messing around with + and – signs isn't your thing, you might do better with an online directory, where you can just click through various directories and sub-directories in search of the subject you want (and the links to the sites that cover it). Take the opening page of Yahoo **http:// www.yahoo.co.uk**. Here you'll see fourteen or so general headings – Arts and Humanities, Business and Economy, Education, News and Media, Reference, Society and Culture and many others. Under each general heading is a selection of sub-headings. So under Society and Culture, you see People, Environment, Royalty and Religion. Each of these headings and sub-headings is a click-able link. Click it and you move to that area of the directory, where you find more links.

As an example, let's look at Yahoo's list of web search tools. Look for the *Computers and Internet* heading. Underneath you'll see several sub-headings – *Internet*, *WWW*, *Software*, *Multimedia*. Click on

< 139 >

WWW. That will take you to the general *World Wide Web* section. At the top you'll see links which take you to UK or Ireland-only sites in the general category. Below is another set of general categories to do with the web, from *ActiveX* and *Announcement Services* to *Web-based Entertainment* and *XML*. By some of these categories, you may notice the @ sign. This indicates that this section cross-references with another general category. So if you click *ActiveX@*, it will take you to the *Computers and Internet: Software* section.

Actually, the exact location of this section is shown at the top in a list of all the directories it is nested within, as in *Home > Computers_and_Internet > Software > Operating_Systems > Windows > Windows_95 > Information_and_Documentation > ActiveX*. This kind of directory chain appears at the top of every page in Yahoo. If you follow a wrong turn, you can just click the previous term in the chain to go back or click *Home* to go the Yahoo homepage. Alternatively, click the *Back* button. Do that here and go back to the *WWW* section and click *Searching the Web*. This takes you to a page that features more categories – from *All-in-One Search Pages* to *Web Directories* and *Weblogs*. By each heading is a number that tells you

Tips – An Alternative to Yahoo

For a less commercial directory, try The Open Directory Project **http://www.dmoz.org/**, which borrows its methodology from Open Source software programming. The idea is that individuals add links and reviews as they can. It's surprisingly good. And there are no ads to put up with. ▲

< 140 >

how many links are in that section. Click ***Indices to Web Documents*** and you access a page with more categories (***Best of the Web*** to ***What's New***) along with a general list of links to different types of web index sites. At the top of each page, incidentally, there's a search engine that lets you search the whole web, UK sites or just sites in the particular category you're investigating.

Good online directories are like well-designed libraries. In real-world libraries, you often arrive at a shelf stacked with scores of titles relating to a particular field. Unless you know beforehand the title you're after, the only way to find out if a book is suitable is to have a look. Similarly, when you're faced with thirty links to sites offering to tell you 'What's New on the Web', you don't have much choice but to click the links and have a look. And that can be a bit hit and miss. Yahoo is great at cataloguing sites, but it isn't in the business of quality control. A slightly different, more personal approach is offered by About.com **http://about.com**. Here guides put together lists of sites in a particular area and write regular features on the subject. It's worth a look, as are several British directories, which claim to do a better job of classifying homegrown content than the UK version of Yahoo. Try UKPlus **http://www.ukplus.co.uk** or Yell **http://uk.yell.com/home.html**, the web site for the Yellow Pages.

If Yahoo seems too big, try one of the specialist directories. These are laid out like Yahoo but confine themselves to specific subjects and hence can usually deliver more information about the sites they list. As you might expect, Yahoo is good place to go to find specialist directories (there's a section in the ***Searching the Web*** category we were looking at earlier). You'll find that there are online directories covering pretty much everything you can think of. Here's a few to be going on with:

< 141 >

The Media UK Internet Directory **http://www.mediauk.com/directory/** A useful collection of links to British TV and radio stations, magazines and newspapers and much else besides.

Seniors Search **http://www.seniorssearch.com/** The Internet directory for the over-fifties, laid out like Yahoo but with categories like 'Just for Grandparents' and 'Seniors Personal Homepages'.

WWWomen **http://www.wwwomen.com/** Bills itself as the 'premier search directory for women online'. Again, set out like Yahoo but with categories like 'Women in Business' and 'Personal Time for Women'.

FIND **http://www.find.co.uk** The Financial Information Net Directory, this has links to all sorts of UK-based financial services resources online.

Shopsmart **http://uk.shopsmart.com/** A shopping directory with links to and reviews of online retail outlets in the UK that offer secure shopping.

Listings, weblogs and web rings

One of the first things people used to do when they got on the web in the early days was make a list of the sites they found, then group them under a heading – cool sites, new sites or underground links. Presumably it was a way of helping them get to grips with the growth of the web. And perhaps they weren't quite sure what to put on a web page. So they created helpful lists of links, which soon became lists of links to lists of links, and so on. Listings sites aren't serious search tools, but they can point you towards sites you might otherwise never find. Yahoo has lots of links to listings sites – look in the *Searching the Web* directory as before. The best listings sites take a particular angle on the web. Take Steve Baldwin's Ghost Sites of the Web **http://www.disobey.com/ghostsites/**, which links to sites that are still online but no longer breathing; in other words, they haven't been updated in ages, but live on,

< 142 >

a relic of earlier web times. Listings are dogged by the online trash aesthetic. For every linkmeister dutifully logging his cool sites of the day, there's another one totting up the web's worst pages – for example, the Useless Pages **http://www.go2net.com/useless/**.

Weblogs are an interesting extension of the listings idea. These sites consist of links, usually updated on a daily basis, to stories and articles on the web. Where old listings pages linked mainly to sites, weblogs tend to link to good pieces of writing. According to Jorn Barger, whose Robot Wisdom is one of the most popular web logs **http://www.robotwisdom.com**, the name refers to the fact that these sites simply log someone's surfing. Certainly, a weblog is often a very personal edit of the web, featuring comments on the material linked to. But that isn't always the case. One of the best weblogs, Memepool **http://www.memepool.com** is a collective effort. Taking things even further, Slashdot **http://www.slashdot.org** links out to stories about Linux and other 'news for nerds' and on its own pages features discussions about those stories. Often weblogs focus on one subject or industry. For example Jim Romanesko's Obscure Store and Reading Room **http://www.obscurestore.com** links to offbeat stories from America's myriad local papers. Overall, weblogs are a great way of finding interesting material online. At CamWorld **http://www.camworld.com**, itself an excellent weblog, you'll find links to some of the best.

For more fuzzy searching, try web rings, which are loose collectives of sites all devoted to the same basic subject. In a web ring, sites are connected so that you can move from one to the other by clicking the *Next Site* link at the bottom of a page. Alternatively, the starting-point of the ring usually offers a link to a master list of all the sites involved. There are web rings devoted to all sorts of subjects – from Afro-American issues **http://www.halcon.com/halcon/1ring.html** to the 'Rugrats'

< 143 >

Read about it online - Blogger

If you fancy having a go at doing your own weblog, Blogger **http://www.blogger.com** makes the whole process very easy. You can basically set up a weblog and update it via the site. It's also a good place to find other weblogs – there are thousands online now. ▲

TV show **http://www.geocities.com/Hollywood/Set/9404/webring.html**. Web rings can get very big (there are almost 800 sites in the Afro-American web ring) and they're a bit hit and miss. Some amateur/fan sites seem deranged, but others are brilliant mini-archives of useful material. Try Yahoo Webring **http://dir.webring.yahoo.com/rw** for a guide to existing rings and help with starting one of your own.

Research online

Most search sites are good for moving you on to other locations. But what about sites that are destinations in their own right and offer searchable databases of information? There are plenty of these online – look under the *Reference* category on Yahoo. As you might expect, you can research all sorts of things online, from films at the Internet Movie Database **http://uk.imdb.com**, to technical terminology at the PC Webopaedia **http://www.pcwebopedia.com/**. One of the areas in which the net is strongest is archives devoted to itself. Try the Usenet newsgroup archives at Deja.com **http://www.deja.com/usenet**. Alternatively, take a look at the excellent Research-It **http://www.itools.com/research-it/research-it.html** – a 'one-stop reference desk' which features dictionaries, a thesaurus, collections of quotations, maps and much else, all on the same page.

< 144 >

Also worth a look are the so-called 'knowledge sharing' sites, where ordinary people and professional experts answer questions on all sorts of subjects. The longest running of these sites is probably Allexperts.com **http://www.allexperts.com**, which got started in 1998. In the last year it's been joined by the likes of AskMe **http://www.askme.com**, Keen **http://www.keen.com**, Expert Central **http://www.expertcentral.com** and Epinions **http://www.epinions.com**. On some of these sites, you'll find product reviews written by ordinary people. On others, you can submit specific queries to experts. On some sites, you have to pay. On others, you just rate the answer you get. The pay-off for the people answering your question seems to be some kind of ego boost. They compete to make it into the regular charts of the site's best experts. As research resources, these sites can be surprisingly useful (as well as fun to browse). Wired Magazine ran an interesting piece about this new web fad, called 'Revenge of the Know-It-Alls', which is online at **http://www.wired.com/wired/archive/8.07/egoboo.html**. ▲

Using your browser to download files from the net

Go to the right places online and you can download software programs, sound files, video clips and animations, even text versions of classic novels. And you can do it in the much the same way that you browse the web. Just click on the appropriate link and after a while you'll have something potentially useful/entertaining on your hard drive. To do this, you'll actually be using FTP, one of those bits of net jargon that the acronymically challenged love to hate. The letters stand for File Transfer Protocol, something which

< 145 >

enables you to shift files around a network – either upload them to another computer or download them to your hard drive. A few years ago, you had to use a specialist FTP program and go to an FTP site – a sort of online file library – to download something. But these days, though FTP sites are still around, pretty much everything you need is on the web and you can get it with your browser. And much of it is available for free.

How free is free software?

You may have heard the internet described as a gift economy. It's a nice idea, though it seems to mean rather different things to different people. For some, it just means that there's lots of stuff up there you don't have to pay for. On one level, that's true. There is plenty of 'free' stuff online: Shakespeare plays, customised levels from computer games like Doom, all sorts of software – screensavers, personal organisers and pretty much everything you need for the net. And, if you don't count telephone charges, you can get much of this without handing over any money. Giving away product is now standard practice in the computer software industry. The idea is to build market share quickly and get people attached to a particular free product in the hope that they will ultimately pay for upgrades or add-ons. However, whilst you may be getting something for free, you are also agreeing to pay attention to a particular company's software. And you're locking yourself in to using it – once you get used to something, you're less likely to try something else. In the past, some American net service companies even gave away computers to build market share. However, to get your free PC, you had to sign up with a particular subscription-based ISP for a lengthy period of time. Usually, you also had to agree to look at certain ads and hand over personal data about what you did on the net.

< 146 >

That's a good illustration of the way most 'free stuff' has some kind of price. Consequently, some people say we shouldn't really think about money when we hear the word 'free'. According to Richard Stallman, the founder of the Free Software Foundation **http://www.fsf.org**, free software is 'a matter of freedom not price – the freedom to modify the software, redistribute the software and release improved versions of the software'. The idea here is that free software is open, that its source code – the stuff that makes it run – is freely available and can be modified. That's a big attraction for other programmers. If they find a problem with a free program, they can mess around with the code, come up with a solution and pass their new, improved version on to other users, who can also do their bit to make it better. As a result, say enthusiasts, where it has a chance to flourish, this kind of free software ends up more reliable than commercial alternatives. Idealistic programmers like this (hackers in the old sense of the word) have a more high-minded interpretation of the internet gift economy. Their idea is that you give away your time and the fruits of your intellectual labour. But you don't lose out, because you benefit from the efforts of numerous other idealists who also do their bit. In the end, nobody gets 'paid' but everybody gets by.

Read about it online – Eric Raymond

One of Open Source's prime movers is Eric Raymond. His homepage **http://www.tuxedo.org/~esr/** has the latest news and his influential essays. For more on Linux, try **http://www.linux.org** or **http://www.linux.org.uk**. Read about the Apache Project at **http://www.apache.org**. ▲

< 147 >

Obviously, this is a world away from a company like Microsoft, which keeps its Windows source code secret because it sees it as the rock on which its empire is founded. If you have a problem, you're supposed to call the Microsoft support line. They sort it out for you and then charge you all over again for a new version of the program in which all the old bugs have been fixed (and a whole set of new ones have been introduced). It's easy to be snide. And the idealistic vision of the internet gift economy does sound great. However, ordinary punters generally prefer the commercial way of doing things. They don't have the ability or the desire to fool around with source code. As a result, free software is more of a techie pursuit and has had more of an impact on the back end programs that keep the net running – for example, one of the more popular web server programs is a piece of free software called Apache.

That said, the Free Software movement, or rather the Open Source movement, as many now prefer to call it, is becoming more influential. As the net is increasingly dominated by business concerns, Open Source has become the repository for the idealism about individual empowerment and collective effort that used to cluster around the net in general. It's been described as the net's first political movement. Most of the attention now focuses on Linux, the free operating system developed in

Read about it online - Neal Stephenson

In 1999, the SF author Neal Stephenson published 'In the Beginning was the Command Line', a fascinating essay about different computer operating systems (Windows, the Mac OS and Linux). You can find it at **http://www.cryptonomicon.com/beginning.html**. ▲

< 148 >

part by Linus Torvalds. This isn't really for beginners – you still have to enter text commands to use it properly. But it is fast, robust and not as buggy as the commercial competition. People are working on a point and click interface for it, which may help it cross over to the mainstream.

In the last few years it's become clear that Microsoft is keeping tabs on the movement. You can too, via Salon's Free Software Project **http://www.salon.com/tech/fsp/index.html**. Salon contributor Andrew Leonard is currently writing a book about Open Source. In the spirit of his subject, he's making chapters available for comment prior to official publication. Feed did a special edition on Open Source **http://www.feedmag.com/oss/ossintro.html**. It's a little dated now, but does reflect the idealism the movement inspires.

To bring all this down to a more basic level, when you download something that calls itself 'free software' you need to be aware of what you're actually getting. There are three basic types of free software you're likely to find yourself downloading.

Freeware

You don't have to pay anything for this, though sometimes the creators ask for a kind of forfeit. You might be asked to send them a postcard of where you live. There are fully-fledged freeware programs but often many commercial software companies also release free patches.

Shareware

One of the more misunderstood terms in computer culture. Shareware is actually a 'try before you buy' thing. You're supposed to use an evaluation copy of a program for a given period. When that's over, if you want to keep using it, you have to register it and pay something. Some pieces

< 149 >

Read about it online – Literary Freeware

The SF author and critic Bruce Sterling made his book about hackers, 'The Hacker Crackdown', freely available online, arguing that since no one would actually download the whole book, his giveaway worked as a kind of ad for the print version. You'll find a web version of the book at **http://www.mit.edu/hacker/hacker.html**. ▲

of shareware 'time out': you can't use them after a certain point. Others continue to work but with certain features disabled. The makers can't force you to pay up if you continue to use their program. They rely on you being honest. So, if you like a program, you really should pay your shareware fees. Plus, shareware is a clever way of keeping software prices down. It bypasses the regular commercial channels and their built-in overheads. And it only works if everyone plays the game.

Beta versions

These are test versions of software currently in development and due for eventual commercial release. Betas let you see what's coming, but you also have to put up with bugs and crashes. Some betas time out after a given period. Companies don't charge for them, but neither do they offer technical support. Some run competitions in which you can pick up rewards for identifying bugs.

Getting started

Your web browser will do a fine job of downloading files, especially if you have Internet Explorer 5.x or Netscape Communicator 4.x. If you're

< 150 >

going to use your browser, you can get moving straight away. But before you do, it's worth spending some time sorting out your computer so you know where to put all those files. Create directories or folders on your hard drive called *Download* and *Program Files*. When you download a file, stick it in the *Download* directory or folder.

Downloading files from the Web

Start your browser and go to WinZip **http://www.winzip.com**. To speed up download times, files are often 'compressed' into a smaller form – known as archives. Before you can use them, you need to decompress them. WinZip is the leading compression/decompression program for the PC. You can't really get by without it and you can get an evaluation copy from the web site. Mac users should go to Aladdin Systems **http://www.aladdinsys.com** where they can get versions of Stuffit/Stuffit Expander, programs which will decompress/compress Macintosh files. Once the page comes up, click on the *Download Evaluation Version* link. On the *Download* page, look for the link to the appropriate program for your machine. Click on that and the download process will start. A dialog box will come up asking whether you want to open the file or save it. Pick the latter. You then have to specify where you want to save the file. Pick the *Download* directory you created, then click *Save*. The program will begin downloading. Once it's done, yet another dialog box will appear telling you so. Click *OK*. Incidentally, during a long download you don't have to wait around doing nothing. You can open a new browser window and get on the web. In both browsers, select the *File* menu, then *New*.

< 151 >

Downloading files from an FTP site

You can also access stuff from an FTP site, which is a little more complicated. If you want to keep things simple, go on to page 154. You can
come back to FTP when you are feeling more confident. Accessing FTP
sites with a browser is similar to accessing web pages. You key in an
address, click a button and go. FTP addresses are roughly similar to web
site addresses. However, they don't begin with **www** but with **ftp** and
when you enter them you start with **ftp://** rather than **http://** (although
with some browsers you don't have to bother). If they're for a specific
file they can be rather long, since they specify all the directories and
subdirectories it is stored in – for example **ftp://ftp.gamesdomain.
co.uk/pub/patches/**. That will take you to the FTP site run by Games
Domain, to a directory of patches, little add-on programs that tweak
computer games to make them run faster or look more gory.

FTP sites are slightly trickier to deal with than web sites. Some sites
are private. To get in, you need a username and password. Public sites
are accessed via what's known as anonymous FTP. You still have to enter
some details but you don't have to give your real name. When asked for
your username, enter anonymous, and for your password, enter your
email address. If you're using a browser, it will take care of anonymous
FTP automatically. FTP sites show you what the web was like before all
those corporate logos and flashy graphics we know and love: grey
backgrounds, spidery text and long, impenetrable lists of links to files.
It's enough to make an old geek get a little watery-eyed. That said,
Internet Explorer seems to make them all look like directories and folders
on your own computer. When you first arrive at an FTP site, you should
see something called the *Root Directory* – basically a welcome message,
general information about the site and a list of the main directories.

< 152 >

Tips – Shakespeare

You can download some e-Shakespeare from the SUN site at Imperial College **http://sunsite.doc.ic.ac.uk/media/literary/authors/shakespeare**. Click on the comedies directory and you'll be able to download the play that sums up your feelings about the net – 'A Comedy Of Errors' perhaps, or 'Much Ado About Nothing', perhaps. You can download even more free classic lit at Project Gutenberg **http://promo.net/pg/**. ▲

Some anonymous sites allow you access to everything. Others restrict some of their contents. The files that are open to all-comers are usually in the *pub* directory.

Click on a directory name and you'll see the contents of the directory – perhaps a series of sub-directories, which you click to open until you find the file you want. By a particular file you may see details of when it was uploaded on to the site and how big it is.

If you follow a set of links and can't find what you want, retrace your steps with the *Back* button. Alternatively, look for a link that says *Up to a higher level directory*, which is usually at the top of the page. On some sites you may see the following links – "*.*" and "*..*". Click on the former and you will go back to the root directory. Click the latter and you'll go up a directory level. All this becomes easy after a while, rather like moving around in the files and directories on your own hard drive.

When you first access an FTP site, look around for a text file called *Index* or *ReadMe*, which should tell how the site is laid out. When you find a file you want to download, click on it and the download process will start. Direct the file to your *Download* directory as before.

< 153 >

FTP troubleshooting

▶ *You can't get into the FTP site of your choice*
If you entered the exact location of the file, check that you got it right.
If you did, the site may be busy. Like good web sites, the best FTP sites
can get incredibly crowded.

▶ *The file you want isn't where it's supposed to be*
The site may have been reorganised and the file you want moved. Look
for the index file and check there.

▶ *You're halfway through a lengthy download and you lose your*
   connection
Both Navigator and Internet Explorer now have features that let you
resume downloads – i.e. log back on and pick up where you left off.
Alternatively, get a plug-in program called Get Right **http://www
.getright.com**. This boosts your browser's in-built FTP capabilities, adding
lots of useful features – you can resume downloads or automate them.
Of course, if you start getting plugs-ins (more on this on page 161), you
may as well get a proper FTP program – try Cute FTP **http://www.cuteftp.
com**. If you become more serious about the net, if you want to create
your own web page, you'll need a decent FTP program. It will make
uploading your homepage files to your ISP's server easier.

Working with downloaded files
So your Download directory is now bulging with all sorts of different
files. Most likely, you've got a selection of files tht when listed on your
computer will have a **.exe**, **.zip** or **.txt** suffix or extension. The latter

< 154 >

Jargon file - Extension

As in File Extension. A group of letters that come after the file name and identify what type of file it is. ▲

present no problem. Click on them and an application on your computer should open them for you. Files with the **.exe** extension are also easy to handle. **.exe** indicates a PC executable file. Click on one of these and it should start to run automatically. *Setup* will kick in and you'll be asked where you want to install the program. Pick your *Program Files* directory. Before you do this, run a virus check. Always virus-check **.exe** files you get from the net before you install them. **.zip** archives are a little more complicated. These are collections of files that have been compressed, using WinZip or something similar. You need to 'unzip' these archives before you can work with them. Get yourself the latest version of WinZip **http://www.winzip.com**. That's an **.exe** file, so it should be easy enough to install, then check out the *Help* files for directions on how to unzip the files. Once you've unzipped and installed, you could delete the original archive from your *Download* directory. If you want to keep them (just in case something goes wrong and you need to re-install), create a directory called *Archive* and put them there. Incidentally, you can use WinZip to compress files (perhaps before attaching them to email, or just to save space). Archives compressed on the Mac using Stuffit come with the extension **.sit** – you'll see a fair amount of them. As mentioned before, to deal with these, you'll need to get Stuffit/Stuffit Expander from Aladdin Systems **http://www.aladdinsys.com**.

< 155 >

File types

You're most likely to come across **.exe** and **.zip** online, if only because PC users are in a majority on the net. However, there are loads of other file types available online, either at web sites or FTP sites. Here's a few you may encounter, with details of the programs you need to view/open them.

.arc   An older type of PC compressed archive. Stuffit Expander can handle this

.arj   Another older PC compressed archive. Stuffit Expander also works here

.au, .aif Macintosh sound files. The Windows Media Player should play them

.avi   Video for Windows file. Again, the Windows Media Player will play these once downloaded.

.bin   MacBinary files. Macintoshes can cope with these automatically

.bmp   Bitmap files. Windows has something (e.g. Paintbrush) which displays these

.cpt   Mac Compact Pro archive. Stuffit Expander can decompress this

.doc   A Word file. WordPad on Windows 95/98 will cope with this

.exe   A PC executable file, to give it its official name. This will self-execute or extract itself when you double-click on it

.gif   As in Graphic Interchange Format, an image file found on web pages. Your browser displays this automatically

.gz, .gzip A Unix compressed archive. Stuffit Expander and WinZip will deal with these

.hqx   A Mac BinHex file. Stuffit Expander will convert it

.htm, .html As in Hypertext Markup Language. Your browser takes care of it

< 156 >

Tips - Compression

You occasionally come across files with double-barrelled extensions –
e.g. **.tar.gz**. This indicates that two levels of compression or encoding
have been used. A good program like Stuffit Expander should
automatically cope with both levels. ▲

.jpg, .jpeg Another type of compressed graphic found on web pages.
Browsers display these automatically

.lha, .lzh Yet another type of compressed archive. You can add an external
program to Winzip so it can cope with these. For more information,
go to **http://www.winzip.com/xextern.htm** on the WinZip site

.mid, .rmi As in MIDI sound files. You may need a external player/plug-
in to handle these

.mov, .qt QuickTime movie files. You can get a QuickTime player/plug-in
to play these

.mpg, .mpeg Compressed video files. You can get a separate player/plug-
in for these though your PC or Mac should have something that
can cope

.mp2, .mp3 An MPEG sound file. You can get an external player for these
(e.g. WinAmp). Windows Media Player will handle these too.

.pdf As in Portable Document Format. You need Adobe's Acrobat
viewer to open this

.pict Macintosh graphics file. Macs handle these automatically

.ra, ram Real Audio sound files. You'll need the RealPlayer plug-in for these

.sea Macintosh self-extracting archive. Just click

.sit Macintosh compressed archive. Use Stuffit Expander

< 157 >

Read about it online - Extensions

If you're puzzled by a particular file extension, what it means and what kind of program you need to handle it, you'll find some help at the Extensions Encyclopedia on the File Format site **http://fileformat.virtualave.net/ext_a.htm**. ▲

.tar Another compressed archive you occasionally come across. WinZip will open it

.txt, .text ASCII text files

.uue, .uu UUencoded files. Winzip and Stuffit Expander can convert these

.wav Another type of Windows sound file. The Media Player will handle this

.z Another Unix compressed archive. Stuffit Expander will open it

.zip PC compressed archive. Winzip or Stuffit Expander will unzip this

Once you've got WinZip and Stuffit Expander, you can cope with most of these. Browsers can also handle many of them. However, for some multimedia files you need to augment your browser with various plug-ins. Find out more on page 160.

Finding files on the net

Searching for files, especially from FTP sites, can be a bit hit and miss. It's fine if you know the exact name of the file you want. Then you can use an old piece of net software known as Archie to locate an FTP site that contains your file. FpArchie combines Archie with an FTP program (i.e. it finds the file, then downloads it). You should still find it at

< 158 >

http://tucows.technet2000.com.au/adnload/dlfparchie.html. It's probably easier to use the general FTP Search site at **http://ftpsearch.lycos.com**. You could also try the big search sites. If you're looking for software, try the 'software warehouse' web sites. Here are a few to be going on with. If you want to see what other programs you could use for mail, news, FTP and chat, these are great places to look.

Download.com **http://download.cnet.com/** Huge site maintained by ClNet. With a Quick Search and links to the top ten, newest and recommended downloads.

Shareware.com **http://shareware.cnet.com/** Another huge ClNet site with lots of stuff for PCs and Macs. Again, easy to navigate and search.

Stroud's **http://cws.internet.com** The full name is Stroud's Consummate Winsock Applications, which is a bit of a mouthful and not strictly accurate any more. Links to lots of useful internet apps plus reviews and information.

Tucows **http://www.tucows.com** Another huge repository of net software for PCs and Macs and lots of other stuff to download.

When you go to a download site, you're usually offered the choice of downloading from a local mirror site – i.e. a copy of the site maintained at another computer, usually on a different continent. The idea is to go somewhere less busy and save download time. Think before you pick a site. Don't immediately pick the nearest UK site. Trying to download something from the Demon Internet site in the early evening would be asking for trouble. Instead, find a site in a part of the world that's asleep, and hence unlikely to be online. Alternatively, pick a site in a country that's unlikely to have a huge net population. US sites can be fine if

< 159 >

you're downloading in the morning, UK time, when most Americans should be asleep.

Using your browser to access multimedia

Your browser will be able to play some of the audio/video files you find on the web. If it can't, it will tell you that you need an extra piece of software, most likely a plug-in. Plug-ins are booster programs that enable your browser to handle specific types of web multimedia. You don't need to know how to use a plug-in; you just click a link and it goes to work, usually playing the multimedia content within your browser window. The plug-in idea was first developed by Netscape. You can get plug-ins for Internet Explorer, but, just to be helpful, Microsoft introduced its own way of handling multimedia within the browser – ActiveX. ActiveX controls are a bit like plug-ins in that they are integrated with your browser and enable it to play multimedia within its main window. There are all sorts of other booster programs you can use to either handle media files or help with other browsing tasks. Because they aren't completely integrated into your browser, these are sometimes referred to as browsing companions or helper applications or helper apps or utilities

Tips - Older Computers

To get the best out of web multimedia, the old PC you bought five years ago won't really do. The minimum you need is a soundcard, a good graphics/video card with at least 2 Mb of memory (more will make video look better), a reasonably speedy Pentium processor and a 56.6Kbps modem. ▲

< 160 >

or add-ons. In the end, though, the terminology is neither here nor there. All you need to know is that there are some more programs you might find useful when it comes to dealing with online multimedia.

Getting plug-ins, ActiveX controls and browsing companions

The new versions of Navigator and Internet Explorer come with lots of the more popular plug-ins and ActiveX controls pre-installed – things like RealPlayer and Shockwave. Navigator, in particular, makes it easy to check what you've got. Select the *Help* menu, then *About Plug-ins* and you'll see a handy list. Often web sites that use multimedia provide links to the appropriate plug-in. If you're using Navigator and you visit a page with a multimedia file it can't handle, a dialog box will appear, directing you to the Netscape plug-in page **http://home.netscape.com/plugins/index.html**. Incidentally, this is a good place to find out more about plug-ins in general. There's also a useful search engine that helps you find the right plug-in to play a particular type of media file.

Some plug-ins install themselves. With others, you may need to close your browser (and any other applications you're running) and start the installation process yourself. Generally plug-ins are executable files with the extension **.exe**: just click on them and the installation process will start up.

If you're using Internet Explorer and you come across a page that uses an ActiveX control you haven't got, your browser will start to download it. It may flash up a *Security Warning* screen to check that it's OK. Some ActiveX controls go to work once you've downloaded them. Others need to be installed. Find out more at Microsoft's Active X page **http://www.microsoft.com/com/tech/activex.asp** or CNet's ActiveX

< 161 >

section **http://download.cnet.com/downloads/0-10081.html**. Plug-ins and browsing companions are available at the software warehouse sites mentioned on page 302. Download.com runs a special sub-site **http://www.cnet.com/internet/ 0-3773.html**, where you'll find a vast list of plug-ins and browsing companions (plus lots of useful browsing tips for both big browsers).

The plug-ins you need

The key plug-ins you need are RealNetworks' RealPlayer, which handles streaming audio/video/animation (the files play as you download them, you don't need to wait until they're completely downloaded) and Macromedia's Shockwave and Flash Players, which are the standard tools for interactive multimedia and animated graphics on the web. Your browser will probably come with all of these pre-installed. If it doesn't, or you want to get the latest versions, you can download RealPlayer from Real Networks' UK web site at **http://uk.real.com** – RealPlayer Basic is the free player. You can get the players for Shockwave and Flash – both are free – from Macromedia **http://www.macromedia.com/shockwave/**. You have to enter some personal details – your computer's operating system and processor, your connection speed, your name and email address – and then click the *Download* link/button. If you read the section on downloading (page 151), it should be straightforward.

RealPlayer will handle most audio/video files. If you fancy an alternative, Internet Explorer comes with the Windows Media Player, which does something similar. You could also try Apple's QuickTime. You can download the full version, which includes plug-ins amongst other things and handles sound and 3D visuals as well as video, from **http://www.apple.com/quicktime/**. Read the QuickTime documentation. Once you've

< 162 >

installed QuickTime proper, you may need to locate the plug-ins and then put them in the Plug-in folder of your browser. RealPlayer will play the much-discussed MP3 music files (there's more on these on page 228). But RealNetworks also do a more specialised program called RealJukebox **http://www.real.com/rjcentral/player**, which you can use to play music files, record music you've downloaded from the web onto CDs, create playlists, listen to online radio stations and more. However, the most popular audio player is probably WinAmp **http://www.winamp.com**, which handles most MPEG audio files, specifically MP3s.

Plug-ins and browsing companions aren't just about interactive multimedia. They can do all sorts of things. To see just how many are available, visit CNet's browsers section **http://www.cnet.com/internet/0-3773.html** and look for their browsing companions directory. In the meantime, here's a few you might enjoy:

Adobe Acrobat Reader **http://www.adobe.com/products/acrobat/readstep.html**
  Lets you read documents created using Adobe's Acrobat graphics program.
Babylon **http://www.babylon.com/** An all-purpose reference tool that does instant searches on keywords on web pages, translates and searches dictionaries.
Copernic **http://www.copernic.com/** Search tool that searches up to 80 engines at once, sorts results, eliminates dead links and more.
Even Better Express **http://www.evenbetter.com/evenbetterexpress.html**
  Lets you compare prices instantly while you're browsing online shops without leaving the shop's website.
FlySwat **http://www.flyswat.com/** Click on a word on a web page (or other documents) and get a list of links to related information.

< 163 >

Get Right **http://www.getright.com** Makes downloading files from the web easier.

KatieSoft **http://www.katiesoft.com/** Divide your browser window into four and read four sites at once, or something.

NetSonic **http://www.netsonic.com/index.asp** Probably the most popular web accelerator, this stores your favourite pages in its cache so you can get at them quicker.

NetZip **http://www.netzip.com** Unzip compressed files via your browser and more.

Pulse Player **http://www.pulse3d.com** Lets you view Toy Story-style 3D computer animation online.

SurfSaver **http://www.surfsaver.com/** Lets you store and save web pages directly from your browser into searchable folders.

Third Voice **http://www.thirdvoice.com** Annotate web pages, find information relating to keywords on the page and chat with other users about the pages you're visiting.

uTok **http://www.utok.com** Another program that lets you leave notes on web pages and read what other users have said.

Window Washer **http://www.webroot.com/washer.htm** Protects your privacy by automatically cleaning up your browser's cache, cookies, history, recent document list and more.

Helper applications and browser companions

You can configure your browser so that if you come across the particular file type a browsing companion/helper app handles, the browser will start it up and it will then play the file in a separate window. If you do want a helper app to automatically handle a particular kind of file while you're browsing, you need to associate it with that file type. To do this:

< 164 >

Read about it online - Cartoon Companion

For a rather literal spin on the idea of the browsing companion, try
BonziBuddy **http://www.bonzi.com/bonzibuddy/bonzibuddyfreehom.asp**, a
cartoon purple gorilla who, once installed on your desktop,
accompanies you as you surf, offering suggestions about other links,
cracking jokes and more. ▲

▶ If you're using **Internet Explorer**, you'll need to open **Windows Explorer**, then select the **View** menu, then **Folder Options**, then the **File Types** tab. Use the **New Type** button to add a new file type.

▶ In **Navigator**, select the **Edit** menu, then **Preferences**, then **Applications**, then just fill out the relevant boxes. Use the **New Type** button to add a new file type. Aside from the file extension, you'll be asked for the MIME type – something like audio/x-mpeg or video/quicktime. Don't worry too much about this: it's just another way of identifying and organising files on line. If you don't know the MIME type for a file, check in the documentation for the helper app you're using.

▶ In the **Mac** version of **Internet Explorer**, select the **Edit** menu then **Preferences**, then, in the **Receiving Files** section, click on **File Helpers**. Here you can change the various helper apps your browser works with.

This process can be a bit fiddly but you can get a free program which does it all for you – WAssociate **http://www.xs4all.nl/~wstudios/Associate/index.html**.

< 165 >

Tips - Java Security Problems

Unscrupulous types can also use Javascript to snatch your email address while you browse their site. You can then find yourself on the receiving end of a lot of spam. You'll find tips on how to avoid this on page 337. ▲

Java

Java is a programming language developed by Sun Microsystems which, amongst other things, can be used to deliver interactive web content. Programmers use Java to create applets, small programs that are placed directly on web pages. They can also add interactivity to their pages with something called JavaScript. If you're using an older browser (version 3.X or before), you may have problems with JavaScript and Java applets. Otherwise you'll be fine. Often you probably won't be aware when your browser is running a Java applet. But sometimes you have to wait for one to download before you can do anything. Java is mostly used to create little animations on web pages and interactive games/routines – everything from calculators to real-time chat. Most web chat rooms now use Java applets rather than plug-ins. If you want to see what applets can do, try the demos at **http://gamelan.earthweb.com/**. Alternatively go to Sun's own Java page **http://java.sun.com** for more applets and updates on Java in general.

Next step

Your browser's kitted out with plug-ins and add-ons – you're ready to check out online multimedia. For advice on where to find it, go to page 227. Alternatively, if you feel like using the net to communicate, head straight to the next section. ▲

< 166 >

Email

Email has been around almost as long as the net proper. When ARPANET (a trial network that was essentially the beginning of the net) was set up in 1969, the idea was that it would enable the sharing of scarce computing resources. But the researchers using it soon began sending messages across the network, first about official business, then about office gossip, then about the science-fiction novels they were reading. Email is an accepted part of our lives now. Today, every major business and institution has an email contact address. TV shows, radio stations, newspapers and magazines can't do without them. Email regularly features in films and novels and the media often run stories about email leaks and mail viruses.

It's not hard to see why email has caught on. For the cost of a local telephone call (or less), you can quickly send messages to someone on the other side of the world. It's easy to save email and keep track of your correspondence. It's cheaper than faxing and you don't have to worry about paper and ink. You can send more than plain text – attaching image and sound files to mail is simple. For no extra cost you can send mail to lots of people at the same time, building up informal

Jargon file – ARPANET

ARPA stands for Advanced Research Projects Agency, essentially the Pentagon's R&D department during the cold war So, as you might expect, the ARPANET was the network it set up to test out new computer communications technology. ▲

< 167 >

Read about it online - Email Fiction

To sample an experiment in email fiction, try Carl Steadman's Two Solitudes **http://www.freedonia.com/ts/**. Subscribe and over the next few days you'll receive a series of emails in which two people play out an online romance. ▲

mailing lists where you can thrash out political problems or discuss last night's TV (more on this on page 194). Email makes it easier to stay in touch with friends and business colleagues abroad. And thanks to the rise of web mail and the spread of cybercafes, it's becoming the preferred way of staying in touch with home while you're travelling for business or pleasure.

There's more to email than speed, convenience and ease of use. Perhaps because it sits somewhere between speech and writing, because it's like a letter with the immediacy of a telephone call, it seems to encourage directness and intimacy. Email can also be less potentially embarrassing than face-to-face contact, which might be why it's finding favour as a way to ask people out on a first date. It's also being used by some to dump boy or girlfriends. When it is, this intimate form of communication can seem very impersonal and much harder to bear for the person on the receiving end. This is a good reminder that there is a downside to email. Sure, it can help us communicate more effectively. At the same time, we're now swamped by vast amounts of email that we're supposed to deal with straightaway. You don't just need to learn how to send and receive email. You need to learn how to cope with it too.

< 168 >

What software do you need?

All you need really is your web browser. Netscape's Communicator/
Navigator and Microsoft's Internet Explorer both come with mail
packages (called Messenger and Outlook Express, respectively). Both
are now as good as most of the specialist mail programs. So save yourself some time and use your browser. Incidentally, to find Messenger,
start up Communicator first, then select the *Communicator* menu,
then *Messenger*. Both these programs are fine. If you have the disk
space, you could install both and switch between them to see which
you prefer. However, you will have to nominate one as your default, so
that when you click an email link on a web page (for example, to send
mail to the person responsible for the page), the computer knows
which program to start up. All very simple, or it ought to be. However,
rather irritatingly, Netscape have made it difficult for you to use their
Navigator browser and have Microsoft's Outlook Express as your
default mailer. For similar reasons, Microsoft don't make it easy for
you to use the Explorer browser with Netscape's Messenger mail software. As ever, the Mac version of Outlook Express is slightly different.
It's still easy enough to figure out, but where there might be potential
for confusion I've tried to include specific instructions for Mac users of
Outlook Express.

Tips – Try Eudora

If you want a specialist mail program, go for Eudora **http://www.eudora.com**.
There are two versions – Light, which is free and fine for most people's
purposes and Pro, which has lots of snazzy extra features. ▲

< 169 >

Configuring your mail software

The mail program that came with the browser supplied by your ISP may have been configured during the general installation process. However, if you're installing something from scratch, you'll need to enter a few details before you can send any mail.

You may have to enter any and all of the following:

Your name: As in Jim McClellan

Your email address: Your ISP will have given you this when you signed on – something like **yourname@yourserviceprovider.net**

Your return email address: Usually the same as above, though you can enter something different if you're going to be picking up replies at another location (e.g. work)

Your user name (also known as the account name): The first part of your email address – i.e. **jim.mcclellan**

Outgoing Mail Server (SMTP): The computer at your ISP that handles the mail you send to other people. This will usually be something like **mail.yourserviceprovider.net**

Incoming Mail Server (POP3): The computer on which the mail sent resides. Again, this will be something like **mail.yourserviceprovider.net**

Password: The password your ISP gave you when you signed up.

▶ With **Outlook Express**, the first time you use it, the **Internet Connection Wizard** should take you through configuration. If it doesn't, start it up yourself by selecting the **Tools** menu, then **Accounts**. Click the **Add** button, then **Mail**. If you need to change existing account information (you might change ISPs and email address), pick your account then click on **Properties**.

< 170 >

▶ In **Messenger**, select **Edit**, then **Preferences**. Then click on **Identity** and **Mail Server** in turn to enter the relevant information.

▶ In the **Mac** version of **Outlook Express**, click the **Tools** menu, then **Accounts**, then **Mail**. With a new Mac/iMac, you can do this via the **Apple** menu. Select **Control Panels**, then **Internet** and you'll call up a dialog box where you can enter details about your email account.

Your first message

Now's the time to bug your friends with one of those 'Hey, I just got on the net' messages. (If you really want to wind them up, call them repeatedly to see whether they've got your mail yet.) If you want to avoid irritating your friends, send a message to the Guardian instead. We've set up a program that automatically replies to all mail sent to **guidetest @guardian.co.uk**. It may be a touch impersonal but it will let you check whether your first mail reached its destination. Open your mail program and click the **New Message/Compose Message** button. A window will open which is split into two parts. The bottom part is where you write your message. The top part is where you write the address and the subject. Click in the **To:** field to move the cursor there, then enter the address – **guidetest@guardian.co.uk**). Don't add an extra period at the end – however they may appear in the media, email addresses do not end in full stops. If all this looks rather confusing, go back to page 24 for more information.

Your own address may already be in the **From:** field. In the **Subject:** field, put a brief description of your message – My First Message or some such. Pretty soon you'll discover how useful the **Subject:** field is and you'll curse people who don't bother entering anything there.

< 171 >

Ignore the other fields in this window for the moment. Click in the bottom part of the window and write your mail. What you put here is up to you – you might want to tell us whether you think this book is any use. On second thoughts, perhaps you should just say what sort of day you're having.

Email style

At school, you may have been taught how to lay out a letter. None of what you learnt really applies to email. You don't need to write your address in the top right-hand corner. When people get your email, their mailbox will show them who sent it and what it's about (if you enter something in the *Subject:* field). Some people don't bother opening their mail with a 'Dear Jim' and just get straight to the message. Email purists also don't sign off with a 'Yours, Dave' or whatever, but instead include a personal 'signature file', aka 'sig file'. This usually contains your contact details – name, email address, perhaps snail mail address and telephone number(s) – plus a jokey/deep quotation that shows what an interesting/deep/sexy individual you are. A few years ago, 'So long and thanks for all the fish' from Douglas Adams' Hitchhiker's Guide to the Galaxy was a popular sig file choice, so popular that it has now been

Tips - Email Conventions

Don't be intimidated by people who insist that email should look a certain way and should end with a sig file. If you want your email to be like your snail mail, fine. The only principle you should stick to is to keep things brief wherever possible. ▲

< 172 >

Jargon file - Snail Mail

Snide slang for old-fashioned mail that comes in envelopes, is delivered by the Post Office and takes a lot longer than email to arrive. Usually. ▲

officially outlawed, along with all quotations from Monty Python, Blackadder and The Fast Show.

Your mail package will let you compose a signature file and save it. When you write mail, you will be able to automatically to paste it in at the end of the message.

▶ In **Outlook Express**, select the **Tools** menu then **Options** then the **Signatures** tab. You can then compose your signature and choose to add it to all messages.
▶ In **Messenger**, select **Edit** then **Preferences**, then **Identity** in the **Mail and Newsgroups** section.
▶ In the **Mac** version of **Outlook Express**, select the **Tools** menu then **Signatures**. When you compose a new message, there's a **Signature** toolbar you can use to add your sig file or not.

With email, brevity and directness are key. People are paying to download your mail, so the idea is not to add to their bills, in however minuscule a way. Perhaps because it's somewhere between speech and writing, email tends to be more informal and slangy than snail mail. In theory, you don't need to take quite as much care with your grammar and upper and lower cases. Of course, sending illiterate pieces of doggerel isn't good email style either. Both Messenger and Outlook Express have spell

< 173 >

checker programs that will automatically go over messages before you send them.

TLAs and smileys

You can compress messages even further by using TLAs, as in Three-Letter Acronyms. This includes things like WRT – with regards to; IMO – in my opinion; LOL – laogh out loud; OTOH – on the other hand; RTFM – read the f- manual. (OK, so they don't always have three letters.) Most of these can be understood quickly, without resorting to some kind of TLA dictionary. That's the theory, anyway. The TLAs above are all capitalised, though people tend to write them in lower case. Capitals are used for emphasis in email – they're the online equivalent of shouting. Shy away from them unless you really need to make a point. It can look rather rude and people do get the hump.

You can also use emoticons, aka smileys, in your online communications. These are little sideways-on faces constructed from keyboard characters, which are used to indicate emotion – :-) means happy; :-(indicates sadness, and ;-) is supposed to signal irony. The idea here is that it can be hard to pick up the tone or spirit of a piece of mail, especially if it's supposed to be funny/sarcastic. Hence smileys, which supply the kind of facial cues you'd get if you were talking face to face. However, most people over the age of fourteen don't pepper their ordi-

Read about it online - TLAs

For a pretty comprehensive list of smileys and TLAs (and a useful glossary of general net jargon), try Netlingo at **http://www.netlingo.com**. ▲

< 174 >

nary paper letters with little faces to help the recipient understand when they're being ironic. So smileys may be a product of the novelty/strangeness of email, something that we'll see less and less as the years go by.

HTML or plain text mail?

Email used to be plain text. But now we also have HTML mail, which means letters with pictures, links and more. Most new mail programs – e.g. Messenger and Outlook Express – automatically use HTML mail for email unless you tell them otherwise. Some older mail programs may have difficulties with this. If you send HTML mail to someone whose software can't handle it, it will appear in their inbox as text plus an attached HTML file. If the person you are sending email to does have problems receiving HTML you can choose which type you send:

▶ In **Outlook Express**, once you've opened a **New Message** window, select the **Format** menu then either **Plain Text** or **Rich Text (HTML)**.

▶ With **Messenger**, when you're writing your mail, click on the **Message Sending Options** button in the bottom-left corner of the **Address** window. Then look for the drop-down **Format** menu on the left that will let you pick text or HTML or both.

Sending your first message

You're happy with your message. You can now choose to go online and send the mail straight away. Alternatively, you can stay offline and send your mail later. It will be transferred to your **Outbox** or **Unsent Mail** folder, depending on which mail program you're using. You can then write more messages and stack them up in the **Outbox** to send all at

< 175 >

once. If you close your mail program without sending your mail, you may get a brief reminder asking whether you want to send it now. With unsent or queued mail, most mail software will send it automatically the next time you check your own mail. To send it straightaway, just get online then press the **Send** button.

Most mail software is set up to save a copy of mail you send, usually in the **Outbox** or in the **Sent Items** folder. If you don't want to save your mail:

▶ In **Outlook Express**, select the **Tools** menu, then **Options**, then click the **Send** tab, then remove the tick in the box next to **Save copy of sent messages in the Sent Items folder**.

▶ In **Messenger** select the **Edit** menu, then **Preferences**, then select **Copies and Folders** (it's under **Mail and Newsgroups**). Then remove the tick in the box next to **Place a copy in folder 'Sent' on 'Local Mail'**.

▶ In the **Mac** version of **Outlook Express**, select the **Edit** menu, then **Preferences**, then click the **Compose** tab and look for the relevant text box.

After you've sent your mail to **guidetest@guardian.co.uk**, if everything's working, you should get a reply from us in a couple of hours – perhaps quicker, though don't hold me to that.

Troubleshooting

Occasionally, email might be bounced back to you unsent. Usually, the problem is caused by errors in the address. Don't add spaces or extra periods. If you've checked everything and it appears ok, the person you're

< 176 >

mailing may have changed address. Alternatively, the problem may be at the ISP where your intended recipient has his or her mailbox – their computers may be down – in which case, try sending your message later.

Getting your mail

Email sent to you sits in your mailbox on your ISP's mail server until you go and get it. To pick up your mail:

▶ In **Outlook Express**, click **Send and Receive**.
▶ In **Messenger**, click the **Get Message** button

You'll connect to the net and your messages will be downloaded. Log off. A window may open showing the new mail in your Inbox. If not, click on your **Inbox** icon or button. For each piece of new mail, you'll see a line of information, telling you who sent it and when and what it's about. Double-click on that and the message will open in a new window. Most people prefer to check their mail manually. You can get your mailer to pick it up automatically at regular intervals. This is mainly of use if you (a) get an awful lot of mail and (b) if you have an always on connection or unmetered access. If that sounds like you:

▶ In **Outlook Express**, select the **Tools** menu, then **Options**, then click the **General** tab. Make sure there is a tick in the box next to **Check for new messages every X minutes** and change the figure to suit your requirements.
▶ In **Messenger**, select the **Edit** menu, then **Preferences**, then **Mail Servers**, then click the **Edit** button, then tick/change the line **Check for mail every X minutes**.

< 177 >

Tips - Multiple Identities

Outlook Express lets you create a different "identity" for each person that uses it. Each user can then maintain separate messages, contacts, and personal settings. To create a new identity, select the *File* menu, then *Identities*, then *Add New Identity*. You can also choose to password this. To switch to a particular identity, select the *File* menu, then *Switch Identity*. ▲

▶ In the *Mac* version of *Outlook Express*, select the *Tools* menu, then *Schedules*, then *File*, then *New* then *Schedule*, then enter the necessary information.

Most programs remove or trim down email headers – i.e. the technical information about when the message was sent and by whom, the path it took on its way to you and other bits and pieces. Headers can sometimes useful if you're on the receiving end of junk email or abusive messages and want to find out where they're coming from. To display the full header:

▶ In *Outlook Express*, open the mail you're interested in, select the *File* menu, then *Properties*, then click the *Details* tab.
▶ In *Messenger*, click on the message, select the *View* menu, then *Headers*, then *All*.

Replying to your mail

A friend has emailed you and you want to reply. Just click on the *Reply To* button. This will open a *New Message* window with

< 178 >

your friend's address already filled in. In the **Subject:** field, it will say 'Re: whatever your friend entered in the Subject line'. When replying to mail, it can be helpful to quote from the previous message. If you use the **Reply To** button on some mailers, when the message window opens it will display the past message – indented with 'quote tags', as in:

```
>Jim
>blah blah blah
>Wally
```

You can then edit this, selecting the bits you want to keep and adding your own contributions, as in:

```
On the 10th March, Wally wrote
>blah blah blah
See what you mean, Wally.
Jim
```

The end result simulates a kind of conversation and helps to keep track of ideas over several messages. But make sure you edit the previous message so that only the appropriate bits are included. Don't send people

Tips - Reading Mail Offline

Perhaps this sounds a bit obvious, but whenever possible work on your mail offline. Once you've downloaded mail sent to you, disconnect and then read it. It's easy to forget to log off and end up paying BT or whoever for all that time puzzling over the right smiley. ▲

< 179 >

back a complete copy of their previous mail when replying – it can get irritating, especially if the first mail was rather long.

Conventional wisdom says you should reply to email quickly, if only to confirm you received the message. Sometimes, if a reply doesn't appear for a while, you do start to wonder whether your mail actually reached its destination. Then again, just because email goes a lot faster, you don't have to as well. One of the few bad things about email is the way it often carries a kind of implicit pressure to be more productive, to speed things up and write back NOW!

Carbon copies and forwarding

Email makes it easy to send the same message to groups of people. You can do this either by using carbon copy (CC) or blind carbon copy (BCC). If you use the **Cc** option, recipients will see who else got your message. If you use **Bcc**, they won't.

▶ In **Outlook Express**, you'll see a **Cc:** line underneath the **To:** line. Type in the addresses you want here. If you want to use the Bcc option but can't see it, move your cursor over the **Cc:** – it will turn into a button. Click on it and you'll be able to access the **Bcc:** line.

▶ In **Messenger**, to add Cc and Bcc addresses, just click the **To:** button in the **Address** window.

It's also easy to forward mail. Once a message is open, just click the **Forward** button and a **New Message** window will open with the old message in quote tags. Then enter the address of the person you want to forward it to and add any comments.

< 180 >

Address books and email directories

If someone sends you mail, you can add their contact details to an address book for future reference – helpful if you find it difficult to remember email addresses or type them out without making mistakes. You can also enter more information – whether they prefer HTML mail or text, for example.

▶ In **Outlook Express**, click the **Address book** button. To add a new entry to the book, click the **New** button, then select **New Contact**. To send a message to someone, click on their name then click the **Action** button, then select **Mail**. To add more information to their entry, click on their name then the **Properties** button. Outlook Express also keeps an easy-access **Contacts** list on the bottom left of the screen. To write to someone on this list, double click on their name.

▶ In **Messenger**, select the **Communicator** menu, then **Address Book**. To add someone to the book, select **Personal** from the browser bar on the left, click the **New Card** button then fill out the relevant details. To send a message, click on the person's name then click the **New Msg** button. To add more detail to their entry, click on the name then the **Properties** button.

Both Outlook Express and Messenger are set up to allow you to search various online directories for email addresses. These are a bit hit and miss. Some rely on submissions from users. Others use software that trawls the net for addresses. They all have a definite American bias. All of them will turn up plenty of results – especially if you do a simple search on a name. But you then have to figure out which, if any, might belong to the person you're trying to contact.

< 181 >

Once you're online:

▶ In **Outlook Express**, click the **Address Book** button then click the **Find People** toolbar button. A **Find People** dialog box will come up. Click the **Look in** drop-down window to pick a directory to search, then enter the name of the person you're searching for and click the **Find Now** button. (This works slightly differently in the Mac version but it's easy enough to understand).

▶ In **Messenger**, get online, then select the **Communicator** menu, then **Address Book**. In the dialog box that comes up, you can click on a directory in the left frame, then write a name in the text box, then click the **Search For** button

Email and attachments

You can attach all sorts of different files to your messages – everything from images and sounds to video and programs. However, most files you might want to send are binary (8 bit), whilst email is all 7 bit ASCII text. So before files can be sent, they have to be converted into ASCII. Then they'll be converted back to their proper form by the person who gets your mail. In theory. Attaching files has been made easy by modern mail software. In Outlook Express or Messenger, just click the **Attach** button on the toolbar (the one with the paperclip on it), then find the file you want to send in your directory, then click on **Attach**. However, problems are caused by people not checking whether recipients of their mail can cope with particular types of attachments. A few years ago, most PC mail programs converted attachments using something called UUencode. That was replaced by something called MIME which is now the standard. Mac mail programs also used something called Bin Hex. Modern mail programs

< 182 >

can cope with all of these. However, when it comes to email, many people are happy chugging along with the old program they've always used. Until they get a chunk of indecipherable gibberish in their mailbox.

So before you send an attachment to someone, find out what conversion method their mail program uses. If they use a newer mailer, there should be no problem. If they have an older program, you'll have to use UUencode. To use UUencode for attachments:

▶ In **Outlook Express**, select the *Tools* menu, then *Options*, then the *Send* tab. The *Mail sending format* will be set to *HTML*. Click the box by *Plain text* to change it, then click *Settings*. You can then specify either MIME or UUencode.

▶ In **Messenger**, click the *Message Sending Options* button in the bottom-left corner of the *Address* section of the *Composition* window then click in the box next to *UUencode instead of MIME for attachments*.

▶ In the *Mac* version of **Outlook Express**, select the *Edit* menu, then *Preferences*, then select *Compose* and make the changes as required.

Tips - Viruses

Be wary of Microsoft Word attachments. They can be host to various macro-viruses. Mail-borne viruses spread by sending themselves to all the addresses they find in the contacts book on a particular machine. If you open the attachment, they infect your machine. So even if the document was sent by a friend, check it before you open it. ▲

< 183 >

If you receive mail with an attachment, both Outlook Express and Messenger will usually show picture attachments in the body of the message. Otherwise, there should be a paperclip icon at the top of the message when you open it. Click that. The file's name will appear. Click that and you'll be asked if you want to open it or save it.

Managing your email

Email doesn't clutter up your office like the stuff that comes on paper. But it can get out of control. So try to read messages as soon as you get them and reply reasonably quickly. Messages in your *Inbox* will probably be sorted according to the date they were received. You can order them in another way – by sender, subject, etc. In Messenger or Outlook Express, select the *View* menu, then *Sort* or *Sort By*. Be ruthless when it comes to deleting messages. It's easy to save your mail, but often you don't need to. If you do want to keep mail, file it when you've read it. You can set up specific folders for mail from different people, organisations, mailing lists or subjects, then transfer it easily as you read it. To create new folders, select the *File* menu, then *Folder* or *New Folder*. To file a piece of mail:

▶ In **Outlook Express,** select a message, then select the *Edit* menu then *Move to Folder*.
▶ In **Messenger**, click the *File* button on the toolbar.
▶ In the **Mac** version of **Outlook Express**, select the *Message* menu, then *Move To*.

You can create filters that automatically direct incoming mail into specific folders rather than the *Inbox*.

< 184 >

▶ In **Outlook Express,** select the *Tools* Menu, then *Message Rules*, then *Mail*.

▶ In **Messenger**, select the *Edit* menu, then *Message Filters*. Click on the *New* button to create a filter.

▶ In the **Mac** version of **Outlook Express**, select the *Tools* menu, then *Rules* then click on *New Rule*.

Next you need to specify what your software should look for and what it should do with a message that fits the parameters you set. Say you get a lot of mail from a particular business colleague. You can put his or her email address in the *Sender* category, then arrange to transfer it to a special mailbox/folder. Alternatively, if they never say anything interesting, you could get it diverted straight to the trash. Outlook Express can be set up so it won't bother to download certain messages – i.e. junk mail – from your ISP's mail server. Actually, there are now many programs specifically designed to block spam. For more on this, go to page 339.

Web mail, redirection and other mail services

In the last few years, web mail – email you read and send via a web page – has gone from being incredibly popular to being totally ubiquitous. Many industry analysts failed to predict this, though perhaps you can't blame them. Their thinking must have been that since most people online already had an email address (courtesy of their ISP), they wouldn't need an extra one. With hindsight, the appeal looks obvious. Web mail makes it very easy to get your mail whilst travelling. All you need is a computer with a connection to the web. You can also change your ISP without having to inform friends and colleagues of your new email address. You can create multiple email addresses and use them for different things.

< 185 >

You can 'maintain your independence' from work or college, according to one Free Mail site. Translation: if you have an official mailbox at work and if that's your only connection to the net, you can set up something more personal on the web. If you share an account at home and want to keep some mail private, a web mailbox is a good option.

Web mail isn't problem-free. Usually it doesn't cost anything, but often you have to look at ads while you get your mail. Sometimes your mail may also contain ads. Given the way web mail works, you'll end up composing some of your mail online – which may mean a bigger telephone bill. The web can be slow, which means getting your mail will be slow too. Some web mail services – in particular Microsoft's Hot Mail – have had problems with spam. Security is also an issue. Hot Mail was hacked into in 1999. So it's probably sensible to use web mail mainly for personal chat. If you need it for business purposes, have a look at some of the web mail services that encode your mail to keep it private – for example Hushmail **http://www.hushmail.com** – there's more on this on page 332.

Here's a list of some of the biggest web mail services:

AOL Mail	**http://aolmail.aol.com**
Email.com	**http://www.email.com**
Eudora Web-Mail	**http://www.eudoramail.com**
Excite	**http://www.excite.co.uk**
Hot Mail	**http://www.hotmail.com**
iName	**http://www.iname.com**
Juno	**http://www.juno.com**
Lycos Communications	**http://comm.lycos.com**
Mail.com	**http://www.mail.com**
Net@ddress	**http://www.netaddress.com**

< 186 >

Tips - Global Net Cafes

Web mail is a great tool for staying in touch while you're globe-trotting. Of course, you need to know where the cybercafes are in the city/country you're headed to. Do a bit of advance research at the Internet Café Guide **http://www.netcafeguide.com/**. ▲

Talk 21   **http://www.talk21.co.uk**
Yahoo Mail   **http://mail.yahoo.co.uk**

There are loads more web mail services to choose from – for a more complete list, go to Yahoo **http://www.yahoo.co.uk** and do a search on Free Email. Alternatively, the Free Email Providers Guide **http://www.fepg.net/** lists 1400 different operations around the world, along with reviews and guides to the different services. You'll find more advice on which web mail service to pick at Free Email Address **http://www.free-email-address.com/**.

Some web mail services are designed to work in tandem with your ISP mail account. Take Big Foot **http://www.bigfoot.com**, where you can create an email address for life – **jim.mcclellan@bigfoot.com** or some such.

Read about it online - Self-Destructing Web Mail

Some web mail services offer encrypted secure mail that 'autoshreds' after a set time, so that you can preserve your privacy. Try ZipLip **http://www.ziplip.com**, Safe Message **http://www.safemessage.com** or 1on1mail **http://www.1on1mail.com**. ▲

< 187 >

You give this to people. Mail arriving at this address is redirected to your ISP mail account. Once again, this reduces hassle when it comes to changing ISPs. Other companies (e.g. iName) let you pick a name that sounds better than your ISP address (in certain cases, charging you for it). Once again, this address is the one you give out and mail is redirected to your ISP mail account. Bigfoot offers some other useful services. It's good at blocking spam. It sends you reminders when important birthdays or anniversaries are looming. When you go on holiday, it automatically sends messages to people who mail you, telling them you're away.

Other web mail services – particularly those put up by the big portals – set out to be all-purpose communication centres, where you can handle a variety of messages. At Lycos Communications **http://comm.lycos.com/**, you can do standard email, but you can also set up a voicemail account that lets you handle messages over the net and arrange to pick up mail via your mobile phone. Excite **http://www.excite.co.uk** offers a similar service – you can get faxes and voicemail sent to one online address. If you're really serious about staying in touch wherever you are, try the unified messaging services, which provide you with a single email address and telephone number to which all your communications – voicemail, fax, email etc – can be sent. Try J2 **http://www.j2.com** or Unified Messaging **http://www.unified-messaging.com**. Incidentally, most ISPs now offer similar email services – from reminders and forwarding to unified messaging. If you think a particular service might be useful, check with them before you sign up.

Web mail services aren't just about business. Some are more focused on amusing you while you're at work. For example, Another.com **http://www.another.com** lets you set up a mail account with a funny/topical address – as in **jim@westlifeblowchunks.com**. At Funmail **http://www.funmail.com**

< 188 >

Read about it online - Entertainment by Mail

Various email services will deliver regular newsletters tailored to your interests. Try Shagmail **http://www.shagmail.com**. Sign up with Zap Spot **http://www.zapspot.com** and they'll send you little video games via the mail. ▲

you can create animated messages and mail them to your friends. Similarly, the horrendously popular Pass This On **http://www. passthison.com** creates images and little video clips – either 'comic' or sentimental – that you can send to your friends. You can also send email greetings cards – many portals and online shops offer this service for free. Otherwise, try Blue Mountain **http://www.bluemountain.com**.

Don't be a slave to your email

Email is a wonderful thing but it will take over your life if you're not careful. When you first get online, you may find yourself checking for new email every thirty minutes and feeling floored and friendless when you don't have any. Then suddenly there's too much of the stuff. You have to clear fifty messages in the morning before you can get on with your work. Worse still, the important ones are often hidden under a mini-mountain of junk mail. Actually, spam may turn out to be the least of your problems. People don't always get irony or sarcasm in emails. As a result, it's easy to annoy people with email without really meaning to. It's also easy to send email to someone without meaning to, email that may contain comments you don't want them to see. So although you're supposed to answer email quickly, think before you press **Send**.

< 189 >

The early belief that email would improve workplace efficiency hasn't really held up over the last few years. For every useful communication in your office inbox, you'll find twenty mails trying to arrange a post-work drink, ten lame email jokes and, if you're really unlucky, several files of stupid animated cartoons. Incidentally, if you really need to write to a friend about what a fool your boss is, do it on paper. Your bosses can probably have a look at your email if they feel like it. You may end up thinking they're the least of your troubles if your steamy messages to the marketing manager get sent to all and sundry by your office colleagues. So remember – email in the office environment is not private and could be saved and used against you. ▲

Online communities

The net makes one-to-one communication incredibly easy. However, its real strength is many-to-many communication. After all, if you want to contact a friend, a standard paper letter will still do the job. But what about contacting a group of friends? And what about circulating their replies so that everybody can read what everybody else has said. That kind of group communication doesn't come easily to the world of paper and stamps. The net, on the other hand, was made for it. It's easy to send a message to a group of people. It's just as easy for each group member to then send their responses to everyone else.

As a result, the net is home to thousands of ongoing discussions covering all sorts of subjects and bringing together all sorts of people. Many of these discussions have lasted long enough to make the people involved feel part of a community. Of course, the 'c' word is much

< 190 >

abused online. Dodgy web sites often try to sell themselves as 'community spaces' because they have a discussion board which is used by a couple of cranks and a company employee. But there are some spaces online where people have shared ideas and feelings for long enough to build up a genuine sense of belonging. These group spaces may not be the same as real world communities. In contrast to the real world, they tend to be composed of like-minded people who share the same particular interests and hobbies. But nevertheless, they can be amusing and affecting places to hang out. You can find out more about a particular subject that interests you. You can build up friendships with people you've never met. And more often than not, these friendships can end up enriching your off-screen life

Internet discussion groups

'Internet discussion group' is a catch-all term that covers several different forms of group communication. First, there's mailing lists, in which email from list members turns up every day in your mailbox. Then there's web discussion boards – bulletin board-like spaces on web sites where you can go to read people's messages about a particular idea or theme, then add your own thoughts. Then there's Usenet newsgroups – yet more bulletin board-style discussions circulated through a global network of news servers. Here you subscribe to a group, then download the day's messages, read them, then post back your thoughts.

Each of these groups works in roughly the same way. You send a message about a particular topic. It goes to everyone in the group. Someone responds and over time, a kind of delayed-action discussion, builds up. Each type of group has its own strengths. People tend to be on mailing lists because they want to be, so discussions are often more

< 191 >

productive. Usenet newsgroups, on the other hand, are wilder and more freewheeling. Web discussion boards are often a great way for people to take issue with, or expand on stories written by the mainstream media. Many big content-based web sites now have discussion boards, or they let readers add their thoughts to the end of certain pieces. As a result, readers can generate conversations that are both longer and more interesting that the original articles. As you get used to the net, you'll discover which one works for you best. But they're all worth a look when you're starting out.

Discussion group netiquette

There is a general code of conduct which applies to all of these spaces. So we might as well get it out of the way now. In a way, it's an extension of email netiquette. When you're contributing to an online discussion group, keep things brief and to the point. Use smileys and TLAs if they speed things up and are easily understood – and if they seem to fit the group. Using capitals is the equivalent of shouting and should be avoided. When you first join a particular group, lurk for a while and see what the group talks about and how they behave generally. When you want to have your say, don't post a message to an ongoing thread about something completely different. If you want to go off at a tangent, start

Jargon file - Lurkers

Net slang for those who hang around in discussion groups (and chat rooms), read what other people have to say but don't actually post anything themselves. ▲

< 192 >

a new thread. Quote the relevant portions of a previous message if you're adding to an ongoing thread. But don't quote the whole message, or the whole previous thread. Most importantly, don't send advertising or junk mail. However, it's OK to include references to your homepage in your sig file. Most discussion groups are public forums, so you may want to remove some of the more personal information from your sig file.

Don't post private email to a group without permission. You're alright re-posting material that has appeared in a group already: it's deemed to be in the public domain. It's beginning to be accepted that posting a message to a public discussion space online is equivalent to publishing it. So don't post illegal or libellous material. The most important thing, though, is to remember that there are people on the other side of the screen. Try to be constructive. Some people in discussion groups do spout the most incredible rubbish. But you can point this out without insulting them – sometimes. Before you start a flame war, think about the rest of the group. Sometimes it's amusing to watch two people slugging it out. But mostly it's a bore. So think a bit before you type, especially with mailing lists. Sending to a message to the whole list which was intended for one person only is easily done, and can have very embarrassing consequences.

Web discussion boards

All sorts of web sites – from the big portals and webzines to online shops and auctions – now feature discussion boards. There are also plenty of sites devoted specifically to hosting discussion groups. At Smart Groups **http://www.smartgroups.com** you can click your way through a variety of publicly accessible discussion boards or you can set up your own private board, an online meeting place for your real world club or business.

< 193 >

For an example of how a standard web discussion forum works, have a look at The Loop, the community area of the webzine Feed **http://www.feedmag.com/loopindex.shtml**.

This is where Feed's readers can respond to the articles the site has run. The authors of the pieces usually drop in to the board to read and respond to criticism. Often a general Feed editor will also be involved, either to stimulate discussion or manage potential conflicts. Feed often highlights particularly lively discussions on its front page. Click one of the links, and you go directly to the relevant discussion in the loop. When you do, you'll see a list of different messages. Some will have a number in brackets next to them. This indicates the number of responses that particular message has generated. If you click on the message, it will come up on the screen, and you'll also see links to the responses it's generated. At the end of a message, you'll see a form you can use to post a reply or send a new message. You just need to enter your email address and a subject line, then your thoughts, then press *Send*.

Feed's Loop section is fairly typical of the way web discussion boards work. It's easy to access and read, easy to send in your own contributions. However, web discussion spaces can feel less intimate and involving than other groups. Often, they're places where people can talk back to the media. And you can read some very stimulating stuff. But in general, they don't build up a group of regular users or a sense of group identity. As a result they can feel less satisfying than some other online group discussions.

Mailing lists

There are thousands of mailing lists online. Some are one-way only. You subscribe and everything from fanzines to product information is sent to you via email on a regular basis. With two-way lists, the content of the

< 194 >

list is generated by the subscribers. Some can be pretty serious affairs. Others are more relaxed and the ostensible subject – a local pop group, gardening, whatever – takes a back seat to general chatter. Two-way lists can either be moderated or completely open. The former are controlled by a moderator who keeps discussions on track, and weeds out insulting or off-topic posts. The latter are completely open. Everything anyone sends to the list goes out to everyone else, which can lead to huge amounts of mail. I prefer moderated lists – so long as the moderator is accountable in some way.

In the early days of the net, mailing lists were run using one of two software programs, Listserv or Majordomo. Once you subscribed to this kind of list, the day's messages were sent to your mailbox. Sometimes, they were archived later on a web site. In the last few years, mailing lists have moved on to the web. Sites like Topica **http://www.topica.com** and eGroups **http://www.egroups.com** host thousands of mailing lists and offer a little more flexibility than the old style lists. You can choose to have a list sent to your mailbox or you can read it on the web, discussion board-style. You can also decide whether to get a digest sent to you, rather than every message. It's easier to search the list's archive and research other lists too.

Tips - Access

Remember that most lists are public forums. They're easily accessible and easily searched. In other words, the things you write might be found by someone using the net to check you out. So you might want to watch what you say. ▲

< 195 >

If you're looking for a list to subscribe to, have a look around on Topica or eGroups. Alternatively, if you want to try one of the old style lists, try the directories at Liszt **http://www.liszt.com/** or Publicly Accessible Mailing Lists **http://paml.net/**. Subscribing to the lists maintained on Topica and eGroups is easy – you'll find lots of information on the sites. Subscribing to lists maintained using Listserv or Majordomo is slightly trickier. The general information about a list at a site like Liszt.com will tell you what to do. Generally, you send mail – usually with 'subscribe' in the body of the message – to the computer where the list is based. You will then receive mail telling you you're on the list. Save this message. It will contain details about how to post to the list and how to cancel your subscription. One thing to look out for: these old style lists have two addresses – one to which you send messages for the list proper and one for administrative queries. Don't get the two mixed up.

Whatever list you choose, joining is pretty easy. Dealing with the number of messages it can generate might prove problematic. If you're going on holiday, sign off from high-volume lists before you go. Don't stay on the list and then use a service that automatically sends people a note saying you're on holiday: if you're on a high-volume list, in your

Read about it online – Setting Up Your Own List

If you want to start your own list, it's easily done at Topica or eGroups. If you fancy running an old-style list, you'll find information about Listserv at **http://www.lsoft.com**, along with a Listserv list search engine too. You can find out more about Majordomo from **http://www. greatcircle.com/majordomo/**. ▲

< 196 >

absence you will end up replying to every message – and you may make the list unworkable. If you're on a high-volume list that's interesting but overwhelming, ask the administrator if there's a weekly digest of the list you can get instead. To avoid messages from a high-volume list clogging up your Inbox, use a mail filter to divert it to its own box. Set the filter to look for the list address or the list name, which is usually in the *Subject* line of messages.

Usenet newsgroups

Usenet newsgroups are probably the most demanding of the various online discussion forums. There are around 30,000 of them, covering just about anything you'd ever want to talk (or argue) about. Most are standard discussion groups. Some are one-way affairs, for announcements only. Others are primarily for exchanging files (anything from images to software). A few are strictly moderated, but most are pretty free and easy. Usenet is one of the more controversial areas of the net, mainly because a large chunk of it is driven by uncensored human desire. There are groups where pornography is available for free. There are also groups devoted to child pornography and paedophilia. Your ISP won't carry these. A few years ago, British ISPs came under police pressure not to carry newsgroups that contain illegal material. As for newsgroup porn, be aware that it is there (especially if you have children who use your net connection), but don't get it out of proportion. For more on dealing with it, go to page 319.

So how does Usenet work? Your ISP keeps a database of newsgroup postings on its news server, a computer running the Usenet news transfer protocol. Your ISP's news server is connected to others and a steady flow of postings to the newsgroups is passed between them. You connect to

< 197 >

the news server to access the various groups and read the latest postings. When you send a post to a particular group, it goes to your ISP's news server and is then passed on to others. Consequently, it can sometimes take a while before everyone on Usenet gets to see your witty deconstruction of David Beckham's haircut. If they don't access Usenet on a regular basis, they may miss it altogether. There are so many messages on Usenet that ISPs clear out their databases fairly frequently.

People often say the newsgroups aren't as good as they used to be, though they've been saying it since the mid-nineties. Certainly, many groups have been made unworkable by bulk junk messages. A bigger problem, though, is that people can now sample public group discussions more easily on the web. So many can't be bothered with Usenet. However, you should give the newsgroups a try. Techno-gurus say the net is a new public realm where everyone can have their say. Usenet is one of the things that lives up to the rhetoric . . . sort of. It also shows you the consequences of that rhetoric. If you want to see what a people-driven info-anarchy actually looks like, visit the newsgroups. They can be both heart-warming and kind of scary. They aren't always pretty, but they are interesting.

Choosing a newsreader

To access the newsgroups, you need a newsreader. Both Microsoft's email package Outlook Express and Netscape Communicator's mail software Messenger are newsreaders. If you're just starting out, they'll be fine. To access your browser's newsreader:

▶ Start **Outlook Express** then look for the **Read News** link on the introductory screen once you've launched the main program.

< 198 >

Tips - Standalone Newsreaders

For an alternative to the big two, PC owners should try Free Agent
http://www.forteinc.com/getfa/getfa.htm. Mac users could try
Newswatcher **http://charlotte.at.northwestern.edu/jln/progs.ssi**.
For more newsreaders, try **http://www.newsreaders.com/**. ▲

Alternatively, click on your news server's name in the *Folders*
window on the left

▶ Start *Navigator*, then select the *Communicator* menu, then
Messenger.

Configuring your newsreader

You need to enter details about yourself and the address of your ISP's
news server – the computer that maintains a database of newsgroups.
Your news server address is usually something like **news.yourisp.net**.

▶ In *Internet Explorer*, select the *Tools* menu, then *Internet
Accounts*. Then click the *News* tab. To add a new news account,
use the *Add* button, then *News* then the **Internet Connection
Wizard** will start up and walk you through it. To change an old one,
click the *Properties* button and follow the directions.

▶ In *Messenger*, select the *Edit* menu, then *Preferences*. Then go
for the *Mail and Newsgroups* section and add in details of your
news server address. Use the *Newsgroup Servers* category to add in
new servers or edit details on existing entries.

▶ In the *Mac* version of *Outlook Express*, select the *Tools* menu,

< 199 >

then *Accounts*, then *News*. Click on the account you want then *Edit* to change any details. Click on *New* to add a new server.

Getting started

The first time you start your newsreader, it should automatically download a complete list of newsgroups from your ISP's news server. Once you've got the list, you need to find the groups that match your interests. There is an order to the newsgroup list – an address system of sorts, though it refers to subject matter, not actual locations. Groups are arranged in hierarchies – fairly wide-ranging thematic categories – followed by more specific detail about what the group discusses. For example, **uk.politics.censorship** would, as you might expect, be devoted to discussing the politics of censorship in the UK only. There are plenty of hierarchies – some easy to decipher, others rather mystifying. Here are a few of the more popular ones.

alt As in alternative – discussions with a non-conformist/anarchic/funky flavour

biz You can send your commercial messages here

comp Discussions about everything to do with computers

microsoft Get your product support advice here

misc Catch-all category for stuff that doesn't seem to fit in elsewhere

news Home to announcements about Usenet and debates on what's wrong with it

rec Recreation, as in sports, hobbies and the like

sci Science

soc For socio-cultural discussion (and a bit of religion as well)

talk The place to argue more controversial issues – gun control, for example

uk Devoted to UK-specific discussions

< 200 >

When it comes to finding a newsgroup, you could browse the general list. Alternatively, most newsreaders let you search the list.

▶ In **Outlook Express**, select the **Tools** menu, then **Newsgroups**. A **Newsgroups Subscriptions** dialog box will come up. There's a search box at the top. You search via simple key words – comics, 'The Simpsons', shopping. Once you find a group you like, click on it then click on the **Subscribe** button.

▶ In **Messenger**, select the **File** menu, then **Subscribe**. A **Subscribe to Newsgroups** dialog box will come up. Then click the **Search** tab. You can then search on simple key words you're interested in. Once you find a group you like, click on it then click on the **Subscribe** button.

▶ In the **Mac** version of **Outlook Express**, just click on the name of your news server in the left-hand window. The newsgroup list will come up in the main window with a search box above it. Then highlight a group and click the **Subscribe** toolbar button.

Your ISP might not provide access to all the available newsgroups. ISPs often don't carry specialist or foreign-language groups. If you want access to those groups, ask them. They will usually oblige. ISPs also don't carry groups that might contain illegal material (i.e. child porn or pirated software). Some ISPs and online services specifically target the family market and as a result block whole chunks of Usenet, for example, all of **alt.sex**. There are problems with this kind of blanket censorship. Some of the **alt.sex** groups are devoted to worthy nattering about sexuality and aren't particularly salacious or pornographic. However, your ISP gets to decide which newsgroups it carries. If it's an issue, try someone else. Of course, with the net, there's always a way round censorship. You can

< 201 >

Tips - Finding Newsgroups

You can't seem to find a group devoted to Namibian woodworking technique. That doesn't mean it doesn't exist. It may be that your ISP doesn't carry it. At Newzbot **http://www.newzbot.com** you can search for such a group. Someone may be trying to start such a group. To find out, look in **news.announce.newgroups** to see which new groups are being proposed and to vote on whether they should be accepted. ▲

always try a publicly accessible news server – go to Newzbot **http://www.newzbot.com** for more information.

Reading newsgroups

Once you've subscribed to a few groups, you need to download the most recent messages. Once you're connected:

▶ In **Outlook Express**, there will be a list of groups you've subscribed to in the window on the left of the screen. Connect to your ISP then click on one of these groups. Outlook Express will download the headers from the newest messages. Click on a header and the whole message will be downloaded. Outlook Express is set to download 300 headers by default, usually enough to get a feel for most groups. You can change it to a higher or lower figure. Select the **Tools** menu, then **Options**, then click the **Read** tab and change the line **Download 300 headers at a time**. In the **Mac** version, to find a similar section, click the **Tools** menu, then **Accounts**, then **News**, highlight the relevant account, then click on **Edit**, then **Options**.

< 202 >

▶ In **Messenger**, to the left of the window, under your news server's name, there should be a list of the news groups you've subscribed to. Double-click the one you want to read. Messenger is set by default to ask before it downloads more than 500 message headers. To change this, select the *Edit* menu, then *Preferences*. In *Newsgroup Servers* change the figure in the line *Ask me before downloading more than 500 messages*. Once you've decided how many headers you want, a window will open, showing the headers in the top part of the screen. Click on a message on the list and its contents will appear in the bottom part of the window.

The most sensible way to consume Usenet is offline. Once you've subscribed to a few groups, you should get the latest messages, log off and then read them.

▶ In **Outlook Express**, download the headers from your newsgroup, then log off. Set Outlook Express to work offline, via the *File* menu. In the main window, you'll see a list of headers, some with a + sign next to them. Click on this and you'll see the thread (i.e. the various replies) this particular message has generated. Next you need to mark the postings you're interested in. To the left of the headers, click in

---

Jargon file - Headers

In this context, headers are the basic details about the message: what it's about, who sent it and when. They are not the message itself. You'll need to go back online to get that. ▲

< 203 >

the column underneath the arrow pointing downward. A little blue arrow will appear to the left of the header. Once you've marked the messages, then select the *Tools* menu, then *Mark for Offline*, then *Download Message Later*. Then go online, select the *Tools* menu then *Synchronize Newsgroup*. Outlook Express will then go online and get the stuff you want.

▶ In *Messenger*, select the *File* menu, then *Go Offline*. Select the newsgroup you're interested in, so that the headers are displayed in the main window. Then mark the messages you want. There are several ways you can do this. The easiest is probably to hold down the *Control* key, then click on each of the messages you want. Once that's done select the *File* menu, then *Offline*, then *Get Selected Messages*. Your newsreader will connect and download the messages. Then you can log off and start reading.

Both newsreaders offer several ways of reading messages offline. It might be worth trying each out to see which you like best. For more information, look in the help files.

It can take a while to get into some newsgroups. Stick with a group over a few days and it should start to make sense. After a while you may realise that some group members are complete time wasters. You can get your newsreader to block their messages. This is one area in which standalone newsreaders have the edge, though Outlook Express isn't bad.

▶ In *Outlook Express*, highlight a post by the offending individual, then select the *Message* menu, then *Block Sender*. Alternatively, to create more versatile filters, select the *Tools* menu, then

< 204 >

Message Rules, then *News*. You can then choose to delete messages from certain people or messages that have certain words in the title.

▶ In the *Mac* version of *Outlook Express*, you can block certain messages by selecting the *Tools* menu, then *Rules*, then *News*, then *New*. You can then specify the criteria for blocking messages.

You can also sort the messages in a group according to date or sender. Don't bother with that unless you're trying to keep track of a particular person. The best way to view newsgroups is by thread – most newsreaders have that as the default option. If you want to change it:

▶ In *Outlook Express*, select the *View* menu, then *Sort By*.
▶ In *Messenger*, select the *View* menu, then *Sort*.

To find a particular message:

▶ In *Outlook Express*, select the *Edit* menu, then *Find Message*.
▶ In *Messenger*, select the *Edit* menu, then *Search Messages*.

Posting messages

If you do something wrong in a newsgroup, or just ask a silly question, you will be flamed by someone. So before you send in a message, do some research. That way you won't present too big a target. Read the newsgroup for a while. Each group has an FAQ – a file of Frequently Asked Questions, which details what the group discusses and how. Read it – you should find it at the Internet FAQ Archives – **http://faqs.org/**. That way, you should be able to avoid sending

< 205 >

Read about it online - Netiquette Guide

You can find a lengthy guide to newsgroup netiquette, as well as some amusing parodies and useful information on the UK Usenet homepages **http://www.usenet.org.uk**. ▲

messages or questions which people will dismiss as obvious or already dealt with.

OK, so you've read a message you want to reply to.

▶ In **Outlook Express,** click either the **Reply to Group** button (to send your thoughts to the group) or the **Reply to Sender** button (to send your message to the author of the post you're responding to – it's considered good netiquette to do this). You can do both by at the same time by selecting the **Message** menu then **Reply to All**. Whatever you choose, a new window opens, with the address filled out and the previous message quoted. Edit it and add your response. Then click the **Send** button on the toolbar.

▶ In **Messenger,** click either the **Reply to Group** button (to send the message just to the newsgroup) or the **Reply to All** button (this simultaneously sends messages to the newsgroup and the original author of the post. A new window will open, with the address filled out and the previous message quoted. Edit it and add your response. Then click the **Send** button on the toolbar.

< 206 >

Messages to newsgroups are often cross-posted, i.e. they're sent to several groups that share some interest in a general subject. When you reply to a cross-posting, your message will be sent to all the groups the previous message was cross-posted to. You'll see them entered in the address field.

To post an original message:

▶ In **Outlook Express**, in the window on the left side of the screen, where your subscriptions list is, click on the group you want to post to. Then click the **New Post** button on the toolbar. Write something suitably pithy in the **Subject** line, write your thoughts in the text box at the bottom then click the **Send** button.

▶ In **Messenger**, select the group you want to post to from the list on the left side of the browser window and then click the **New Message** button. Write something in the **Subject** line and click **Send** when you're done.

When you send an original message, don't cross-post it to groups you don't know. It's a good way to annoy people. Remember – they have your email address and they will let you know how they feel. If all this sounds a bit daunting, try a test post first. Some ISPs have their own test newsgroups and there's also an **alt.test** group you can try. Don't send a test post to a regular newsgroup, another sure-fire way to upset people. Incidentally, if you do send a message to a group by mistake, you can retrieve the situation by sending a cancel message. This will remove the posting (although it takes time and if someone downloads the message before your cancel message reaches the group, there's nothing you can do).

< 207 >

▶ In **Outlook Express**, highlight the message you posted, then select the **Message** menu, then **Cancel Message**.

▶ In **Messenger**, select the offending message, then select the **Edit** menu, then **Cancel Message**.

Getting answers from newsgroups

Newsgroups are, so people tell you, packed with experts who are desperate to help you. All you have to do is ask. On one level, this is true. But there is a correct way of asking. If you have a question, tell people to answer with private email and then post a summary of responses. That way, the group won't become clogged with people sending the same answer. Students shouldn't assume that newsgroup users are just dying to help out with their dissertations. Don't send a questionnaire on a particular subject to a series of groups. This annoys newsgroup users (understandably) and you won't get any useful replies. Instead, hang out in relevant newsgroups, identify the more knowledgeable members and send them private email asking if they have time to answer a few questions. Then send your questionnaire. If you're looking for answers, your best bet may be to tap the archived collective wisdom of Usenet via the archives at Deja.com **http://www. deja.com/usenet**. You can also access the newsgroups via Deja.com. However, the web can be slow – slower than downloading messages from your ISP's server.

Attachments and HTML

There are plenty of newsgroups where people exchange files, not ideas. These files could be anything from images and sound samples to share-ware games. But mostly they're images, often pornographic. Groups

< 208 >

devoted to exchanging porn (e.g. many of the alt.binaries groups) do account for a sizeable amount of newsgroup traffic. Remember this, especially if your kids are using Usenet. But don't assume that's all there is to newsgroups that swap files.

In the past, dealing with files attached to Usenet postings could be tricky, but the latest newsreaders make the whole thing easy. They work in exactly the same way as email attachments – go to page 182 for general advice. UUencode was the standard way to convert attachments on Usenet. It's been replaced by MIME. Outlook Express and Messenger can handle both, but if you're using an older newsreader you may have problems. A group FAQ might have advice on how to convert attachments posted to the group. Alternatively, hang out in the group see what everyone else does.

Usenet newsgroups used to consist of text postings and UUencoded attachments. Now the new generation of newsreaders let you send HTML messages that come with links, graphics and embedded images. Both Outlook Express and Messenger can handle HTML. When you're composing a reply or a new message to a newsgroup, you can format it in HTML. However, before you send your flashy message, think about whether it's appropriate. Many groups prefer plain text. Again, see what seems to be acceptable in the group in question. For information on how to change the format of your newsgroup postings from HTML to text or vice versa, go to page 183 in the email section.

If you decide to configure Messenger to send postings to newsgroups in plain text, it will send all your email in text as well. If you want to send text to a newsgroup, you could do it on a message-by-message basis. In the *Composition* window, click the *Message Sending Format* button in the bottom left of the *Address* window and then look for the *Format*

< 209 >

> ### Read about it online - Starting Your Own Newsgroup
>
> There's an easy and a hard way to do it. You can start an alt group –
> that's the easy way. You'll find some advice in So You Want to Create
> an Alt Newsgroup at **http://www.visi.com/~barr/alt-creation-guide.html**.
> Alternatively, you can start an official Usenet group – for advice on this
> go to the UK Usenet homepage at **http://www.usenet.org.uk**. ▲

drop-down menu in the bottom right. You don't need to worry about this
with Outlook Express. You can choose to send text to newsgroups and
use HTML for your mail. To check on this, select the *Tools* menu, then
Options, then *Send*.

Next step
If you're worried about privacy and the newsgroups, go to page 335.
Alternatively, now you've done discussion groups, you're ready for the
real-time rough and tumble of online chat, so go to the next section. ▲

Online chat

If you're not actually talking yourself, or rather typing, online chat can
look a bit silly. Sure the idea sounds good – people from all around the
world having a conversation that scrolls out in real time text across
their computer screens. But often the reality is a disjointed stream of
gibberish that ends up going nowhere in particular. At least that's the
opinion of sarcastic journalists, who, a few years ago, loved to write off

< 210 >

chat as a modern Citizen's Band radio. What they didn't realise is that the net is not a spectator sport. Online chat is very dull to watch. But do it yourself and, even if you're only exchanging banalities, it can be surprisingly exciting.

Conversations in chat room do tend to towards the trivial, though not always. In the past, people stuck in war zones have used chat to get frontline reports out to the rest of the world. However, for the most part, chat is just a fun way of passing the time. Some chat does revolve around sex, though not as much as newspaper reports might lead you to think. It's true that a fair few people do meet up in private chat rooms to type dirty to each other. Nothing wrong with that, of course, if they're both consenting adults. However, many men do try to force their virtual attentions on women in chat rooms. This is obviously a drag, though if you do encounter problems, you can set your chat software to block idiots from your screen.

And men who hit on women should be aware that you can never be sure who you're chatting with online. Those who make a big deal of presenting themselves as women are often men goofing around. If nothing else, this ought to help them see what women have to put up with in online chat rooms. Indeed, many women choose to keep their

---

Read about it online – Chat Theory

MIT professor Sherry Turkle **http://web.mit.edu/sturkle/www/** had some interesting chapters on chat and chat worlds in her book, Life on the Screen. You'll find more information at **http://www.uiowa.edu/ ~commstud/resources/digitalmedia/digitalpeople.html**. ▲

< 211 >

gender secret while chatting. Sexual deception is one thing. In some chat rooms, you might find yourself talking to something non-human, as in a chatbot, a program designed to greet new arrivals or even hold a sort of conversation. Some chat rooms are also home to hackers who indulge in silly but usually harmless mischief.

Chat can take over some people's lives. And some teenagers find it as compelling as the phone. There is also evidence that paedophiles frequent chat rooms trying to engage children in conversation. So parents should try to supervise their children's chat in some way. They need to set guidelines and offer advice on what to look out for or avoid. For more on this, go to page 323. But don't get too hung up over the potential problems. For most people, online chat is an entertaining way to pass the time, make friends and build a sense of community. Take all those stories about online relationships that turned into real-world marriages. They usually started in chat rooms.

Places to chat online: Online services

Chat has always been important to online services like AOL. In fact, it paid their bills in the early days. AOL in particular still hosts thousands of rooms, devoted to all sorts of subjects. Chat in the online services is a

Read about it online – Celeb Chatbots

For some chatbot fun, try the Robbie Williams site **http://www. robbiewilliams.com**. In the chat rooms here, you can shoot the digital breeze with various Robbie fans. You might also find yourself talking to a Robbie chatbot, programmed to talk/type like him. ▲

< 212 >

Read about it online - katie.com

Children and teenagers do need to take care online, especially in chat spaces. For a cautionary tale try **http://www.katiet.com**, the web presence of Katie.com, Katherine Tarbox's book about how, as a teenager, she was lured into a relationship by a paedophile she met in an AOL chat room. ▲

pretty organised thing, with regular events in which users can get advice from experts and put questions to celebrities and politicians. It's also subject to some control – in theory. If someone bothers you, you can report them to a moderator. Though AOL likes to sell itself as a family operation, things can get pretty steamy in a lot of their chat rooms. However, parents who want to make sure their kids aren't exposed to dirty typing can block their access to certain rooms.

Internet Relay Chat, aka IRC

To chat using IRC, which was created by the Finnish programmer Jarkko Oikarinen in 1988, you have to connect to a chat server. Groups of chat servers around the world are hooked up into networks, known as nets. Much like an online service, a particular net will host a bewildering amount of chat spaces (known as channels), each in theory devoted to a particular subject. Though not as organised as AOL, IRC nets do host celebrity chats, special events and even games. In general, IRC is free and easy – which may attract some and worry others. Compared to the online services, it is more confusing. However, it does feel less American.

< 213 >

Jargon file – Java, Javascript, Applet

Java is a programming language which, among other things, can be used to create interactive multimedia effects on the web. Javascript is a similar sort of language. An applet is a small program written in Java which can be placed on a web page. ▲

Web chat

Many web sites – from the big portals to webzines – now feature chat rooms. The basic format is the same as IRC and AOL – various rooms devoted to different topics. Again, they sometimes host special events. The main attraction of web chat is that it's happening on the web, so you can use your browser without resorting to separate software. To access many web chat rooms, you generally need an up-to-date browser – i.e. one that can run Java or Javascript. When you enter the chat room, your browser loads a Java chat applet. However, many web chat rooms now also run in HTML too.

Chat style and netiquette

Chat style is similar to email style. If anything, the TLAs and smileys people use in their mail are more useful in real-time chat. Once you get used to them, the former can speed up your typing; it still won't be anything like normal spoken conversation, but it helps. The latter can help resolve misunderstandings caused by bad typing or delays on the line. As with discussion groups, when you enter a room, lurk for a while and find out how the group works. However, in a chat room, everyone knows you are lurking; your arrival is always announced to all the other

< 214 >

Read about it online – Chat Netiquette

For an exhaustive (and somewhat specialist) guide to chat/IRC netiquette, which advises you to 'Consider the lag factor', avoid 'attention-seeking gimmicks' and much else, go to **http://mirc.stealth.net/misc/chanrule.html**. ▲

users. So if someone does say hello, it's bad form not to respond. The basic idea with chat is to keep the conversation going and to remember that it is a conversation. Don't change the subject of an ongoing chat or start talking about something unconnected with the room's designated subject. If you have a lot to say, break it down into shorter chunks. Keeping things short is always the best policy with chat. Capitals are the equivalent of shouting and should be avoided. Similarly, always think a bit before you type. Don't immediately kick off a flame war in response to something that seems like an insult. It may not be intended that way.

Never give out personal information in a chat space, especially your ISP password. The person asking may flash apparently authoritative credentials. Don't believe them. (This scam has been particularly common in the American chat rooms on AOL). Most chat programs let you create a personal profile. Including information about your hobbies is fine. Don't include anything important or personal. Think about the nicknames you pick for yourself. If you call yourself 'Hot Hunk', you're asking for a certain kind of attention. Women should go for chat room nicknames that don't indicate their gender. Otherwise, they will be hassled by the troglodytes who populate some chat rooms. Finally, don't believe everything you read in a chat room. People are often not really what they say they are.

< 215 >

Chat on the web

The web is probably the best place to start with online chat. If you decide that chat is your thing, you can always move on to IRC. Perhaps the only difficult thing is finding the right place to chat. There are chat spaces all over the web these days and most work in roughly the same way. Why not start with Yahoo Chat UK **http://uk.chat.yahoo.com/**. You'll need to register first. Before you do, you'll have to read their extended terms of service and code of conduct. There has been some trouble in the Yahoo Chat rooms recently – the police caught a paedophile who was trying operate there. Clearly the company is now going out of its way to improve security and anticipate problems. Next you go on to registration proper. Once you've chosen your screen name, password and the rest, you'll go to the *Chat* front page.

Here you'll see links to currently featured chat rooms, along with a link to a complete room list. You'll also see a *Favourite Rooms* list, which lets you access certain spaces quickly, and a *Friends in Chat* list – once you assemble this, you can see when your friends are online and go directly to chat with them. Pick a room – either from the *Featured Rooms* list or the *Complete Rooms List* – and click on it. When the chat window proper loads (which may take a while), it will be packed

Read about it online - Web Chat Listings

A good place to chat on the web is Talk City **http://www.talkcity.com/**, a kind of chat community site which features all sorts of themed rooms (accessible via a directory) and various celebrity chats and advice forums. ▲

< 216 >

with frames. To the right of the window, you'll see a *Chatters* list of people in the room. To the left, taking up the bulk of the window, is the chat. Yahoo uses a colour-coding scheme to make it easier to follow. People are shown in red type, what they say is in black. Below the buttons, you'll find the text box. Type your contribution in here then hit *Return* to get involved. You can determine how your contribution appears. There are buttons to colour it, bold it, underline it or italicise it at the bottom left of the chat window. The *Emotions* button calls up a list of emotions you can send with your chat message, things like 'cackle', 'cringe', 'snicker' and 'snivel'. Just select one from the scrolling menu then double-click on it. It will appear on the screen next to your name.

To send a private message to someone, click on their name in the *Chatters* list then on the *PM* button below the list. Then fill out the pop-up box that appears. If you want to send an emotion to another user, click on the *Emotions* button, select an emotion from the list, highlight their name in the *Chatters* box, and then press *Emote User* at the bottom of the *Emotions* box. To see if any of the friends on your list is currently chatting somewhere on Yahoo, click the *Friends* button below the main chat window. Below the main chat frame, in the bottom left-hand corner, is a general navigation menu. The buttons are generally

Read about it online - Yahoo Voice Chat

Yahoo now offers voice chat. You obviously need a computer with a sound card and a microphone. But you can vocalise in real time, or something, with people hanging out in a Yahoo chat room. For more information, go to **http://help.yahoo.com/help/uk/chat/cjava/cvoice/**. ▲

< 217 >

pretty easy to understand. Clicking on *Who's Chatting* calls up a vast list of everyone currently on Yahoo, along with the chat room they're chatting in and some information from their personal profiles. Click on *Create A Room* and a menu comes up that lets you choose a name for your chat room, specify whether it is public or private and more. If you create a public user room, it appears on the general *Rooms* list. A private room won't. The only way people can enter it is if you invite them. Just click on the *More* button under the *Chatters List*. Type in the name of the person you want to invite and click the *Invite* button. Alternatively, you can invite other chatters to your room through the *Who's Chatting* list. Locate a name in the list and click the *Invite* link.

Web chat rooms don't seem to draw crowds of regulars or build up a real sense of community. They often seem to be populated by people there on a whim. As a result they can be chaotic. Since they are so easy to access, people do drop in just to shout rude words or wind people up. You can choose to ignore them. Click on their name in the *Chatters* box then press the *Ignore* button. If someone is hassling you with private messages, you can also click the *Preferences* button and uncheck *Pop Up New Private Messages*. Now, when other chatters try to send you a private message, it should appear instead on the main chat screen with *(PRIVATE)* before the message and a *Reply* link after it. If you want to respond to the message, click on the *Reply* link. There are lots of other things you can do in Yahoo's chat rooms – for more tips, try their Help section **http://help.yahoo.com/help/uk/chat/**.

Internet Relay Chat

Once you're used to chat on the web, why not give IRC a try. You'll need a special IRC program. PC owners should go for mIRC **http://www.mirc.co.uk;**

< 218 >

Mac users should try IRCLE **http://www.ircle.com/**. Whatever chat software you choose, you'll need to take some care setting it up. First, you'll probably need to specify an IRC server to connect to. As mentioned before, chat servers are hooked up in nets. Whatever chat server you connect to, you'll be able to access the channels being hosted on the net that it's a part of. There are all sorts of different nets, each with their own distinctive flavour – for more information, go to **http://www.irchelp.org/irchelp/networks/**. In the meantime, here's a few you could try.

Undernet **http://www.undernet.org/**
Dalnet **http://www.dal.net/**
KidLink (an IRC net for kids) **http://www.kidlink.org/rti/IRC/**

When you're just starting out, don't worry too much about which net to use. Chat programs like mIRC have lists of chat servers/nets you can use. Pick one reasonably close to home. Next you need to enter your name, email address and nickname. As mentioned before, women in particular might want to enter a fake name. There are various computer commands which let IRC users look at the information you enter – they might discover you are actually a woman, for example. You should also enter a fake email address, if that reveals your real name. Nicknames are fairly straightforward. Don't pick something provocative if you can't stand the potential heat. In addition, some names won't be acceptable in some IRC channels. Some chat programs let you take measures to retain a degree of privacy on IRC – you can set things up so people won't be able to find you online unless they know your exact nickname.

    Once you're ready to chat, click the *Connect* button (or something similar). You'll then connect with the server you chose when you configured

< 219 >

Tips - IRC Setup

You can add all sorts of information when setting up chat programs like mIRC. For a more detailed guide, try the excellent New IRC Users **http://www.newircusers.com/** and look for the mIRC section. ▲

your software. A screen should come up with general information – a message of the day and some details about the person responsible for the server. A list of the channels available on this particular net should then open automatically. If it doesn't, you can usually call it up via a toolbar button. To join a channel, just click the **Join** button. When you're just starting out, look for channels like **#newbies**, **#newusers**, **#beginners** or **#ircbeginners**. (Note that all IRC channels start with the # sign.)

Most new IRC programs feature plenty of user-friendly toolbar buttons. But you can also use text commands to get things done. You type the command then press **Return**. Hardcore IRC types probably prefer using commands (there are hundreds of them). Anything preceded by a **/** is interpreted by chat programs as a command. To join a channel, type **/join #newbies** in the main text box, then hit **Return**. Always remember the **/** sign. If you miss it out, your software will assume you've typed some chat and will broadcast it to the channel. Once you've joined a channel, you should see a listing of the people currently on the channel. Below the main chat window, you'll see the text box where you enter your contributions. When you first arrive, it's polite to say hello to everyone. Type 'Hello' in the text box then hit **Return**. After that, lurk for a while and see what's happening. If this channel really isn't you, leave by typing **/part**. Alternatively, just close the window.

< 220 >

Read about it online – Chat Circuit

For more IRC speak and lots of, ahem, newz and viewz, see Chat Circuit **http://chatcircuit.com/webzine/**, which started out as a webzine but has grown into a kind of chat network. ▲

If you want to chat privately with someone in an IRC channel, double-click on their nickname in the people list. A query window should open. Alternatively, right-click on a nickname in the list and you'll get a mouse menu that lets you open a private query window with that person. If you want to find out if a friend is on the system chatting, type */whois*, then their nickname. Chat programs now let you chat more securely with individual users (and even exchange files). Basically, it connects directly to their IRC program – in mIRC, it's called DCC Chat.

There's all sorts of things you can do in an IRC channel, from sending coloured text to creating a new channel. Look in the mIRC help files for a list of commands you can use. To set up your own channel on an IRC net, think of a name, then type */join*, then the name you came up with, as in */join #mychannel* (always remember the # sign). Since it's your channel, you might as well make yourself the 'op' (as in 'operator', the person in charge). Type */op*, then your nickname. Everyone who enters the channel will now know that you're in charge. To invite other users to your channel, type */invite*, then their nickname and the name of your channel, as in */invite dave #mychannel*. To set the subject for your room, type */topic*, then details of what you want to talk about. As channel op, you're in charge. If necessary, you can kick troublemakers off the channel. Type */kick*, then the channel name, then the name of the troublesome user.

< 221 >

Read about it online – IRC

For more information about IRC and what you can do, try the web.
IRC Help **http://www.irchelp.org** is good place to start, particularly the IRC
prelude. Alternatively, try the mIRC homepage – **http://www.mirc.co.uk/**. ▲

For a few bored computer teens, IRC is a wonderful playground.
Some seem to like nothing better than trying to take over certain IRC
channels. You aren't likely to run into the more malevolent kind of IRC
user unless you go looking for them. However, there are precautions you
can take. First, if someone asks you to type a particular computer
command, don't ever do it, whatever they say. It will do something nasty
to your PC and may even let someone else control it. Remember that you
don't have to accept private messages. If someone hassles you via private
messages, raise the problem in the public part of the channel or get help
from the channel op. Alternatively, type **/motd** to get the Message of the
Day which should feature contact details for the system administrator.
You can set your software to ignore certain users. Type **/ignore** then the
nickname of the user. (mIRC allows you to be much more specific when
it comes to ignoring people and messages, so look in its help files).

Graphic chat and MUDs

Chat isn't just a text thing. There are places online where people can
represent themselves on screen as characters in 2D or 3D space – their
speech appears in comic-strip style bubbles. Microsoft Chat was one of
the first programs to offer this kind of thing. Now you can find it in lots
of places on the web. At Dobedo **http://www.dobedo.co.uk**, once you've

< 222 >

signed up, you can design yourself a cartoony avatar (your visual representation on the net). When people are chatting with you, they'll see that image in a particular space. Dobedo is an amusingly colourful, comic book place. At Cycosmos **http://www.cycosmos.co.uk** the avatars you design have a more realistic look. You can also specify a personality for your online self. You can then search for other users with particular character types and chat with them or mail them. There are also discussion boards and other community features.

Both Cycosmos and Dobedo have borrowed ideas from a very old form of online chat – MUDs. These are alternative worlds spun out of text, where users can play out ideas, theories and fantasies. MUDs started out as online extensions of Dungeons and Dragons-style role-playing games. People competed to become wizards and kings. But then some MUDs dropped the gaming side and became more social, more like digital communes where people explored alternative identities and lifestyles. If you want to find out more, there's a MUD FAQ at **http://www.lysator.liu.se/mud/faq/faq1.html**. There's a good list of MUDs at the

Read about it online – Chatbot Assistants

Artificial Life Inc **http://www.artificial-life.com** is developing chatbots that come with a graphic animated interface – i.e, they look like people and they move when they talk. The idea is to create on-screen guides who can help people round the networks of the future. For more of the same, try Stratumsoft **http://www.stratumsoft.com** and look for their EVAs (as in Electronic Virtual Assistants) or Kiwilogic **http://www.kiwilogic.com**. ▲

< 223 >

MUD Resource Collection **http://www.godlike.com/muds** and MUD Connector **http://www.mudconnect.com** has a list of currently active MUDs. People can get very involved in MUDs, spending hours in them building alternative selves. For an example of just how serious things can get, have a look at Julian Dibbell's A Rape in Cyberspace **http://www. levity.com/julian/bungle.html**, a fascinating account of a 'sexual assault' that took place in LambdaMOO, a particular well known, determinedly bohemian MUD.

Traditional MUDs are text-based. But now some computer games companies are attempting to introduce graphic MUDs, in which you can see the world you're playing in. Ultima Online **http://www.uo.com** was the first graphic MUD-style game – it provided an online extension to an existing computer game. According to fans, it's now been outstripped by Sony's Everquest **http://www.station.sony.com/everquest/**. Janelle Brown of Salon wrote a fannish appreciation of the site at **http://www.salon.com/ tech/feature/1999/06/15/everquest/index.html**. These worlds have spawned a new type of commerce. Skilled Ultima Online/Everquest players are now creating game characters, earning them special powers by what they do in the game, then selling those characters via eBay to people who presumably aren't as good. Once again, Salon ran an interesting piece on

---

Read about it online - Made in the UK

MUDs are another online British invention. Richard Bartle and Roy Trubshaw created the first MUD, while studying at Essex University at the end of the seventies. Their new MUD (called MUD2) can be accessed via the web at **http://www.mud2.com**. ▲

< 224 >

this, which you'll find at **http://www.salon.com/tech/feature/1999/07/13/ultima_ebay/index.html**.

Instant messages

The most popular chat-like tools on the net at the moment are instant message programs. When these first appeared, they were a bit like intelligent online pagers. They told you when friends came online and let you message them to say hello and chat a little. Now the most popular instant message program, ICQ **http://www.icq.com** (as in 'I seek you') is an all-purpose communications tool. It lets you send voice messages as well as text to friends. It lets you send text messages to mobile phones. You can use it to surf the web with friends and swap ideas about the sites you see. You can use it to access different content channels and get news headlines and sports results. You can use it to swap files and play online games.

ICQ is the biggest instant message tool – at the time of writing, it had 82 million users round the world. The competition includes Microsoft's Messenger **http://messenger.msn.com**, Yahoo's Messenger **http://pager.yahoo.com/**, AOL Instant Messenger **http://www.aol.co.uk/aim/**, PowWow **http://www.tribal.com**, HotJabber **http://www.hotjabber.com/** and Odigo **http://www.odigo.com**. AOL's Instant Messenger lets you message AOL users, anyone else who has registered the software and ICQ users. It's bundled with Netscape Communicator so you'll probably already have a copy. Obviously with messaging systems, the number of users you can reach is one of the key things to look for. ICQ and AIM are the two leading programs and they can talk to each other. So they're the ones to go for.

AOL Instant Messenger lets you message friends and send them images. It also lets you block certain users and includes a Warn feature that sends a warning to abusive users (and the AOL authorities). It's also

< 225 >

just added a voice feature, so that you can talk to friends. But if instant messaging is your thing (and it's proving incredibly useful as a business tool), you'll probably want to use ICQ. You can do more things with it – from sending files to browsing the web with friends. It also still does the basic paging job really well. For example, if you instant message someone and they're offline, it holds on to your message and sends it when they come online. And it has reasonable privacy controls – your authorisation is required before people can add you to their buddy list and you can block messages from certain users. You can download ICQ from **http://www.icq.com**. Once you install it, you need to register and get a password and a screen number. This is what you pass on to friends who want to message you. You can create a 'buddy list' of friends who also use the same software, so that when they come online you're notified, via a small window on your desktop (obviously you have to be online too). You can do an awful lot more besides this – the best place to find out more is the ICQ site, where you'll find lengthy guides to the software. For more news and lots of tips, try CNET's ICQ section **http://www.cnet. com/internet/0-3782.html**.

Next step

If you want to find out more about what you can do on the web, go to the next section. However, if you've had more than enough of the web, go to page 319 for some tips on security online. ▲

< 226 >

4 TAKING THE WEB TO THE NEXT LEVEL

●●

I hope you now feel as if you know your way around the net. You should do. You've done the work, slogged your way through the basics. You know your **ftp** from your **http**. This section is designed to point you towards some of the more interesting things you can find online. It starts with web multimedia – everything from film clips and music to net radio stations and web cams, along with the broadband connections you probably need to take full advantage of online media content. It then covers shopping on the web, online auctions and personal finance. There's some advice on using the net to organise your life and work, which includes tips on mobile net access and WAP phones. It closes with a quick guide to putting up your own web site. By now, I'm assuming you're more comfortable with the net and net software (and know how to find a Help file), so there isn't so much detail about how to work individual programs.

Multimedia on the web

A few years, the web was really just words in a row and some well placed graphics. Press coverage may have suggested otherwise. Indeed some of it gave the impression that the web was a full-on MTV-style multimedia

< 227 >

experience. It never was. And it still isn't, quite. But now the web does let you listen to music and watch video in real time. You can play games or watch animations bounce around web pages. All very wonderful, except when it gets in the way. Example? Tedious Shockwave introductions to sites, which make you wait while they download, then stop you actually getting the information you want. Web multimedia can still sometimes feel like a programmer's high-tech self-indulgence. However, as with lots of things online, it's getting better all the time. And a broadband connection does lessen the pain.

Music on the net

According to Search Terms **http://www.searchterms.com**, a site which tracks online searches, MP3 is one of the most used search terms on the net (Last time I looked, it was number two in their charts, behind 'travel', but ahead of 'sex' and 'pokemon'). This is a good an indication as any of just how big MP3s have become in the last few years. The letters are short for MPEG Layer 3, a technique used to compress music or video files stored on a computer to about a tenth of their normal digital size, without a huge loss of quality. Software for playing MP3 files is freely available online, as are the programs you need to convert ordinary CDs into computer files and then compress them.

Consequently, it's relatively easy to convert tracks from your CD collection into MP3s and upload them to the net, where they can be downloaded for free by other fans and then played at home on a computer. And all this can happen without any money beyond the original CD purchase price going to the record companies – or the artists. In effect, MP3 files have re-booted bootlegging for the digital age. That said, two years ago, finding and trading MP3 files was hard work. You

< 228 >

had to go to the chat rooms, where people told each other about FTP sites where they could download music files. These sites often disappeared after a few hours, to avoid the music industry's watchdogs.

There were lots of web sites that claimed to feature MP3 files. But they were usually advertising scams. Links apparently pointing to well known tracks just took you to another page with more supposed links to MP3s, and lots of ad banners, often for porn web sites. If you did find a site with genuine MP3s, it often took ages to download them. And the MP3s available tended to reflect the tastes of the more prominent members of the scene – American students. So there was lots of stuff by alt.rockers like Rage Against the Machine or metal bands like Metallica.

All that changed with the arrival of Napster **http://www.napster.com**. Designed by 19 year old Shawn Fanning, launched in the autumn of 1999, Napster is a file-sharing network which makes it easy for users to swap the MP3s currently sitting on their own hard drives. First you need to install the Napster software, which you'll find on their web site. Start it up and you log on to the Napster network. When you search for a particular track, Napster searches the hard drives of everyone else currently logged on to the network to see if they have what you want. It then shows a list of results, with details of the size of the file and the

Read about it online - Napster History

For a thoughtful introduction to Napster and the issues it raises, try Charles C. Mann's essay 'The Heavenly Jukebox', which appeared in The Atlantic Review in Autumn 2000 **http://www.theatlantic.com/issues/ 2000/09/mann.htm**. ▲

< 229 >

connection speed of the computer on which it's stored. Downloading a particular MP3 is just a matter of clicking on a link. Once downloaded, it's stored in your Napster directory and made available for others to download whenever you're online and logged on to Napster.

Napster made searching for MP3s as easy as searching for something on the web. And by putting ordinary users in touch with each other, it removed advertising conmen from the equation. So it's not hard to see why it became so popular, so quickly. In September 2000, around a year after it started, it had 30 million users worldwide. Of course, the more people that get involved with a network, the more valuable that network becomes. Because so many people began to use Napster, it became easier to find less mainstream tunes. Hence it becomes ever more attractive as more people log on.

The record industry had already been cracking down on MP3 trading in chat rooms and FTP sites. Napster took things to another level completely. It turned MP3 trading into a mainstream pursuit. And it made it very visible. It also showed that most MP3s circulating online were copies of music made by well-known bands. Previously, there'd been talk about how MP3s would let unsigned bands get their music out to a wider public. That is beginning to happen, on a small scale. But Napster made it clear that most people want MP3s by bands they've already heard of.

However, the architecture of the site made legal action problematic for the record companies. Napster doesn't actually have any illegal MP3s on its servers. Instead, it brokers relationships between ordinary users, who have the illegal files on their computers. The music business could, in theory, prosecute individuals who were trading MP3s. But there were so many of them. And many were still the industry's best customers –

< 230 >

Read about it online – Anti-Napster Action

Some anti-Napster musicians and activists have tried to sabotage the site by uploading mislabelled files and the like, for example, The Cuckoo's Egg Project **http://www.hand-2-mouth.com/cuckooegg/** and Stop Napster **http://www.stopnapster.com/**. The New York Times covered their activities earlier this year in a piece called 'Taking Sides in the Napster War' **http://www.nytimes.com/2000/08/31/technology/31naps.html**. ▲

music-loving students, who, even though they packed their hard drives with MP3s, continued to buy CDs. It doesn't always look good to take your customers to court, however naughty they've been.

In the end, the Recording Industry Association of America (RIAA) took Napster to court. Their argument is that Napster is abetting mass copyright infringement, depriving artists in the process. It's true that some musicians were anti-Napster. Metallica famously began a suit against the company – and the likes of Eminem and Dr Dre don't like it much either. Others – Limp Bizkit, Fatboy Slim and Radiohead – seem more relaxed about the site. Many critics pointed out that record companies have generally made sure they give artists as little as possible of the money their work generates. That said, they do give them something – which is more than the big nothing they get from Napster.

Napster's champions say musicians can benefit from the site, because people who download MP3s often go on to buy the official CD. Indeed, there have been suggestions that Radiohead's album 'Kid A' went to the top of the charts as a result of general buzz built by early exposure on

< 231 >

Napster – see MP3 Newswire's story **http://www.mp3newswire.net/stories/2000/radiohead.html**. Napster supporters point out that, overall, record sales have been up over the last year. However, other surveys seem to indicate that sales at record stores in college towns are down (students are amongst Napster's biggest fans). For Napster supporters, the fact that so many law-abiding people are defying the copyright restrictions around music is crucial. It shows that the law needs to change, they argue. People want to take advantage of the flexibility permitted by the net. They want to access music in different ways. They don't want to be tied to buying a whole CD rather than the four good tracks it contains. They want to be able to listen to their collections wherever they are.

The music business is also keen on the net, but they want to keep the lucrative current copyright system. So to counter MP3s, they've championed the Secure Digital Music Initiative (SDMI), an attempt to develop a file format which uses digital watermarks and encryption to block copying. The SDMI project has yet to really get anywhere. And some music business gurus argue that there's no point in pursuing it. They say that MP3 has become the de facto standard and the record companies should work with it.

Read about it online – Secure Digital Music Initiative

For more on SDMI, visit the web site **http://www.sdmi.org**. Salon also has a useful set of articles on the subject, focusing in particular on the efforts of various hackers to crack the supposedly secure format **http://www.salon.com/directory/topics/sdmi/index.html**. ▲

< 232 >

They argue that we're moving from a time when music was a product you owned. According to this theory, we're heading for a future in which music is a service you subscribe to, a future in which people will access the music they want wherever they are (thanks to fast wireless networks). Imagine a kind of ubiquitous personal jukebox. Hence the more radical music gurus think that the industry should embrace Napster as a step on the way to that future. Despite this, for most of 2000 it looked like the RIAA court action would close the site down. This wouldn't have achieved much, since there are all sorts of Napster clones ready to take its place. The best known is Gnutella **http://gnutella.wego.com/** (more on this shortly), but there are plenty of others – try the page of links connected to The Atlantic Review's Napster piece **http://www. theatlantic.com/issues/2000/09/mannlinks.htm**.

However, as this book was going to press, the Bertelsmann Music Group broke ranks with the other major record labels, dropped their court case and signed a deal with Napster. The plan seems to be to start a kind of Napster 2, to run alongside the existing network and contain BMG's musical output. Users will pay a monthly subscription to access this network. The details of the deal had to be worked out and the other record companies were still pushing ahead with their court case against Napster. But we seem to be moving to a future in which each major label runs their own subscription-based file-sharing network. That said, everything could change again. So if you want to keep track of what's happening with Napster, why not try the special sections devoted to it at Salon **http://www.salon.com/directory/topics/napster/index.html**, Wired News **http://www.wired.com/news/mp3/** or MP3 Newswire **http://www. mp3newswire.net/**.

< 233 >

Napster and peer to peer networks

Napster is the biggest thing to happen to the net over the last year – and not just because it has encouraged millions of people to break the law. It's also introduced a big new net idea – peer to peer networking, or P2P, as jargonauts call it. Net idealists have worried for some time now that the net is becoming too corporate, too centralised and too commercial. File-sharing networks like Napster seem to be a move in the other direction. They do the thing the net was always supposed to do – let ordinary people communicate with each other, without central control. Hence peer to peer networking.

There are now lots of sites attempting to extend the Napster idea. Gnutella, mentioned above, is a general file-sharing network where people can swap more than just MP3s. It was designed to avoid the weaknesses of Napster. There's no central directory and no organisation behind the site, so there's no one to sue or shut down. However, searching is slower and more difficult. When it looked like Napster was going to be shut down, there were suggestions that Gnutella would take over. Since then critics have argued that it's not robust enough to cope – see Janelle Brown's Salon piece at **http://www.salon.com/tech/feature/ 2000/09/29/gnutella_paradox/print.html**.

Read about it online – P2P Directories

There are now all sorts of peer to peer networks online. Wired Magazine recently put together a useful directory of links to the main sites **http://www.wired.com/wired/archive/8.10/p2p_pages.html**. ▲

< 234 >

Because Napster annoyed the big corporations and allowed ordinary people to network with each other, pundits have been musing a lot about its political implications. In the New York Times, Andrew Sullivan used it as the hook for a piece about the rise of digital socialism and dot communism – it should still be on his site **http://www.andrewsullivan.com**. This is interesting, within limits. Napster is a business first and foremost, as demonstrated by its deal with BMG. And all sorts of businesses (not least Intel) have talked up P2P as the next big e commerce idea. CNet ran a good piece on the scene that put things into perspective **http://news.cnet.com/news/0-1005-201-3248711-0.html**.

Others have cast doubt on the idealism surrounding file sharing. Xerox PARC researchers Eytan Adar and Bernardo A. Huberman recently published a survey **http://www.parc.xerox.com/istl/groups/iea/papers/gnutella/** that seems to show that most Gnutella users are takers, not givers and that most of the files on the service are provided by a small number of committed users. Now that Napster is getting into bed with the record companies, net radicals will probably move on to the much more hardcore Freenet **http://freenet.sourceforge.net/**. Created by Irish programmer Ian Clarke, it's a decentralised network designed to let people distribute information anonymously and without fear of censorship. Feed recently ran an interesting interview with Clarke **http://www.feedmag.com/re/re369_master.html**.

One good place to catch up with the ideas generated by the P2P idea is the homepage put up by American net theorist Clay Shirky **http://www.shirky.com**. He talks about Napster ushering a 'content at the edges' model for the net of the future. Over the last few years, he argues, we've gradually turned the net into a centralised, increasingly one-way network. People treat their computers as terminals they use to access a

< 235 >

limited number of big media web sites. In contrast, file-sharing networks like Napster use the power people have on their desktops to enable them to work together on the margins.

P2P casts doubt on the idea that in the future we'll all use slimmed-down network computers or information appliances. Instead, says Shirky, we'll see the rise of the desktop server – a cross between the PC and the server, which will let people network with each other in all sorts of ways. Napster works by aggregating the disk space on individual users' PCs to create an enormous online storage system. But you can also pool the unused processing power of individual computers to create a huge, distributed supercomputer. The first project to try this was SETI@Home **http://setiathome.ssl.berkeley.edu/**, which uses distributed computing to analyse radio signals from space for evidence of alien communication. New companies are attempting something more practical – both Parabon **http://www.parabon.com** and Popular Power **http://www.popularpower.com** suggest they will use distributed computing power for medical experiments (finding cures for the common cold and

---

Read about it online – Mojo Nation

Mojo Nation **http://www.mojonation.com** tries to combine a file-sharing network with distributed computing and anarcho-capitalism. Users can earn 'Mojo' by renting out unused processor power. They can then use this to buy files on the network. And they can upload files of their own. It's a bit more complex than this suggests, however. Find out more from Salon's profile of founder Jim McCoy **http://www.salon.com/tech/view/ 2000/10/09/mojo_nation/print.html**. ▲

< 236 >

cancer). The GOLEM Project **http://golem03.cs-i.brandeis.edu/** wants to use distributed computing to conduct an experiment in artificial intelligence. There have been suggestions that distributed computing might help improve search engines in the future. Whatever happens to Napster, it's clearly only the beginning for peer to peer networking

Music download sites

As mentioned above, the MP3 scene has been home to a lot of idealistic chatter about the empowerment of musicians, or something. The big idea is that unsigned bands can use the format to route around the hated record companies and sell direct to the fans. It's hard not to have doubts about this. Most new bands are using MP3s to create some buzz in the hope of scoring a more conventional record company deal. In addition, downloading an MP3 file still takes a while. Most people aren't willing to waste that kind of time on bands they don't know.

For that reason, the artists most likely to use MP3s and the net to liberate themselves from record companies are big names who already have a sizeable fan base. Long term it might make sense for the likes of David Bowie (who started his own service offering net access to fans) to cut out the record companies and deal directly with his fans. Many famous artists – from The Beastie Boys **http://www.beastieboys.com** to Radiohead **http://www.radiohead.com** and The Offspring **http://www. theoffspring.com** – now give away MP3s as a way of generating PR. MP3s also seem well suited to bands who used to be big and retain a fan base that is committed but not large enough for the big record companies. Many are starting to set up their own web sites and sell directly to their fans. Small independent record labels are doing the same thing (for example, take a look at the leftfield British dance label Ninja Tune

< 237 >

Read about it online - MP3 Players

If you want something nice to play your MP3s on, you could try an MP3 player – first on the market was the Rio **http://www.riohome.com** – the Rio online audio portal **http://www.rioport.com/** is also worth a look. Also worth a look is the portable Nomad Jukebox, which stores around 150 CDs (in MP3 form) **http://www.nomadworld.com**. ▲

http://www.ninjatune.net or the American indie Matador **http://www.matadorrecords.com/**.

That said, some unknown bands are beginning to make money from circulating MP3s on the net. MP3.com runs a program called 'Payback for Playback' **http://www.mp3.com/payback/**, which rewards bands according to the number of times their tracks are downloaded. Some of the top earners, which include previously unknown outfits like 303infinity and reasonably famous bands like The Cowboy Junkies, have been making up to $15,000 per month from the scheme.

Before Napster got started, MP3.com **http://www.mp3.com** dominated the online music scene. Michael Robertson's site started out as a vigorous critic of the record industry. MP3.com didn't feature any illegal material – just MP3s willingly uploaded by unsigned bands. But it did have links to MP3 search engines and the software you needed to convert your CDs to MP3s and to play them on your computer. Then the site was floated successfully on the stock market (at one point, it was valued at $7 billion) and it started to look more corporate, with ads for well known bands and MP3s willingly made available by big names.

< 238 >

MP3.com's transformation from net subculture champion to online record company in the making led to criticism from hard core fans. However, the site managed to get caught up in its own lawsuit, thanks to its MyMP3.com service. Basically, this was a central database of CDs designed to let users listen to music from their own record collections on the net. MP3.com went ahead with the service without sorting out a proper license agreement with the big record companies. They were able to agree terms with four of the big five, but Universal Music Group held out and took them to court. As this book was going to press, MP3.com still hadn't settled with UMG and seemed likely to be stuck with pretty crippling financial penalties. It had begun to agree deals with the other labels and publishers. For an update, visit the site.

Other sites are also setting up 'online music lockers' – for example MyPlay **http://www.myplay.com**. And there are also plenty of sites where you can download MP3s. Most sites now offer a mix of files by name bands and newcomers. Most give away music, though some are trying to introduce different revenue models – everything from paying for specific tracks to regular subscription charges. Try Vitaminic **http://www.vitaminic.co.uk**, Epitonic **http://www.epitonic.com**, PeopleSound **http://www.peoplesound.com**, iCrunch **http://www.icrunch.co.uk** and Emusic **http://www.emusic.com**. MP3 isn't the only music file format online. There's also Liquid Audio, which offers more control for the music industry. Visit **http://www.liquidaudio.com** and you can download a special player and access plenty of legal music files made by big names. When it comes to finding music online, one of the better search sites is Listen.com **http://www.listen.com**.

The technology news site ZDNet.com does a good job of tracking the whole scene – it's a good place for tips on new sites **http://music.**

< 239 >

gamespot.com/index.html. It is mainly focused around rock and dance, like most media discussion of online music. Other genres are available online. The Global Music Network **http://www.gmn.com/** concentrates on classical and jazz and features webcasts and downloads. Online Classics **http://www.onlineclassics.net/** showcases classical webcasts, most of which are online and available for viewing when you want. The American political magazine The New Republic covers classical music online – go to **http://www.thenewrepublic.com/cyberspace/index.html** and look for pieces by Adam Baer.

Radio on the net

Radio is, if you believe the techno-pundits, poised to become a boom area online. They've been saying that for a while. But this time they may be right. Sound quality is beginning to improve, with many sites now streaming MP3 quality audio. Breaks in transmission caused by net congestion are a problem, though broadband connections should improve things. Beyond that, online radio stations are now experimenting with the new possibilities offered by the net. Some sites now let

---

Read about it online – Spoken Word Online

Net audio isn't just about music. You can also download audio books and files that features authors reading their work – some put up by publishers, some by literary webzines. The online audio portal Voquette **http://www.voquette.com** has links to what's out there. Salon also has a good audio section, formerly known as MP3Lit.com **http://www.salon.com/audio/index.html**. ▲

< 240 >

Tips - Unmetered Access and Net Radio

Unmetered access makes listening to net radio as cost effective as switching on a transistor radio. However, some unmetered deals won't let you tune in online. So check the fine print. ▲

users determine the musical output and are edging towards the universal jukebox idea mentioned previously.

In the UK, net radio hasn't yet developed the way it has in America and Europe, thanks mainly to the difficulties involved in obtaining a license to broadcast music online. However, the record companies have begun to relax their regulations, which should allow UK companies to catch up. For the moment though, UK net radio means either terrestrial stations, like Radio 1 **http://www.bbc.co.uk/radio1** and Capital **http://www.capitalfm.com**, who stream their output over the net as well as over the airwaves, and pirates like Interface **http://www.pirate-radio.co.uk**, an online dance radio station that has been up and running for a few years now.

There is a point to listening to 'Today' on Radio 4 on the net, if you're living on the other side of the world. It keeps you in touch with your home. But otherwise, if you've got a transistor radio, it seems peculiarly pointless to tune in online. Instead, why not try one of the countless stations round the world that now broadcast via the net? You can get everything from American shock jocks and East European news outlets to stations specialising in West Coast rap, Brazilian samba and Finnish tango. For an guide to what's out there, try the Internet Radio List **http://www.internetradiolist.com/** or Live Radio **http://www.live-radio.net/info.shtml**. Yahoo's Broadcast.com has a good selection of mainly

< 241 >

American stations **http://radio.broadcast.com/**. Similarly, on general media portals like iCast **http://www.icast.com** and Akoo **http://www.akoo.com**, you'll find links to 150 radio stations. To listen to most stations online, you need standard plug-ins like Real Player or something like the Windows Media Player. However, at some sites, you do need to download special software – for example Spinner **http://www.spinner.com**.

The big UK stations are about to expand their online operations. Virgin **http://www.virginradio.co.uk** is planning a series of specialist net radio channels. The BBC is about to launch digital stations aimed at particular markets that you should be able to hear online. Other net radio sites are experimenting with personalisation. This isn't just a matter of picking a channel that specialises in the particular musical micro-genre you like (hardbag ethno-techno or whatever). Instead, once you've chosen a particular channel, you're invited to rate the tracks you hear. The site then customises the audio stream appropriately. These channels can also look at the music you like, cross-reference it with other users' tastes and then recommend artists they think you might like.

For an example, try Launch.com and its Launchcast service **http://www.launchcast.com**, where you can also customise your own music video channel. The big US music site Sonic Net **http://radio.sonicnet.com** offers something similar, as does Tune To **http://www.tuneto.com**. The latter delivers high quality audio, but it does it by downloading several dozen megabytes of sound files on your hard disk. If space is tight, this may be an issue. Of course, once you're tracking what a listener is choosing to hear, you can do more than just change the soundtrack. You can also send ads their way, special online offers and the like. Apparently, Chrysalis Records are about to launch a personalised net radio channel over here, called PureMix **http://www.puremix.com**.

< 242 >

Read about it online - Personalised Radio

Critics have suggested that personalisation gets rid of one of the great things about radio – that people are listening to something together. Michelle Goldberg recently thrashed out these issues for the US magazine The New Republic **http://www.thenewrepublic.com/cyberspace/goldberg071000.html**. ▲

Many general music sites offer a net radio service. Try Tunes.com **http://www.tunes.com**, which along with reviews and MP3 downloads, also has a radio channel. Alternatively, there's BeSonic **http://www.besonic.com**, a UK outfit that's set up in Europe. Here you can download MP3s and listen to net radio, amongst other things. More UK net radio stations are on the way. Ex-Radio 1 DJ Bruno Brookes has just set up Storm **http://www.stormlive.com**, which is aimed at the over-40s. More interesting are sites that give ordinary people, as opposed to dreary old DJs, the chance to set up their own net radio stations. Try Live 365

Read about it online - Net Radios

According to some, the future of net access is the specially designed information appliance that does one thing well. Example – the net radio receiver, which looks like an ordinary set but picks up stations from around the world. Early versions are already out, courtesy of Sonic Box **http://www.sonicbox.com**. Also worth looking out for is the Kerbango **http://www.kerbango.com**. ▲

< 243 >

http://www.live365.com, which, along with access to more standard channels, lets you set up your own radio channel or listen to those set up by other amateur DJs. The pioneers in this area were Shoutcast **http://www.shoutcast.com**. Their site has a useful list of the sites using its technology to broadcast online. Alternatively, try Gogaga **http://www.gogaga.com**, which regularly features 'Solid Steel', the radio show by UK DJs and multimedia pioneers Cold Cut or Radio Spy **http://www.radiospy.com**, which offers tools for creating your own channel or searching channels set up by other users.

Video on the net

Film industry types worry that they will soon face the same problems online as the music business. Copies of popular Hollywood films are beginning to appear on the net – things like the SF action film 'The Matrix' and 'The Phantom Menace'. The files involved are massive, so at the moment this kind of thing is restricted to people with high-speed connections – i.e. people in the net business and students. But as bandwidth increases and as compression technology improves, bootleg film files may become more widespread. Unsurprisingly, the film industry has moved quickly to act against Scour **http://www.scour.com**, an excellent online media search site that looked like it might turn into a Napster for film.

There's lots of video you can check out online without facing legal action and lengthy downloads (relatively speaking). It's still low quality and very small screen, but there are some interesting things if you look. Incidentally, I'm using video as a catch-all term for various kinds of visual material – everything from mainstream TV broadcasts streamed onto the web to short films and animations put up by independent film makers and unedited live feeds from webcams.

< 244 >

To get a sense of the variety of stuff that's online, try one of the 'entertainment hubs' set up by the big media/technology companies. Real Networks' showcase page **http://realguide.real.com** links to different video sites that use its technology. There are pages devoted to movies, music and much more. Via the site, you can check out film trailers and music videos and even watch live news (usually American). Alternatively, try Yahoo Events (it's at **http://www.broadcast.com**) where you'll find links to online events, webcasts and multimedia content. The video section **http://www.broadcast.com/video** is worth checking. The Worldwide Broadcast Network **http://www.wwmovies.net** is useful too. Time Warner has set up Entertaindom **http://www.entertaindom.com**, where, again, you'll find music videos, concert webcasts and cartoons (more on this shortly). For a cheekier, more British entertainment hub, try Switch2 **http://www.switch2.net**.

Incidentally, the big media companies haven't found the net an easy ride. In 2000, Pop.com, which was backed by Steven Spielberg's Dreamworks company and Ron Howard's Imagine, closed down. Similarly, the Digital Entertainment Network (aka DEN), which was backed by Microsoft, also had to go offline. There have been suggestions that online video won't really be viable until broadband connections become more widespread. Certainly, at the moment, the technology prohibits showing anything you might see down at the local multiplex. Instead, online video is focused around the kind of short films you don't see on TV. The net is becoming a place for established creatives to test out ideas or for first time filmmakers to get their work out.

So if you want something that features stars and big budget effects, you'll have to make do with Hollywood trailers. Try Trailer Park on the Film Unlimited site **http://www.filmunlimited.co.uk** or the big entertainment

< 245 >

Read about it online – The Blair Witch Project

Hollywood promotional sites are usually pretty dull. In contrast, the indie handheld horror 'The Blair Witch Project' used the web cleverly to embellish on the film's back story. Consequently it pulled in a whole new audience. The sequel 'Book of Shadows' was promoted more conventionally, with a series of webcasts, which you can still see at **http://www.blairwitch.com**. ▲

hubs mentioned above. Alternatively, look out for 'Quantum Project', a film which premiered on the web in the summer of 2000 and stars Stephen Dorff and John Cleese amongst others (you can still find it at **http://www. sightsound.com**). At the time, there was talk in the press about net film coming of age. Much was made about 'Quantum Project's Hollywood-style production values and the quality of the script and the talent involved.

However, another project has a better claim as the real breakthrough for film online – Kevin Rubio's 'Troops', a short 'Star Wars' spoof, made in 1997 and released online a year later. It got a lot of attention in the run-up to the release of 'The Phantom Menace'. You can still see it at the 'Star Wars' fan site The Force.net **http://theforce.net/troops**. 'Troops' was cheeky, clever and short – perfect for the current state of the web, both technologically and demographically. Now, you can see all sorts of short films online. Try the iFilm network **http://www.ifilm.com**, Atom Films **http://www.atomfilms.com**, Reel Screen **http://www.reelscreen. com**, The Bit Screen **http://www.thebitscreen.com**, and The Sync **http://www. thesync.com**. At Alwaysi **http://www.alwaysi.com**, along with new independent films, you can also see old classics – everything from slapstick

< 246 >

shorts starring Charlie Chaplin to old Howard Hawks' films like 'His Girl Friday'.

Online video isn't completely dominated by Americans. British filmmakers and writers are beginning to move on to the web. Take 'The Junkies' **http://www.thejunkies.com**, a no budget sitcom about some hopeless junkies written by established comedy writers David Quantick and Jane Bussman and pumped straight out on to the web. For them, the net is a way to get ideas out quickly, without conservative commissioning editors getting in the way. Some directors are also trying develop stories that take advantage of the net's distinctive properties. For example, 'Running Time' **http://www.itsyourmovie.com/rt**, an interactive film developed by Simon Beaufoy, who wrote 'The Full Monty', let viewers vote on which way they wanted the story to go (the story involved a bike messenger caught up in a high tech criminal conspiracy). Then the filmmakers had to respond. Opinions are mixed as to whether it worked, but it was an interesting experiment. The show's over now, but you can still see the film at the site.

Animation online

Using technologies like MacroMedia's Shockwave and Flash, animators are now putting short cartoons up on the net. Some use speech bubbles and are just one step on from comic strips. Others are full-blown cartoons, though often technical limitations mean that kinetic action takes a back seat in favour of talking heads and witty scripts. Courtesy of technology created by Pulse Entertainment, some web cartoons now feature 3D computer animation. Again, if you want to sample what's out there, start with one of the big entertainment hubs, like Entertaindom and Atom Films.

< 247 >

Alternatively, try Pulse Entertainment **http://www.pulse3d.com** or Macromedia's Shockwave site **http://www.shockwave.com**, both of which showcase cartoons created using their programming tools. On the latter you should find 'Stain Boy', a cartoon created by film director Tim Burton – it's also on his own site **http://www.timburton.com**. He isn't the only creative using the web to avoid dealing with the established film/TV business. John Kricfalusi, the man who created the cult cartoon series 'Ren And Stimpy', now puts his new work directly online at **http://www.spumco.com**. Aardman, the company responsible for 'Wallace and Gromit' and 'Chicken Run', have created a series specifically for the net – 'Rude Kid'. You can find it on the Atom Films site – alternatively, try the link on the Aardman site **http://www.aardman.co.uk**.

Established animators like the web because it's easy, quick and cheap to do something that looks reasonably good. So it's a good place to test out ideas, in particular to try things that stretch the boundaries of taste and decency. Lots of web cartoons are aimed at a young audience and are fairly in your face. It seems to be what people want. Some webtoons are getting good enough ratings to persuade people to give them a go offline.

Read about it online – Virtual Humans

Some sites have been using 3D computer animation technologies to create 'virtual celebrities', like the online newscaster Ananova **http://www.ananova.com**, who delivers the headlines in tones marginally less robotic than Moira Stewart. For an alternative virtual human, try Jackie Strike **http://www.jackiestrike.com**), the first ever computer-controlled virtual presidential candidate (unless you count Al Gore). ▲

< 248 >

Read about it online – Scott McCloud

There are plenty of comics now online – from well-known strips like Dilbert **http://www.dilbert.com** to artier efforts. One of the best comics sites is by Scott McCloud **http://www.scottmccloud.com/**, a comics auteur, whose book 'Reinventing Comics' is about adapting comics for the net. It's been a big influence on web designers, apparently. ▲

'Starship Regulars', a webtoon from Icebox **http://www.icebox.com** is due to be turned into a small screen series. Icebox's popular 'Mr Wong' is also about to be made into a straight-to-video full-length film. For TV execs, web cartoon sites are becoming research and development labs – places where they can see which ideas work. So if you want to look for 'The Simpsons' of the future, try the sites run by the leading web cartoon companies – Mondo Mini Shows **http://www.mondominishows.com** (where you'll find links to their excellent 'Like, News'), Wild Brain **http://www.wildbrain.com** and Dot Comix **http://www.dotcomix.com**, which features a new cartoon everyday.

Webcams

Idealists love to talk about how the web allows ordinary people to put their own ideas up online for the rest of the world to see. Some people now take this idea to another level altogether, via webcams, small cameras that upload images of their everyday lives to the net. Surprising as it may sound, some of these d-i-y docusoaps draw large audiences. Indeed, you could argue that they anticipated reality TV shows like 'Big Brother'. Web cams have been around for quite a while. In the early days,

< 249 >

Read about it online – Webcam Stories

Some sites use web cams to create immersive net fictions, like Online Caroline **http://www.onlinecaroline.com**, which features a web cam that lets you keep tabs on Caroline and her problematic relationships. She also emails you with the latest news. Some people found this so compelling they thought Caroline was a real person. ▲

they were (relatively) low-tech and delivered still images at regular intervals. Now they can handle live video. Back in the mid-nineties, they were something of an indulgence. Geeks began uploading images of their coffee machines – mainly because they could. Things moved up a gear when Jennifer Ringley set up a webcam in her bedroom and began uploading uncensored images of her life. Jennicam **http://www. jennicam.org** was presented as an arty experiment. However, it sparked off a new genre of online porn, countless sites offering uncensored 24-hour feeds from college girls' dorms.

However, there's more to all this than new angles on old style erotica. There are now web cams all over the place – in the middle of cities, out in the country, at zoos, at big sporting events, in radio station studios. Cammunity **http://www.cammunity.com** has links to all sorts of cams (aside from those that might feature sexual content). Alternatively, try the Webcam Resource **http://www.camcity.com/webcamresource/ index.shtml** or the Yahoo webcam section **http://dir.yahoo.com/Computers_ and_internet/Internet/Devices_Connected_to_the_Internet/Web_Cams/**. As computers and connections get more powerful, more people are putting up webcams in and around their homes. There are now American sites

< 250 >

Read about it online – Webcam History

For more on the first wave of web cams, try Salon's 1998 story 'Live From My Bedroom', **http://www.salon.com/21st/feature/1998/01/cov_08feature.html**. Recently, the webzine took another look, via a very snide attack on the dullest webcam celeb, Dotcomguy **http://www.salon.com/tech/feature/2000/08/01/dotcomguy/index.html**. ▲

to help people broadcast their ordinary lives online, like SpotFree **http://www.spotfree.com**.

Jennicam showed how much net traffic a show-all webcam site could generate. It's still running and still moderately successful, though it has a lot more competition now. For example there's Here and Now **http://www.hereandnow.net**, a live, unedited 24 hour feed from a house inhabited by four student buddies (one of them the nephew of Gore Vidal). Of course, the biggest web cam site (at least in the UK) was the online extension of the 'Big Brother' TV series **http://www.bigbrother. terra.com**. While the show was running, the site topped the UK web ratings by a long way. If you believe the people behind it, Nasty Nick's exposure was the biggest thing to happen to the net in the UK, at least in terms of traffic levels.

Broadband connections

To get the best from net multimedia, you'll probably have to move to a broadband connection. At the moment, that usually means cable or ADSL. There are other options on the horizon. Satellite connections can deliver information very quickly – up 35Mbps, but they're one way only.

< 251 >

If you want to upload data, you need another sort of connection. More promising are wireless connections that work via radio frequencies. These offer high speeds too – 11Mbps. There have even been experiments that apparently show that power lines can double as broadband connections delivering data at speeds up to 1Mbps.

However, these are still a way off. For the moment, ADSL and cable are your best bet. That said, there is an alternative, reasonably speedy option that has been put in the shade by newer technologies – an ISDN line (the letters stand for Integrated Services Digital Network). Over the last few years, BT has been pushing ISDN to ordinary users, via its Home Highway service **http://www.bt.com/homehighway**. Basically, ISDN is a digital telephone line that offers connection speeds of up to 128Kbps. ISDN also lets you do two things at once; you can be connected to the net and talking on the telephone at the same time, all via the same line. However, you do need extra hardware – either an internal ISDN card or an external ISDN Terminal Adapter. You'll need to convert your existing BT line – which costs around £50 at the moment (though if you don't have a BT line, the cost can be anything from £150 to £290. Rental and call charges are high too. That said, the price of ISDN lines is coming

Read about it online – Online Gaming

All sorts of net pursuits make more sense with broadband connections, not least online gaming. If you're using a standard 56k modem, playing Quake online is always problematic. But with ADSL it should be a lot better. For more info, try Wireplay **http://www.gameplay.com/wireplay** or Barry's World **http://www.barrysworld.com**. ▲

< 252 >

Jargon file - ADSL

The letters stand for Asymmetric Digital Subscriber Line. ADSL uses ordinary telephone lines to send and receive data to the net at high speeds. ▲

down, mainly because BT now has another high speed connection option to sell – ADSL.

ADSL

This is probably the most talked about broadband option, if only because it seems to involve the least amount of hassle for the user. ADSL uses standard telephone lines to deliver a high speed connection to the net – speeds on offer can go up to 2Mb a second – that's around 40 times faster than a 56K modem. You pay a flat monthly fee and get a connection to the net that is 'always on'. In other words, when you want to get online, you don't need to make a dial-up connection. You're there already, as it were. The highest profile ADSL service currently on offer comes from BT. Called 'openworld' **http://www.bt.com/openworld/**, it was launched in the summer of 2000 and was aimed first at business users, though a home user service did reach the market by the autumn. The first version of the service promised home users connection speeds of up to 500Kbps – around ten times faster than a standard modem. That's download speed. If you're sending information back, the speed promised is 250Kbps.

This connection speed may go up. At the time of writing, the business service announced it was launching its 1Mbps and 2Mbps services in November 2000. Presumably at some point in 2001, those kinds of

< 253 >

speeds will be available to ordinary punters. At the time of writing, the home service is aimed at people who want to hook up one computer. If you want to hook several up in a home network, you'll have to go for one of the pricier business options. At the moment, home users have to pay a one-off installation fee of £150 and then monthly rental of just under £40 per month. If you want to sign up to the 'openworld' home service, you'll need a computer running Windows 98 or Mac OS8.1 or higher, a Pentium 133MHz at least, and 32MB of RAM. If you decide to go for the business service and want to connect up several computers, they'll need Ethernet cards.

For home users, the installation charge seems to include the new bits of technology you need – in particular a USB ADSL modem and a splitter, which lets you use one line for voice and fax calls as well as the net. You also get access to some specially created broadband content – music videos, webcasts of concerts, news, film reviews, trailers and much more. There are currently a few restrictions on the service. You need to sign up for a minimum of twelve months. To get it, your local exchange needs to be ADSL enabled. Your line will need to pass a line test. And BT's 'openworld' is distance dependent. If you're too far away, it degrades consider-

---

Read about it online – Living With Broadband

ZDNet journalist Rupert Godwins took part in BT's 1999 ADSL trial and wrote about how it changed the way he used and thought of the net – the piece is still online at **http://www.zdnet.co.uk/news/1999/29/ ns-9086.html**. ZD Net also has a useful archive of ADSL news at **http://www.zdnet.co.uk/news/specials/1999/07/adsl/**. ▲

< 254 >

Tips – Shop Around

BT's 'openworld' is the highest profile ADSL service currently on offer.
But other ISPs are moving into the market. Find out more about who's
offering what at ADSL Guide **http://www.adslguide.org.uk** or ADSL UK
http://www.adsluk.org.uk. ▲

ably. So you need to live within 1-3 miles from your exchange. Find out
whether you qualify for the service at the openworld site.

Cable

Cable can deliver fantastic connection speeds – up to 10Mbps in both
directions. Unfortunately, the network is still being built and coverage
can be patchy. You're probably alright if you live in or near a big city
in the South. Otherwise, you may have to wait. In addition, you share
a cable with your neighbours. So if everyone uses the service at the
same time, download speeds can fall drastically. That said, cable is
definitely worth investigating. At the time of writing the two main

Tips – Security & 'Always-on' Broadband Connections

Because broadband connections are always on, they are more
vulnerable to potential intruders than the standard dial-up connection.
Your ISP can help configure your computer so that it is more secure
during installation. There are things you can do too – for more
information go to page 345. ▲

< 255 >

Read about it online – Cable Modem News

Things change constantly in the internet access business. For up-to-date information on cable deals – everything from prices to which companies have entered the market, try The Cable Modem Centre **http://www.cable-modems.co.uk/**. ▲

players in the UK were NTL **http://www.ntl.com** and Telewest, via their Blue Yonder service **http://www.telewest.co.uk/hsi/blueyonder.html**. To sign up with these services, you need a reasonably up to date PC or Mac. You'll also need to install an Ethernet Card and you'll need a cable modem. With NTL, you have to buy your own cable modem. Telewest offers free cable modem rental. You also have to pay an installation fee.

At the time of writing, Blue Yonder seems the best service in terms of price. Users pay £33 a month and an installation fee of £50. NTL users pay £40 a month, along with an extra £10 or so for an NTL telephone line and basic cable TV service. They also have to buy their own cable modem – though NTL has a few deals here – you should end up paying £150 or so. There's also a £25 installation charge. With both you have to buy and install your own Ethernet card if you don't have one. So things can add up. But overall, these offers still compare reasonably well with BT's ADSL service. However, before you spend too much time wondering whether you can afford it, visit NTL and Telewest's web sites to see whether they cover your area.

< 256 >

Shopping on the net

Net shopping first reached the British mainstream in 1999, leading many techno-pundits to suggest that pretty soon we would abandon the high street and instead shop online, where buying would be easy, there would be a greater range of choice and everything would be cheaper. Pundits weren't the only people who got carried away. Net businesses rushed to open online shops, often without ensuring they had the necessary back-up to provide a decent service. In a bid to quickly build market share, they spent millions on ad campaigns and publicity stunts in which they gave away products.

As ever, a backlash quickly followed the hype. Shortly after Christmas 1999, the press was quick to point out that net shops hadn't proved as popular as had been predicted. And many net users who did take the plunge and do some of their Christmas shopping online complained about dodgy service and late deliveries. By spring 2000, net shops that had been launched just six months before were experiencing financial difficulties. Customers still weren't there in large enough numbers to cover the massive advertising campaigns the companies had to pay for to ensure people knew they existed.

The highest profile failure was the sports fashion retailer Boo.com, which hyped itself as the future of shopping in the autumn of 1999, but was out of business less than six months later. Boo.com suffered from bad management and from trying to introduce flashy multimedia sales tricks that didn't really work that well. Some journalists decided that the site's failure proved that net shopping would never catch on. It does nothing of the sort. However, people do need to scale down their expectations. Net shopping is going to take a while to reach the mainstream. And the companies pioneering it may not ultimately survive. More than

< 257 >

a few net shops and e commerce companies will go out of business over the next year or so.

But net shopping is going to be around for a while. Why? Because it's easy and convenient and gives you access to a wider range of products than you can find on your local high street. Do it properly and you can save time and money. That doesn't mean that shopping on the net will replace real shops. Most of us enjoy shopping in our favourite real world stores – whether they're bookshops or high fashion boutiques. We're not going to give that up. On the other hand, it is possible to overstate the sensual pleasures of the weekly supermarket shop.

Once you give net shopping a try, you discover that it isn't the same as real-world retail. Some early online shops didn't, and mistakenly attempted to simulate supermarkets and shopping malls. Smarter businesses saw quickly that the net let them experiment with new ways of selling, that you didn't have to mock up shelves full of beans. However, what many are now also realising is that online shopping still has much to learn from offline retail.

In the past two years, all sorts of new ideas have been tried out online. We've had reverse auctions (e.g. Priceline.com **http://www.priceline.com**),

Read about it online - E Commerce Critics

Net shopping has plenty of critics concerned about more than late deliveries. In the journal NetFuture, Stephen L. Talbott argues that shopping isn't just about price but also about supporting a local community **http://www.ora.com/people/staff/stevet/netfuture/1999/may1499_90.html**. ▲

< 258 >

in which customers say how much they'll pay for a flight or hotel room, and companies then decide if they're prepared to meet the price. We've had 'demand-driven' sites (e.g. Respond.com **http://www.respond.com** in the States or the car site Autobytel UK **http://www.autobytel.co.uk**), in which punters says they want something – a book, a CD player, a car – and the site attempts to put them in touch with retailers. There've been aggregate buying sites, in which people club together in order to get better prices. The Swedish site Let's Buy It **http://www.letsbuyit.com** is trying to make the idea work over here. There've been 'zero margin' shops that claim to sell products at cost and hope to make money from advertising. The big US player is Buy.com – their UK operation is at **http://www.gb.buy.com**.

All very interesting, but also potentially confusing to net users who are already a bit uncertain about buying online. The best net shops realise that the shopping experience needs to be familiar as well as different. The leading online retailer Amazon **http://www.amazon.co.uk** gets the balance between innovation and tradition about right. Visit their books department and you find top ten charts, reviews and interviews. You can also post reviews of books you've read. Amazon cross-references its records, so that it can recommend titles purchased by people who bought the same books as you. You can also get email updates about new titles on subjects you're interested in.

However, when it comes to buying something, the process is very simple. You make a list of what you want. You enter your credit card details. The stuff gets sent to you. Perhaps in the future, more complex retail models will become established. But at the moment, most net shoppers are after convenience. They like net shopping because it doesn't take as much time as a trip to the high street, something that sites that are attempting to develop radical new retail models would do well to remember.

< 259 >

Tips - Shopping and Privacy

Amazon can remember what you've previously purchased because it creates a little identifying file on your browser – called a cookie. There are benefits to this. Net shops can tell you about special offers in an area you've shown an interest in. But there are problems too. Will they sell your data it to junk emailers? For more about net shopping and privacy, go to page 335. ▲

With online shopping, you do have to wait for your purchases to be delivered. However, some American sites now offer same day delivery, for example Kozmo **http://www.kozmo.com** and Urban Fetch, who did try to set up over here **http://www.urbanfetch.co.uk**, but, at the time of writing, seem to have closed down. There are no delivery delays if your purchase can be sent electronically. It's been possible to buy software online and download it directly for quite a while. Try Jungle.com's Download section at **http://www.downloadshop.co.uk**. But now you can also buy music and electronic books. Try the E Books section at Barnes and Noble **http://ebooks.barnesandnoble.com/** or Online Originals **http://www.onlineoriginals.com/**.

Products that consist of bits are obviously well suited to online shopping. As for things made out of atoms, some work better than others. You probably wouldn't want to buy a designer suit online. But books, CDs, videos, video games and computer software are another thing entirely. They're portable and you don't need to touch them to know roughly what you're getting. Similarly, with travel and financial services, you don't need to see the thing you're buying. Indeed, some travel sites

< 260 >

are now issuing electronic tickets, so they don't have the hassle of delivering paper tickets. Computer hardware, electronic gadgets and cars are also becoming popular online purchases.

Perhaps the biggest potential growth area is online supermarket shopping. E commerce generally uses low prices to draw in the punters. But many people are happy to pay a bit more to get out of the weekly supermarket shop, as Tesco **http://www.tesco.net**, Sainsburys **http://www.sainsburys.co.uk**, Iceland **http://www.iceland.co.uk** and the other big UK supermarkets have discovered. Doing the weekly shop online isn't without problems. It takes a while at first – you need to set up your standard shopping list. But it's definitely worth a try. Go along to your favourite supermarket's web site to see if they cover your area.

Making an online purchase

This tends to work in the same way at most online shops. You browse for the product you want, then press a 'Buy' button, which adds the item to your online 'shopping cart'. Once you're ready to pay, you press the 'Checkout' button. You go to a page where you enter your details – name, address, credit card number. You also choose a shipping method.

Tips - Check the Delivery Costs

Once you start browsing round online shops, you may be surprised by some of the prices. You'll often find 20% of the standard prices for books, CDs and videos. But before you buy, check the delivery charges (and times). These can add up. You can still come out ahead, compared to the high street. But it pays to check. ▲

< 261 >

The total cost is totted up and you're given an opportunity to confirm the purchase or change your mind. Then it's just a question of waiting for your goods to arrive. Some online retailers email you to confirm the purchase and will also send an update about your order's progress.

Obviously, security is a worry when shopping on the net. This probably has more to do with novelty than with real risks. Giving your credit card number to someone over the telephone is potentially risky, but most of us do it without thinking. To protect yourself online, first make sure that personal information and credit card details are sent to a secure server. Both Navigator and Internet Explorer are set up for secure transactions (they use something called Secure Sockets Layer (SSL) technology to make sure that important information is encrypted when it is sent over the net). If you're connected to a secure server, you should see a little graphic of a locked padlock at the bottom of your browser screen. Some earlier browsers use the image of a key. If it's broken, you aren't on a secure site. You can also check by looking at the address in the browser location bar. If you're on a secure server, the URL should start with **https://**. When you enter, your browser may also flash a dialog box telling you as much (you'll see another one when you leave). You can also check a site's security status by looking at its security certificate.

▶ In **Internet Explorer**, select the **File** menu, then **Properties**, then click the **Certificates** button.
▶ In **Navigator**, press the **Security** button on the toolbar, then click on **Open Page Info** if you want to find out more.

If you are worried about sending details over the net, good online retailers always give you the option of telephoning them in. Don't shop

< 262 >

on a site that isn't secure. Don't send personal/credit details by unprotected email. Don't give out any more information than you would with a standard credit-card purchase via the telephone. Incidentally, if you use a credit card, you are protected in various ways against fraud. Many online retailers also offer protection (money-back guarantees and the like), if you can prove that you were the victim of online fraud. There are a few general precautions you can take when shopping online. First, check out the retailer. Make sure they have a real-world address and telephone number. Don't buy from a company with just an email address. Check the refund and return policies before you buy. Ask for confirmation of your order. At the very least, save and print the order screen when you make your purchase. Use your common sense. Be suspicious of incredible offers. It's worth visiting the pages on net shopping put up by The Office of Fair Trading **http://www.oft.gov.uk/html/shopping/ index2.html**. There's some good basic advice, along with details on your legal rights when you buy on the net and what to do if things go wrong.

So where should you shop online? Many net shops are spending lots of money on advertising. If you see something you like the look of, note down the address and go and take a look. Alternatively chat to friends and find out which shops they use and where they've had a good deal. The net magazines and the papers run regular net shopping columns that review the latest net shops. For example, The Guardian's Consumer page, which appears in the G2 supplement every Thursday, features a regular Cybershopping slot.

The best place to go is to find out about net shops is probably one of the big online shopping directories, where you'll find reviews and links to the sites. ShopSmart **http://www.shopsmart.com** is probably the best known UK online shopping directory and is definitely worth a look, as

< 263 >

Tips - Take It Slow

One crucial tip as far as net shopping is concerned – slow down. Net shops remove the barriers that slow us down in the real world. In a way, that's the point. But sometimes, hauling your purchase to the checkout allows time for you to decide you don't want it. The net allows a new kind of hair-trigger impulse buying. See it, want it, buy it. Point. Click. Shop – as someone's net shopping ad campaign says. Sometimes it pays to hang back a bit. ▲

is Shops on the Net **http://www.shopsonthenet.co.uk**. Shopping Unlimited **http://www.shoppingunlimited.co.uk** is also worth checking. Another good place to look is Which? Magazine's Webtrader page **http://www.which. net/webtrader**. In order to boost consumer confidence in net shopping, the magazine now runs a scheme that checks out online traders to see if they meet certain standards. If you then have problems with one of the shops they've approved, Which? will offer legal support and help. There are now so many shops signed up to the scheme that the pages covering it are now a kind of alternative shopping directory. Alternatively, try the shopping areas on the big UK portal sites – Zoom is quite good here – **http://www.zoom.co.uk**. Yahoo **http://uk.shopping.yahoo.com/**, Excite **http://www.excite.co.uk/shopping/**, Virgin **http://www.virgin.net/shopping/**, and Freeserve **http://www.freeserve.com/shopping/** are also worth a look. However, remember that the sites you see here are the ones who have signed deals with the portals. You're not seeing everything the net has to offer.

< 264 >

Net shopping abroad

It's easy to browse net shops in the US and elsewhere. Actu...
something is more complicated. But there are lots of reasons t... it a
go. Sometimes American net shops are the only place to go for some
items – a book or CD yet to come out over here, a hard to get Christmas
toy. Many products – books, CDs and computer software and hardware
– are cheaper in the States. Even when you pay the shipping costs (and
the duty – more on this shortly), they can still be cheaper than the equivalents on sale here. However, not all US sites will sell to overseas visitors.
Check their policy on this in their customer service/help sections before
you start browsing. In general, shopping overseas requires a little care.
You need to check shipping costs and times carefully. Some shops attach
conditions to international orders (e.g. you have to spend over a certain
amount). You need to check whether guarantees apply. You need to
check on formats (US videos use the NTSC format, whereas here we use
the PAL format) and sizes (American clothes sizes are different to ours).
To keep track of how much you're spending, use the Universal Currency
Converter **http://www.xe.net/ucc**.

Read about it online - Buying from American Sites

Obviously if you buy from an American site and experience problems,
it will be difficult to sort them out. There are US organisations that
monitor commerce on and offline – try the Better Business Bureau
at **http://www.bbb.org/**. The excellent About.com has a page about
net shopping where you'll find some useful tips
http://onlineshopping.about. com. ▲

< 265 >

What you pay at an American site isn't the end of it. You should pay more when your goods enter the country. There are three basic charges on goods imported into the UK – customs duty, excise duty and VAT. There are various exemptions. You don't pay duty or VAT on books. You don't pay VAT on kid's clothes. You don't pay duty on computers or computer parts. You don't pay duty or VAT if the total value of the goods bought on the net, including shipping costs, is less than £18 (so you might just squeeze in two cheap CDs sent rather slowly). But this exemption doesn't apply to tobacco products, alcohol or perfume. You don't have to pay customs duty on stuff you buy on the net anywhere within the European Union. But you do pay VAT. And if you've bought booze or tobacco products you pay excise duty as well. Incidentally, digital products you download direct from a site are considered 'services' and hence are exempt from duty. However, they are liable to VAT. But given that the duty/VAT liable on physical goods sometimes goes uncollected, it's hard to see how the law on VAT on electronic goods will be enforced properly for the moment.

VAT is charged at 17.5%. Duty rates vary from product to product. They can go up to 15% of purchase price. There's a useful guide to the rates at the HM Customs & Excise web site **http://www.hmce.gov.uk/ bus/regions/dutyrate.htm**. You can find detailed information about the whole duty system in Notice 143 **http://www.hmce.gov.uk/notices/143.htm**. Duty and VAT are supposed to be collected by the Post Office on delivery. They may also charge you 'a clearance fee' for collecting them. Often they don't get round to collecting any of these various charges. If you get something sent by one of the big international courier firms, they may collect the duty/VAT instead (and may charge more for it than the Post Office).

< 266 >

Read about it online – Europe Online

Shopping online overseas doesn't just mean shopping in the States. For a glimpse of net shopping across the channel, try the French shopping directory Achetenligne **http://www.achetenligne.com**. ▲

The big portal web sites are good places to start browsing the American net shops. Try Yahoo **http://shopping.yahoo.com**, Excite's Shopping Channel **http://shopping.excite.com** or Alta Vista's Shopping.com at **http://www.shopping.com**. You could also do a lot worse than look round Amazon **http://www.amazon.com**. The UK site has branched out beyond books to cover music, videos and DVD, software and games and more. But the US version has gone a lot further and offers everything from electronics and health and beauty products to gardening equipment and cars. There are plenty of shopping search sites – try Buyer's Index **http://www.buyersindex.com**, ShopNow **http://www.shopnow.com** and ShopGuide (US) **http://www.shopguide.com**. For a more offbeat directory, try Cool Shopping **http://www.coolshopping.com**.

Shopping bots

There are various search tools – usually referred to as shopping bots – that will, in theory, find the lowest price online for a particular item. Techno-gurus think that in the future bots will go online, buy items and arrange shipping all by themselves, leaving us free to get on with our lives. That's a long way off yet. However, price comparison is available now and is worth looking into. Shopsmart **http://www.shopsmart.com** has a useful shopping bot, as does Kelkoo **http://www.kelkoo.com**. DealTime's

< 267 >

Tips - Price Isn't Everything

Shop around for a good price but don't spend too much time on it An evening spent staring at a computer trying to save a couple of pounds is probably an evening that could have been spent doing something more interesting. ▲

price comparison service is also available at Shopping Unlimited **http://www.shoppingunlimited.co.uk**.

There are a couple of things to look out for, though. First, check the number of shops that a particular bot searches. Some bot sites have deals with certain retailers and only search those pages, missing out cheaper competitors. Second, check whether the price served up by the bot includes shipping. If it doesn't, the results may be misleading. The better shopping bots now give you all the information you need to make a purchase, including delivery time. Some shopping bot sites don't update their price comparison databases as often as they should. So it can pay to hunt around on your own after you've done a price search, just to see what else is out there. If you want to try an American shopping bot, have a look at MySimon **http://www.mysimon.com**, Price Scan **http://www.pricescan.com** or Bottom Dollar **http://www.bottomdollar.com**.

Research it online, buy it offline

The net is great tool for researching offline purchases. You can read product reviews online and check out the prices on offer, then head down the high street better equipped to get a good deal. The UK is yet to catch up with the States in this area. But there's more and more information

< 268 >

online. You can read some of Which? Magazine's product tests at **http://www.which.net.** Many specialist consumer magazines are now on the net, from hi-fi guides like What Hi-Fi **http://www.whathifi.com** to car buying magazines like AutoExpress **http://www.autoexpress.co.uk** and WhatCar **http://www.whatcar.co.uk**. Some publishers now pool the reviews from their magazines on their sites – try ZD Net **http://www.zdnet.co.uk** for some useful help with computer buying.

Some sites try to locate the best real world prices for certain items. Free2Look **http://www.free2look.co.uk** claims to sift through ads from newspapers and magazines in search of the best offline deals. Price Offers **http://www.priceoffers.co.uk** serves up something similar, though it focuses more high street sales and special offers. Once you tell Ybag **http://www.ybag.com** what you want, it searches online and offline stores for the best price. For more specific price comparisons, try Buy.co.uk **http://www.buy.co.uk** where you'll find tools that help you find the cheapest rates for gas, electricity and water in your area.

Classified ads are another good source for bargains. They're beginning to migrate to the net, where they make a lot more sense. Once they're put into a database, ads are a lot easier to search. You can also

Read about it online – House Buying

If you know exactly where you want to live, the classifieds in the local paper are still probably your best bet when it comes to buying a house. That said, property sites are useful for checking prices in different areas and seeing what's out there. Try Home **http://www.home.co.uk** or Asserta Home **http://www.assertahome.com**. ▲

< 269 >

set up search tools that send you email alerts when an ad for something you want appears online. Once you find an ad, you contact the seller as usual, either by telephone or email. Many of the UK's major classified ad outlets are online, from the general: Loot **http://www.loot.com** and Exchange and Mart **http://www.exchangeandmart.co.uk**, to the specialist: Autotrader **http://www.autotrader.co.uk**. Several online operations have moved into the area too. Yahoo runs a classified section **http://uk. classifieds.yahoo.com/uk**. Alternatively, try Preloved **http://www.preloved. co.uk** or Local Ads **http://www.localads.net**.

Online auctions

Over the last few years, buying (and selling) at online auctions has become one of the most popular activities on the net. Log on to eBay **http://www.ebay.com**, the place where it all got started (the UK end is at **http://www.ebay.co.uk**) and you'll see millions of auctions in progress – individuals selling everything from remaindered computer parts to modern day collectibles like 'Star Wars' and Beanie Babies. Imagine a global car boot sale and you come close to understanding what's going

Read about it online – eBay Advice and Angst

eBay provides plenty of information for beginners, but if you want more, try the Curioddities eBay Resource **http://www.curioddities.com/ ebayinfo.htm**. When eBay started, many people thought they could make a living selling on the site. Now, as bigger businesses move in, times are getting hard, as one individual seller revealed in Salon **http:// www.salon.com/tech/feature/2000/10/27/doomed_by_ebay/index.html**. ▲

< 270 >

on here. Lots of people now claim to suffer from eBay addiction, not least the media. In the past, press coverage of the site has featured stories about the crazy things for sale on eBay – guns, drugs, companies and people, warnings about the scams at online auctions and interviews with people who run businesses via the site, selling collectibles round the world. Indeed, eBay is now so big, when it has a technical problem and goes offline, it's news.

Unsurprisingly, eBay's success has brought competition from big net names. Freeserve **http://669.fairmarket.co.uk/**, Yahoo **http://uk.auctions. yahoo.com/uk/** and Amazon **http://www.amazon.co.uk** now run their own auctions. The best known online auction site here is QXL **http://www.qxl.com**. They started out selling refurbished computers and then moved in to travel, holidays and much else. They were quick to set up an eBay style operation in which ordinary punters could sell stuff too. The two different strands of their operation are bundled together on the site now – the items that QXL sells are usually labelled as 'QXL Direct' offers. They've been joined by other companies – try Fired Up **http://www.firedup.co.uk** or eBid **http://www.ebid.co.uk**. Even Loot now has its own auctions at **http://auction.loot.com/scripts/lootsite.dll**.

In online auctions, you can either buy direct from the site hosting the sale or from another individual. Bids are sent in via the net and auctions are time-limited, In other words, products go to the person who gets the highest bid in before the deadline. Often people wait until the last minute and things can get a bit hectic. There are other more complicated auctions – for instance the Dutch auction. This is a way of selling multiple identical items – 15 videos, say. The seller sets a minimum price and the number of items available. Bidders bid at or above that minimum for the quantity they are interested in purchasing. At the close of the auction, the highest

< 271 >

bidders purchase the items at the lowest successful bid.

It's easy to see why net auctions are so popular. They do the thing the net was always supposed to do – they allow people with similar interests to pursue those interests together. At their best, they create genuine communities. And they're fun. Seeing the incredible prices at the start of auctions, you can't help but be drawn in. And because online auctions are time-limited, you hang around to see what happens, to see if that laptop is still going for £200.

You should take a few precautions when buying at an auction site. Check on exactly what you're buying. That super-cheap computer is probably second hand or end of the line stock. If you're buying from an individual, check on their past performance. EBay and QXL post reports on sellers from previous buyers, so you can see how they behaved and whether the goods were sent on time. Find out what the item you're bidding on is actually worth. Auctions specialise in items that are hard to price exactly. So you'll need to think about what the thing is actually worth to you. Then set a price you're willing to pay and stick to it. It's easy to get carried away and end up paying way over the odds (that's why sellers like auctions, despite those apparently low prices). Finally, if you're buying from an individual on an auction site,

Read about it online - Auction Search Sites

Bidfind **http://www.bidfind.com** is an auction search engine that covers hundreds of different auctions worldwide. You enter the name of something you want and it finds auctions that have that it currently on sale. I wouldn't try a search on Beanie Babies though. ▲

< 272 >

use an escrow service. Most big auction sites run them – QXL's is called Safe Pay and Safe Ship. The idea is that the buyer pays by credit card into a special 'escrow account'. QXL tells the seller that the money is there. It stays there until the buyer gets the goods. Once the buyer confirms that the goods have arrived and are as described, the money is released to the seller.

Personal finance online

Back in the mid-nineties, there were suggestions that soon we would be using special electronic currencies that would protect our privacy and enable all sorts of micro payments which would eventually build up into a thriving info-economy. E-cash and micro payments have yet to take the world by storm, for various reasons. First, it's a difficult thing to pull off technically, before you tackle the real problem of building trust in it. Second, we already have a kind of secure electronic currency we trust – our credit cards. Third, in general people can't be bothered with such small purchases. As one net theorist put it, do you want to be nickel-and-dimed to death? However, some loyalty points schemes sell themselves as electronic currencies in the making. Have a look at Beenz **http://www. beenz.com** and try to decide whether or not they're a prototype form of electronic cash or just the Green Shield stamps of the net.

E-cash may not have happened yet, but banks are online and will let you manage your real world money via the net. Some financial institutions are online under their familiar names – for example, Barclays **http://www.barclays.co.uk** and Lloyds TSB **http://www.lloydstsb.co.uk**. To avoid confusion (and having to grant real world customers the kind of deals they're offering online), others have launched spin-off net banks. The Co-op has Smile **http://www.smile.co.uk** and the Prudential has Egg

< 273 >

http://www.egg.com. The Abbey National has its own site **http://www. abbeynational.co.uk** but is also behind Cahoot **http://www.cahoot.co.uk**. In addition, there are genuinely new online names like First E **http://www.first-e.com**.

When banks first got online, they often wanted customers to use special software and connect directly with their central computers. Most have now realised that people want to access their accounts via the web. It's quicker and easier. It does, however, open up security worries. There have been some high profile security lapses at online banks over the last year or so. It's something to bear in mind. Before you sign up, explore the security policy and see what they promise to do in case of any problems. If you have an account with a real world bank, once you sign up with their online operation, you can administer your account via the web 24 hours a day – check the balance, transfer money, pay bills and the like. Most offer this service for free.

When they first got started, net-only banks concentrated on savings accounts. But now they're offering the services you get from other banks – current accounts, credit cards, direct debits, loans and mortgages. Net-only banks say that, because they don't have to cope with the overheads

---

Tips - Unmetered Access and Online Banking

Telephone banking makes it quick and easy to sort out your money. Truth be told, it's usually quicker than going online – and some banks offer a 24-hour service too. Once you sign up for unmetered access, things begin to look different, and it can be more cost effective to juggle your money via the net – if you're really counting the pennies. ▲

< 274 >

Read about it online – Financial Advice

If you're looking for some general help with managing your money, try Money Unlimited **http://www.moneyunlimited.co.uk**, where you'll find news stories, financial directories and much more. Another useful personal finance site is MoneyExtra **http://www.moneyextra.com**, which has all sorts of tools for comparing different deals. ▲

involved in running a series of real world banks, they can offer their users better rates and deals. There are some very good offers on their sites. But check the fine print. Online current accounts, for example, don't always offer standard services. For example, at the time of writing, First-E's current account didn't allow direct debits or overdrafts – though they were apparently on the way.

Aside from the banks, all sorts of other financial institutions are now online, from building societies to insurance companies. Financial products are well suited to the net. You don't need to hold them in your hand before you decide to buy. You can scan and compare rates just fine on a computer screen. For an example of what's on offer here, try Screentrade **http://www.screentrade.com**, which lets you compare quotes and buy travel, home and car insurance online. For a similar service focused round loans and mortgages, try E Loan **http://uk.eloan.com**.

Share trading online

Share trading on the net has generated a lot of column inches recently. There've been features about how millions are just waiting to be made, countered by scare stories about stock market crashes and personal

< 275 >

savings meltdown. Several journalists are currently trying to see if they can day trade their way to a fortune (or just pay the mortgage) and are posting regular updates to the papers and the web. And many of the dot com ads you see on TV are for share trading sites. They generally suggest that ordinary people only have to log on to beat the big boys at their own game and cash in big time. They would, wouldn't they? As ever, don't believe the hype.

Online share trading sites say that they cut out the evil old middlemen (real world brokers) and let people buy and sell for less. It's true enough. But never forget that they're still middlemen. They still come between you and the market. And if you become really serious about day trading, you're going to find them way too slow. You'll move on to a more serious source of information that you'll pay proper money for. And you'll look to make most of your money from taking advantage of the slowpokes using the mainstream share trading sites. That may sound cynical, but I'm only giving you a summary of the thoughts of someone who's been there – Joey Anuff, co-founder of the webzine Suck **http://www.suck.com**, who gave day trading a try for a year or so and wrote about his experiences in the very amusing 'Dumb Money'. You can find out more about the book on the web **http://dumbmoney.suck.com/**.

Jargon file - Day Trading

The name given to the kind of jittery trading in which people try to take advantage of the minute by minute fluctuations of volatile stocks. Day traders are not in it for the long term. They get very nervous holding on to a stock overnight, let alone for several months. ▲

< 276 >

Anyone who still thinks there's millions just waiting to be made should read it as soon as possible.

However, if you just want to invest more sensibly, if you want to manage an existing portfolio, or check the current prices of stock you own, the web can be very useful. The big online share trading sites are American. Schwab Europe **http://www.schwab-worldwide.com/Europe/** and E Trade **http://www.etrade.co.uk** are probably the best known. Barclays runs one of the bigger British sites at **http://www.barclays-stockbrokers.co.uk/**. Also worth a look are the Halifax's Share Express **http://www.halifax.co.uk**, SharePeople **http://www.sharepeople.com/** and Selftrade **http://www.selftrade.com/uk**. If you're looking for advice about the markets, you could do a lot worse than try the Financial Times online **http://www.ft.com**.

Netscape 6

Netscape 6 took over two and a half years to develop and the company has declared it to be a radical upgrade on not only Navigator, but all other previous browsers as well. Because it was released officially just as this book was going to the printers, I've not spent that much time using

< 277 >

it. So my opinion may change. But at the moment, though Netscape 6 is good, it doesn't quite live up to the hype. It continues the trend to present browsers as all-purpose integrated net tools. It can handle instant messages and multimedia content as well as email and newsgroups. It also has less tech-y look and feel – similar to the new mainstream post-browsers – i.e. AOL 6.0 and MSN Explorer. However, initial reviews have suggested that Netscape 6.0 is probably better suited to more experienced web surfers, who would appreciate some of its cleverer features.

In general, Netscape 6 loads web pages a little quicker, though some early users have complained that it mangles some pages and crashes too often. As for the new features, the most noticeable is My Sidebar, an extension of the Internet Explorer's browser bars. The latter are a clever interface device – for example, they let you view the History list at the side then call up the pages you want in the main window. In Netscape 6, however, you can use My Sidebar to show slimmed-down versions of active web pages. So you can keep a page of stock info from your favourite financial site up in the sidebar, while you surf elsewhere on the web. At the moment, I'm not hugely convinced by this, but if there are pages you feel you need to keep tabs on all the time, it may be for you.

Netscape 6's communication features are more impressive. Messenger, its email program, is much improved and now lets you check multiple mail accounts, an AOL mail account and web mail too, if you sign up with Netscape's own free mail service at Netcenter. It will also sort these different accounts into separate inboxes, which is useful for keeping track on things. In general, the mail filters work better too. In addition, AOL Instant Messenger (AIM) is integrated into Netscape 6's Messenger. Once you've set it up, you can use AIM to message friends who send you email (if they also use AIM as their instant message client – if they use ICQ,

< 278 >

you're out of luck). When you pick up your mail, you should see an Instant Messenger icon next to the messages. Click this, and if the person who sent you the message is online, you can chat to them.

Netscape 6 also has an improved set of security tools. The Cookie Manager, in particular, is very useful. This lets you specify which sites you want to accept cookies from. So if you're happy taking them from a shopping site like Amazon, you can say so. But otherwise, Netscape 6 will refuse cookies or ask you whether it should accept them. You can access this via the *Edit* menu, then select *Preferences*, then *Advanced*, then *Cookies*. There are a few other features worth checking out – for example the Gist-In-Time translation tool that will translate web pages in a foreign language – sort of. To access it, select the *View* menu, then *Translate*. Netscape also lets you customise its look and feel, via various different 'skins' or 'themes'. It comes with two themes pre-loaded – 'modern' or 'classic' (which is like the old Navigator). You can download more themes from the Netscape 6 home page **http://home.netscape.com/browsers/6/index.html**, which is also a good place to go for news and more general advice on its various features. Alternatively, if you're looking for more reviews and tips on what you can do with Netscape 6, go to CNet's Browsers section **http://www.cnet.com/internet/0-3773.html**. So should you give Netscape 6 a try? It's definitely worth a look, though not the huge step forward that you might have expected. That said, the email/instant messaging tools are impressive and if you are on the move a lot this could be the browser for you.

Get organised online

Online reminder services are nothing new. Most net shops now let you sign up for email alert services that warn you when important birthdays

< 279 >

are coming up (and suggest a few presents from their own stock). But reminder mail is just a fraction of what's on offer these days. Sign up with the US site Lifeminders **http://www.lifeminders.com**, tell them about your life and interests and you'll get free weekly email reminders and tips. Not just the usual 'it's your mum's birthday next week' but mail telling you it's time to fertilise your lawn. Perhaps more useful are sites like Pay My Bills **http://www.paymybills.com**, an American operation, which does what it says on the tin, as it were. It's yet to find its way over here, but Servista **http://www.servista.com** offers something sort of similar. Sign up and the company will try to find you the best deals on gas, electricity, telephone and net access. They'll then send you one monthly bill that covers the lot. Also aiming to make your life easier is I Have Moved **http://www.ihave moved.com**. Sign up here when you're moving house and they will apparently take care of the hassle of letting everyone know where you've gone.

Online personal organisers

Most big portals now offer some sort of online personal organiser. You're given a space online where you can compile 'to do' lists and schedule your work/social life. You can create personalised web calendars, which track online events you're interested in. You might think that people would hesitate before putting lots of personal information online. Beyond that, if you put your diary/contacts book online, you risk not being able to get at it if the site is down – not something that's going to happen with standard personal organiser programs. Fans say that if you use these sites, your personal information will survive systems crashes that might befall your various bits of hardware. And as people access the net while they're out and about, using various wireless devices, sites where you keep your useful personal information will become more

< 280 >

useful. If you're interested, try Yahoo Calendar **http://calendar.yahoo.com**, Excite Planner **http://planner.excite.com**, When.com **http://www.when.com** or Eorganizer **http://www.eorganizer.com**.

This sort of thing perhaps makes more sense if you're trying to organise a group or club. You can use the web to set up a group mailing list and calendar. You can schedule meetings and send automatic reminders to people. These services are the natural off-shoot of online conferences and mailing lists, which is why sites like eGroups **http://www.egroups.co.uk** and Smart Groups **http://www.smartgroups.com** offer them. You can find something similar at Yahoo Clubs **http://clubs.yahoo.com**, Bungo **http://www.bungo.com** and MyFamily.com **http://www.myfamily.com**, which also offers help on building your family tree and space for displaying photos online. EBoard **http://www.eboard.com** lets you create a virtual corkboard where you can post messages and photos online in seconds. You can, suggests the site, use an eBoard as a 'homebase' for your team – a place where they can all put up notices and ideas.

The virtual desktop

According to some people, online personal/group organisers are just the beginning. The real future is the virtual desktop, a kind of catch-all name

---

Read about it online – Virtual Desktop Hype

For a good piece about the virtual desktop idea, try 'Storing Your Life in A Virtual Desktop', which ran in the New York Times at the end of 1999, just as the hype was starting up in the States **http://www.nytimes.com/1999/11/25/technology/25desk.html**. ▲

< 281 >

Read about it online - Password Help

The web can help with one info-management task – remembering passwords for all the different sites you've registered with. Go to Pass Center **http://www.passcenter.com** for more information. Microsoft is offering something similar with its Passport service **http://www.passport.com**. ▲

for web sites that offer the applications you'd normally find on the average personal computer. The big idea here is that soon people will be using slimmed down information appliances to access the net. They won't have storage space on these machines, but they will have an always-on connection to the net. So when they want to get something done, they'll visit an application service provider and use a spreadsheet or word processing program as and when they need them.

A variety of companies are already delivering virtual desktop services. I-Drive **http://www.idrive.com** and X-Drive **http://www.xdrive.com** are self-styled online hard drives – they give you storage space on the net, where you can save documents and much more. Blox **http://www.blox.com** is an online spreadsheet application. My Free Desk **http://www.myfreedesk. com** is an online suite of applications – word processor, spreadsheets, presentations and scheduler. ThinkFree **http://www.thinkfree.com** and Desktop.com **http://www.desktop.com** offer something similar.

Mobile internet

Virtual desktops are, like the more familiar web email services, built for a world where people move around but still want access to their personal

< 282 >

information. In other words, they're built for the world of mobile internet access. As mentioned on page 46, this has been talked up so much in the last year or so, there's already been a backlash, especially as far as WAP phones are concerned. So why should you bother with it? Recently I read a US newspaper story hyping wireless net access. It told the story of a WAP phone user who used his phone to check up on some sports statistics and win an argument in a bar. The attitude of the journalist writing the piece was, hey cool (I'm shortening his argument slightly, but I think I've caught his basic drift). However, most people will probably think that the guy with the WAP phone succeeded only in proving himself a kind of mega-bore, the kind who not only takes arguments about trivia way too seriously, but uses new technology to prove he was right and you were wrong.

So the message is, get a mobile internet device and you will mark yourself out as a crashing bore. OK – perhaps that's overstating things slightly. The anecdote could be interpreted more charitably as showing that WAP phones let you access data exactly when you need it most. That's basically the big draw. Of course, how you define crucial information is up to you. It could be your email, or the latest sports scores, or

---

Read about it online - The Blackberry

One of the most popular wireless net devices in the States – with geeks and e commerce types at least – is the Blackberry, a kind of turbo-charged email-enabled pager that comes with a small keyboard. Find out more at **http://www.blackberry.net**. The NY Times recently ran a good piece about the Blackberry craze **http://www.nytimes.com/2000/09/21/technology/21PAGE.html**. ▲

< 283 >

stock prices, or train times, or directions to a restaurant. But whatever it is, the idea is that you will be able to get it when you need it, wherever you happen to be. However, we're not there yet. The wireless net devices currently on the market are prototypes. If you bear that in mind when you try them out, you may get something out of them.

There are basically three kinds of wireless net currently on the market – WAP phones, handheld PDAs and Pocket PCs. Let's deal with the last two first. PDAs like Palm Pilots **http://www.palm.com/europe/uk/index.html**, Psions **http://www.psion.com/** and Handspring Visors **http://www.handspring. com/uk** have become very popular in the last few years, mainly as personal organisers. Some people also use them to read web content and email offline. In other words, they hook them up to their PCs, download their new mail into their PDA and then read it and write replies on the move. They can then send those replies by hooking their PDA back up to the PC. The web pages you can download onto a PDA are stripped-down affairs you usually access via the special software provided by AvantGo **http://www.avantgo.com**. Lots of big names have signed up to create channels for AvantGo – The Guardian and Football Unlimited, Salon, Wired News, The New York Times, Yahoo! and more. Go to the AvantGo site and look for the Channels section. For details on The Guardian's AvantGo content, look for the link on the main page **http://www.guardian.co.uk**.

It is possible to use your PDA to read web pages online. You need to buy a special modem, then either hook it up to a telephone point or a mobile phone. I've yet to meet anyone who's actually done this. Perhaps I don't get out enough. But if you have to have live net access via your portable device, a PocketPC is probably a better bet – though they are more expensive. Devices like Hewlett Packard's Jornada **http://www.hp.com/uk/**, Compaq's Ipaq **http://www.compaq.**

< 284 >

Read about it online – The Joy of Text

Sending someone an email via a WAP phone is hard work, unlike sending someone an SMS text message, which is why the latter is so popular and WAP is yet to catch on. For an interesting Guardian piece on text messaging, try Richard Benson's The Joy of Text **http://www.guardian.co.uk/Archive/Article/0,4273,4024760,00.html**. You can get news updates (and much more) delivered to your mobile as a text message by Yahoo **http://uk.alerts.yahoo.com/wireless/alert**. ▲

co.uk/products/handheld/ and Casio's Cassiopeia **http://www.casio.co.uk/ cassiopeia** use Microsoft's PocketPC operating system (it used to be called Windows CE). They're more like mini-computers than PDAs, in that they have more memory and processing power and run stripped-down versions of popular applications like Office. They also come with versions of Microsoft's Internet Explorer. They don't usually come with a modem. You have to spend extra to get that, and then you have to hook your device up to a land line or a mobile phone. But when it comes to web browsing, you'll be using a familiar interface and a colour screen – something that isn't yet a standard with most PDAs.

The great advantage of WAP phones is, obviously, that you don't need to buy a modem or hook them up to a telephone point. However, the screen is very small and it's black and white (or rather black and green, gray or brown). And inputting addresses (or writing mail, or simply browsing information) is frustrating when compared to PDAs. If you want a WAP preview, try the emulator at Yahoo! Mobile **http://uk.mobile.yahoo.com/**. Enter a WAP address (not a standard HTML

< 285 >

address) and it should come up in the green screen. This doesn't give that accurate a picture of WAP access. The screen is much bigger than the ones on real WAP phones and entering the long addresses many WAP sites are lumbered with is easier with a keyboard than with a phone keypad. That said, WAP phones are improving. Ericsson's new R380 model **http://www.ericsson.com** is a cross between a PDA and a phone and features a larger screen, a stylus interface and built-in POP3 email software. Nokia's standard WAP phones – for example the 7110 – come with a scrolling wheel which makes browsing sites a lot easier.

When you connect with a WAP phone, you go to the portal run by the service you're using. You'll find links to different services – news, weather, travel etc. You can use these or go to different WAP sites. As mentioned above, entering WAP site addresses is rather fiddly, so bookmarking is essential. The difficulty involved in entering addresses means that most WAP users tend to use what's on offer on the portal – hardly the full-on surfing portrayed by the ads. It's more a mobile phone version of the kind of 'walled garden' networks offered by old style online services and new interactive TV services like Sky's Open. If you do visit other WAP sites beyond your phone company's portal, you're not seeing the same net you access via your PC. WAP sites are written using Wireless Markup Language and are simplified, text-only affairs carefully designed to work with the small screens and kludgy interfaces of mobiles (or so designers claim).

WAP sites wouldn't look quite so bad if they hadn't been so oversold. Businesses are beginning to back away from early claims about surfing the net on your phone. They now say that WAP is more about delivering specific information services to your mobile. Perhaps the real problem for ordinary users is that WAP phones are slow and unreliable.

< 286 >

It can take a long time to access even the simplest bit of information. You often lose the connection in the process and have to start over. As a result, it's hardly surprising that sales of WAP phones have been disappointing so far – leading to lots of dodgy headlines about 'WAPathy' and the like.

Despite this, there are more and more WAP services starting up. As ever, there's a useful directory of WAP sites at Yahoo **http://uk.mobile. yahoo.com/**. Here are a few others to be going on with. (Incidentally, the following addresses are WAP addresses – they won't work with a standard web browser, unless it's capable of handling WML – Opera 4 is up to the job, apparently. If you want to see what they look like, try the WAP emulator at Yahoo! Mobile). You can get news headlines (via The Guardian **http://www.guardian.co.uk/wml**), sports results (from Waparesult **http://www.waparesult.com/index.wml**) and stock updates (from StockSmart **http://agsub.stocksmart.com/ss.wml**). You can access WAP versions of the big search sites (Yahoo! **http://wap.yahoo.co.uk** and Excite **http://mobile.excite.co.uk**) or the new generation of WAP portals (Any Time Now **http://www.anytimenow.com/index.wml**, IoBox **http://wap. iobox.com** and Mviva **http://www.mviva.com/wap/index.wml**). There are various messaging services, which let you pick up email from your main account (Infinite Technologies **http://wap.mailandnews.com**, MobileID **http://wap.mobileid.com**).

You can also access various kinds of travel information. Big travel sites like Ebookers offer WAP services, as do some airlines. However, attempting to book flights via WAP seems perverse, given that a phone call will often sort things out in half the time. More useful are WAP sites that deliver information specific to your location at the time. There are all sorts of city guides – try Citikey **http://wap.citikey.com**. MapQuest

< 287 >

http://wl.mapquest.com/gb/ will give you directions for any location in the UK. Enter a postcode into the WAP version of Somewhere Near **http://www.somewherenear.com/wap/index.cgi** and it lists hotels, restaurants and other places of interest in the location.

You can also access Railtrack's online train timetable via a WAP phone – visit their standard web site for details **http://www.railtrack.co.uk**. Newcomers Kizoom also offer a train timetable WAP service, which delivers basic times and alerts about journey disruptions. Again, find out more at their standard web site **http://www.kizoom.co.uk**. Incidentally there are some WAP sites where you can buy stuff, but I haven't mentioned them, mainly because they're hard to use and they don't allow for secure transactions (at least at the time of writing). Stick to the net proper or the high street. The same goes for the WAP banking sites that are beginning to appear – often it's quicker (and safer) to use a telephone banking service.

Many pundits feel that WAP travel sites and so-called location-based services, which track where you are and deliver relevant information are the future of the mobile internet. They could have a point. That said, others argue that by concentrating on 'content', WAP pioneers are making the same mistake as the first big web sites. Businesses have since

Read about it online - Mobile Fun

The net is a great place to go to find various toys related to mobiles, in particular all sorts of irritating ring tones. Try Your Mobile **http://www. yourmobile.com/default.asp**, The Free Site **http://www.thefreesite.co.uk/ mobiles.htm** or ZapLite **http://www.zaplite.com/**. ▲

< 288 >

learnt that to succeed on the web, you should exploit the fact that the net allows ordinary people to communicate with each other in new and interesting ways. According to this argument, the future of WAP is services like Sketchaphone, developed by Supedo **http://www.supedo.co.uk**, which lets people send each other images via their phones.

Perhaps the interesting thing about WAP is that, at the moment, no one really knows what works best. Everything is in transition. WAP may not even be the standard that survives. There is a competing system up and running in Japan – DoCoMo i-mode **http://www.nttdocomo.com/top.shtml**, which lets people access slimmed-down web pages (i.e. pages written in HTML) rather than WML pages. WAP enthusiasts say things will change as Europe moves to the GPRS mobile phone standard over the next two years. In theory, the General Packet Radio Service standard allows for data transfer speeds of up to 171.2Kbits per second– a big improvement on the 9.6 Kbits currently available. It's also an 'always on' system – you don't need to dial into a system but can download data straightaway.

Hardcore geeks are already looking forward five years or so to third generation mobiles, which will have broadband connections that enable you to access the full multimedia net. Where these will leave WAP is uncertain. After all, it was developed to deal with low connection speeds, small screens and one handed operation. Once mobile devices can cope with the net proper, will it survive? Yes, according to people working on WAP, who say it will develop over the next few years. For more on this, have a look at the site put up by Phone.com **http://www.phone.com**, the company behind WAP.

< 289 >

Putting up your own web page

Looking at some web pages, it's not hard to think that you could do something better. You probably could. But can you keep it up every week, week in, week out? Web gurus say that you need to update your homepage constantly to keep it fresh. If your site becomes a serious business thing, they're right. But if all you want to do is have a bit of fun putting up something your friends can check out, you can safely ignore them. And the beauty of the web is that, if you're prepared to forgo the high-tech tricknology, it's pretty easy to put up a simple page and then forget about it.

More and more net users are taking the time to set up their own homepages. HTML – the language used to format simple web pages – isn't that hard to learn, but now there are plenty of web publishing software packages which make the whole process as simple as creating word-processor documents. It's also easy to get free space for your page – either on your ISP's site or on one of the web communities like Yahoo Geocities. These places will also give you plenty of help with page design and will supply templates and the like. If you want to put lots of pictures up, you will need a scanner of some sort. And if you want to do some

Read about it online – Big Step

People seem to be queuing up to help you take advantage of the net/web these days – and for the moment, they don't seem to want any money. Take Big Step **http://www.bigstep.com**, which will help you take your business online. It will help you set up and design a web page and will host it, all for no money. ▲

< 290 >

Tips - FTP Software

If you do get serious about doing your own web page, you'll need a decent FTP client. The browsers are OK for downloads but if you're going to be uploading your own pages, you need something more flexible. Try Cute FTP **http://www.cuteftp.com** or Get Right **http://www.getright.com** or Gozilla **http://www.gozilla.com**. ▲

---

sort of cutting-edge multimedia extravaganza, you will have to learn some more complex programming (or buy some fairly expensive software). But if you just want to share your thoughts on 'The X Files' with the world, you probably have the software you need already and won't need to do that much research. Most of the information you need is online. Rather than get into detailed description and advice, the next few sections aim to point you to the information you need.

HTML basics

As mentioned above, HTML is the language used to create simple web pages. Basically, it's a set of text commands – known as tags – which determine the way a document is laid out, the line spacing, placement of images, links to other documents and much else. When a document written in HTML is viewed by a browser, you see the content the way the designer intended. If you open the same document in a text editor, you see all the tags around the basic content. Actually, you can view the HTML code for any web page you're browsing.

▶ In **Internet Explorer**, select the **View** menu, then **Source**.

< 291 >

▶ In **Navigator**, select the **View** menu then **Page Source**.

As you'll see, tags are enclosed by < and >. You may also notice that they generally come in pairs – an opening and closing tag. The closing tag usually features a forward slash, as in </BOLD>. Looking at the source code of web pages can give you a few clues about how to use HTML. However, there are several useful interactive tutorials online which let you mess around with tags and see what they do. HotWired does a good introductory tutorial on its web developer site WebMonkey – go to **http://www.hotwired.com/webmonkey/teachingtool/**. Once you feel like you're getting the basics, go to the NCSA's Beginner's Guide to HTML for more in-depth information **http://www.ncsa.uiuc.edu/General/Internet/WWW/HTMLPrimerP1.html**. For a good general introduction to web page design, try the HTML Headquarters **http://webhelp.org**, Mike Smith's Guide to HTML and CGI Scripts **http://snowwhite.it.brighton.ac.uk/~mas/mas/courses/html/html.html** or the excellent Big Nose Bird **http://www.bignosebird.com/**.

HTML editors

Some would argue that beginners don't need to bother learning HTML. There are plenty of WYSIWYG programs (as in 'what you see is what you get') which let you design web pages without ever having to expose yourself to any techno gobbledegook. Professional designers argue that you shouldn't rely on these editors because they don't create 'clean' HTML and that in the end you have to sort out the mistakes they introduce. This isn't really going to be an issue for ordinary users: they could get by with the latest version of Word, Microsoft's word processing package, which features web page templates you can adapt to your own

< 292 >

purposes. It also lets you create documents the way you would normally, then save them as HTML. If you don't have a new version of Word, you should have received something you can use when you downloaded your browser. Internet Explorer comes with Front Page Express. Netscape's Communicator suite has Composer. Both are fine if you're just starting out. In addition, the big homepage hosting sites have templates you can use to put up simple pages – try Yahoo Geocities **http://geocities. yahoo.com/home/** or Tripod **http://www.tripod.co.uk/index-b.html**.

There are plenty of HTML editors/web publishing packages you could try out – Hot Dog Pro **http://www.sausage.com**; Hot Metal Pro **http://www.hotmetalpro.com/**; Arachnophilia **http://www.arachnoid.com/ arachnophilia/index.html**; Coffee Cup HTML Editor **http://www.coffeecup. com**. Mac users could try BBEdit **http://www.barebones.com**. When it comes to creating and formatting the visual content of your page (the graphics should be saved as gifs and any photos as jpegs), have a look at Paint Shop Pro **http://www.jasc.com**. Many professional designers use Macromedia's Dreamweaver **http://www.macromedia.com/software/ dreamweaver/**. In the past, .net magazine has given away Dreamweaver programs on their cover discs (albeit an early version). In general, .net and Internet magazine are useful sources of both software and web site design tips.

Finally, there are all sorts of authoring tools you can use to add features to your page – everything from discussion groups to search engines. Excite UK has some good links at **http://www.excite.co.uk/ computers_and_internet/directory/310132/310148/189743/**. Alternatively try the toolbox at Elated **http://www.elated.com/toolbox/** for advice and some free graphics. At Free Find **http://www.freefind.com**, you'll find tips on adding a search engine to your site. If you start to get more serious, have

< 293 >

a look at Link Exchange **http://adnetwork.bcentral.com/**, a banner ad swap scheme for smaller web sites (which is now owned by Microsoft, like everything else). You show a couple of ads for a page, another site shows an ad for yours.

Some general advice

Mastering the technology isn't the only problem you'll face. Even if you're just doing your homepage for fun, you do need to think about design. After all, you want people to enjoy your site. Good web design isn't just about aesthetics. You also need to think about how people are going to be viewing your page. That big graphic file may seem the perfect front page, but if it takes several minutes to download no one's going to hang around to see the rest of your site. So think about design, who your page is for and how they'll be accessing it. You can get plenty of advice on web design on the net. HotWired's Webmonkey is a good place to start **http://hotwired.lycos.com/webmonkey/design/index.html**. Alternatively, try the pages put up by Philip Greenspun **http://philip.greenspun.com/**, author of the excellent 'Philip and Alex's Guide to Web Publishing' **http://www.arsdigita.com/books/panda/** or Lynda Weinman **http://www. lynda.com/**, a much-respected American web designer. For tips on making your site more user-friendly, visit the Useable Web directory **http:// usableweb.com/** or Use-it.com **http://www.useit.com/**, the site put up by interface theorist Jakob Nielsen. If you want to minimise download times for your readers, have a look at the Bandwidth Conservation Society page **http://www.infohiway.com/faster/**, where you'll find tips and tools for keeping file size low and graphic quality high.

Another good way of picking up design ideas is to look at the source of pages you particularly like. Some people suggest you help yourself to

< 294 >

Read about it online - Web Designers

There are plenty of sites that specialise in advice for professional web designers. Even if you aren't that serious, they can be good places to find out what's new. Try HotWired's WebMonkey **http://hotwired. lycos.com/webmonkey/**, CNet's Builder.com **http://www.builder.com** or Website Garage **http://websitegarage.netscape.com/**. ▲

HTML that you particularly like. In theory, this isn't that big a deal for amateurs. However, there have been cases in which professional designers plundered huge chunks of code from others without crediting them. Even if you aren't in it for the money, there is something a bit cheesy about just helping yourself to someone else's hard work. Look and learn by all means. But try to adapt what you find. Some people even suggest that a good way to learn about web design is to look at bad web pages, although what constitutes a badly designed web page is still open to argument. Decide for yourself and try a site like Web Pages That Suck at **http://www.webpagesthatsuck.com**.

Another 'design' issue you need to consider is your domain name. If you put your page on your ISP's site (or on a site like Yahoo Geocities), you'll be lumbered with a long, slightly clumsy web address – something like **http://www.yourisp.net/freespace/yourname/**. Your pages have more impact (and will be easier to find) if you have your own snappy domain name. Your ISP will probably be able to help you register something appropriate. Alternatively try Net Names **http://www.netnames.co.uk**. You could try using V3 Redirect Services **http://come.to/**. They will help you set up a more interesting name and then will redirect the traffic to your site.

< 295 >

If you're doing your page as part of a business, you need to devote some serious thought to it. You can't just put up a page and expect it to start boosting your profits. You need to figure what you want a site to do: is it going to be marketing/pr-based or a transactional site where you'll actually sell things. You'll need to make sure it's integrated with the rest of your business literature/communications. You'll need to keep it well maintained and updated. You'll need to publicise it. In the end, you may decide that you need to get in a professional designer. However, it's always worth learning a bit about HTML and design: at least you'll have a bit more of an idea about what you're paying for.

Publishing and publicising your page

Once you've laid out your masterwork, you need to upload it to your ISP's server or to the site hosting your page. Get in touch with your ISP to find out exactly how to do this. In fact, it's worth talking to them about your page in general. Though all the ISPs now offer free space for web pages, they have lots of little rules that may come into effect if, for example, your page turns out to be either controversial or incredibly popular. Once your page is up, you'll need to make sure the world knows about it. You can visit the sites of the major search engines and submit the details of your page, though this can be time-consuming. There are sites that let you submit the details to all the engines at once – try Submit It **http://www.submit-it.com** or try the Submission Wizard at Exploit **http://www.exploit.com**. You can also send details to newsgroups or mailing lists if the site is particularly relevant. But be wary of sending anything that resembles spam. You don't want your site to be taken down by anti-spam activists in its first week.

If your site is about a popular topic, try joining the web ring devoted to that subject – for more on web rings, go back to the section on search

< 296 >

engines on page 133. If you create links on your page to your favourite sites, you can always get in touch with them and see if they'll put in a link to your page. If they do, it might drive some traffic your way. You can also add design touches to your page so it can be easily identified by search engines – the meta tags discussed in the section on search engines. Remember that abusing meta tags for a few extra visits is bad netiquette. People are unlikely to enjoy your page if they're conned into visiting it. Of course, the easiest way to get traffic is to do something controversial then alert the newspapers so they can run one of their Internuts stories, but if you don't agree that all publicity is good publicity, you might prefer to rely on gradually building word of mouth.

Next step

If you're looking for some tips on places to visit, go to the next section, where you'll find a list of some of my favourite sites. If you want to find out about protecting your privacy (and more) while you're shopping and generally organising your life online, go to page 319. ▲

< 297 >

5 THE ESSENTIAL CLICKS

● ●

The following section obviously isn't supposed to be a comprehensive net listing. It features two hundred or so sites and there are millions online. The idea behind this book has been to give you the skills you need to find the information you want on the net. We've now got to a stage where everything that happens in the real world is represented in some way online. If you're interested in something – gardening, sailing, fashion – it's on the net. Just go and look. I hope this book has shown you how. That said, there are some things online, a net culture, that you wouldn't know about unless somebody told you. And there are some sites that are so useful or entertaining you can't afford to miss them. It seems sensible to put a few of these into a list. Think of it as a kind of Bookmarks starter pack. As ever with the net, feel free to edit and add your own.

Guardian Unlimited

Before I start plugging other people's sites, allow me a moment to talk about The Guardian's own web pages. Launched in 1999, Guardian Unlimited was designed as a diverse but linked network of sites – News Unlimited, Film Unlimited, Football Unlimited, Cricket Unlimited, Jobs

< 298 >

Unlimited, Work Unlimited, Shopping Unlimited, Education Unlimited, Books Unlimited, Money Unlimited, MediaGuardian, The Observer and Learn.co.uk. The various projects build on and extend specific sections of the paper. But they also stand on their own, as destinations in their own right, something you might find useful and entertaining even if you don't read The Guardian.

Techno-types often insist that old media corporations don't get the net. They accuse them of 'shovelware' – thoughtlessly dumping material that works in print onto the net. This can be overstated. Sometimes 'shovelware' is what you want. If you've been away for a few days, it's nice to get online and catch up with what's been in the paper. That said, the Unlimited sites do supplement the print edition very well. Stories come with extra material and links to other online sources. At Guardian Unlimited you can also read Guardian Eye, a smartly written take on the day's top story, check out the Newslist, a list of the top stories with links to relevant sites and the weblog, a set of links to quality writing at other sites on the web. Incidentally, if you want to keep up with events online, the site has a useful daily section of net news.

As for the rest of the network, the sports sites are packed with statistics and extra material from partners like Wisden. Film Unlimited has a useful search tool that lets you find out what's showing near you. Education Unlimited has a terrific set of links to online resources for parents, teachers and children. Jobs Unlimited lets you set up tailored searches that track only the kinds of job ads you're interested. Books Unlimited hosts a reading group. Media Guardian summarises the latest news and gossip from the trade magazines. OK, I'm biased. I read The Guardian and I do the odd bit of work for them too. But I think all the sites have something going for them. Plus they look good too. Once you've

< 299 >

spent some time online, especially at other newspaper sites, you'll appreciate how important a clear user-friendly net-wise look and feel really is.

The Guardian **http://www.guardian.co.uk**
Football Unlimited **http://www.footballunlimited.co.uk**
Cricket Unlimited **http://www.cricketunlimited.co.uk**
Film Unlimited **http://www.filmunlimited.co.uk**
Education Unlimited **http://www.educationunlimited.co.uk**
Jobs Unlimited **http://www.jobsunlimited.co.uk**
Work Unlimited **http://www.workunlimited.co.uk**
Shopping Unlimited **http://www.shoppingunlimited.co.uk**
Books Unlimited **http://www.booksunlimited.co.uk**
Money Unlimited **http://www.moneyunlimited.co.uk**
MediaGuardian **http://www.mediaguardian.co.uk**
The Observer **http://www.theobserver.co.uk**
Learn **http://www.learn.co.uk**

The essential clicks

SEARCH

About.com **http://www.about.com** A search site that supplements technology with various human 'guides'.

AltaVista **http://altavista.co.uk** Ignore the unmetered access disaster – this is still a good search engine.

Deja News **http://www.deja.com/usenet** Revamped as a shopping site, this still has the famous newsgroup archive hidden at the above address.

Excite **http://www.excite.co.uk** Often loses out to Yahoo in terms of media coverage – but still an excellent search site.

< 300 >

Google **http://www.google.com** The best search engine out there – also still mercifully free of ad overload.

Liszt **http://www.liszt.com** Long running and still worthwhile directory of online discussion groups.

The Lycos 50 **http://50.lycos.com/** Fun listing of the top fifty things people are searching for on Lycos, plus witty commentary.

Metacrawler **http://www.metacrawler.com** One of the best of the sites that let you search all the other search engines.

Spy On It **http://www.spyonit.com** Interesting search site, where you set up agents to track certain things and they contact you with results.

Yahoo **http://www.yahoo.com** Still the leading general net directory/search site.

RESEARCH

Britannica **http://www.britannica.com** The online extension of the famous encyclopedia, with lots of extra content.

Dictionary.com **http://dictionary.com** Dictionaries, a thesaurus, discussion of language, crosswords and lots more.

Epinions **http://www.epinions.com** Weirdly compelling site where ordinary people review things (toasters, MTV, Jeffrey Archer) and you review their reviews.

Internet FAQ Archives **http://faqs.org/** Read Frequently Asked Question files circulated on the newsgroups – surprisingly useful.

Learn2com **http://www.learn2.com** Despite the business revamp, still the place for useful tutorials on everyday problems.

RefDesk.com **http://refdesk.com/** Monster reference site featuring dictionaries, encyclopedias and links to other fact-based sites

Research-It **http://www.itools.com/research-it/research-it.html** Long running

< 301 >

reference site that lets you search dictionaries, maps and more.

Scoot **http://www.scoot.co.uk** Useful real world research tool that lets you track businesses, people, products and films.

UpMyStreet **http://www.upmystreet.com** Enter your post code and get the latest on property prices, crime rates, schools and much else.

SOFTWARE

Download.com **http://www.download.com** Huge software warehouse site maintained by the computer information network CNet.

Stroud's Consummate Winsock Applications **http://cws.internet.com** If Download.com feels too overwhelming, try the more focused selections here.

Tucows **http://www.tucows.com/** Download software and more from this perky but useful site.

ART AND CULTURE

The Alternative Museum **http://www.alternativemuseum.org** A self-style global museum – come here for arty interactive online exhibits.

Art and Culture **http://www.artandculture.com** Simply brilliant site which maps the connections between art, design, literature and more.

Arts And Literature Daily **http://www.cybereditions.com/aldaily/** The highbrow weblog – come here for links to the most cultured writing online.

The Complete Review **http://www.complete-review.com** Book reviews from the media and the net, along with author interviews and more.

Douglas Coupland **http://www.coupland.com** The GenX author may not be everyone's cup of tea but his site looks good and reads well.

Irational **http://www.irational.org** British net art/wind-ups from techno-artist/provocateur/prankster Heath Bunting.

< 302 >

James Gleick **http://www.around.com** Stimulating site from the respected pop science author.

Komar and Melamid **http://www.diacenter.org/km/** Amusing project in which the artists created a people's art in response to online questionnaires.

Levity **http://www.levity.com** Excellent selection of links to post-sixties experimental literature and journalism.

Lisa Jewell **http://www.lisa-jewell.co.uk** Advice on getting published and more from the author of the best-selling twentysomething comic romances.

Malcolm Gladwell **http://www.gladwell.com** Collected articles from the New Yorker writer interested in how ideas catch on and spread.

Salon Audio **http://www.salon.com/audio** A good place to download sound files of big name authors reading their work.

Spike **http://www.spikemagazine.com** UK-based literary webzine that does a great job of covering people, books and ideas.

Steven King **http://www.stephenking.com/** Get the real skinny on King, from the man himself, and buy fiction direct from him.

The 24 Hour Museum **http://www.24hourmuseum.org.uk** A listings page (and more) for over 2000 of the UK's museums and galleries.

GENERAL ENTERTAINMENT SITES

Atom Films **http//www.atomfilms.com** Find short films, animation and Aardman's 'Angry Kid' at one of the better online film sites.

Broadcast **http://www.broadcast.com** Yahoo's guide to streaming audio/video online. Typically comprehensive.

DotComix **http://www.dotcomix.com** A good showcase for all sorts of webtoons – look out for 'Doonesbury' and 'Sister Randy'.

< 303 >

Extratainment **http://www.extratainment.com** Yet more online cartoons and yet more toilet humour – especially from 'Recycle Dog'

Icebox **http://www.icebox.com** More in-your-face webtoons. Some are now heading for TV – look out for 'Mr Wong'.

Mondo Mini Shows **http://www.mondominishows.com/** One of the leading web cartoon studios – 'Like, News' is their best effort, but there's a lot more to check out.

Shockwave **http://www.shockwave.com** Macromedia's showcase for cartoons and game created using Shockwave and Flash.

Switch2 **http://www.switch2.net** The usual mix of cartoons, shorts and games, served up with very British cheekiness.

FILM

The Astounding B Monster **http://www.bmonster.com** The place to find out more about B movie culture and history.

Coming Attractions **http://corona.bc.ca/films/** On set gossip and more from films currently in production.

Dark Horizons **http://www.darkhorizons.com** Excellent film gossip/news site – better than the much praised Ain't It Cool News.

Drew's Script-O-Rama **http://www.script-o-rama.com** Download scripts from all sorts of films and TV shows.

Internet Movie Database **http://uk.imdb.com** Obsessively detailed databases about any film you might care to wonder about.

Jeeem's Cinepad **http://www.cinepad.com** Film site that mixes fannish intensity with buff-ish learning and even finds space for Microsoft.

Popcorn **http://www.popcorn.co.uk/** Carlton's film site is very mainstream, but still useful – reviews, news and a film finder.

< 304 >

MUSIC

All Music **http://www.allmusic.com** A great place to research just about any kind of music

ArtistDirect **http://artistdirect.com/** An American music site that's now home to the old Ultimate Band List – so a good place to research your favourite bands.

Global Music Network **http://www.gmn.com** Music site specialising in jazz and classical – check in here for webcasts and downloads

Listen.com **http://www.listen.com** Very American site, but still a useful online music search site

MP3.com **http://www.mp3.com** Get downloads from unknown hopefuls and big names, or just catch the latest MP3 news.

Music365 **http://www.music365.com** Music given the usual 365 mix – news, reviews and a cheeky attitude, plus lots of user feedback.

Napster **http://www.napster.com** Share files with other users and participate in the net's current big idea.

NME **http://www.nme.com** If anything, the well-known music weekly works better online

Radiohead **http://www.radiohead.com** The uptight art rockers used the net cleverly to push their 'Kid A' album – check in here for news, visual blips and more.

Shoutcast **http://www.shoutcast.com** Links to all sorts of online radio channels, plus the software you need to do it yourself.

Sonic Net **http://www.sonicnet.com** Big US music site that has videos, radio channels, news and much more

Vitaminic **http://www.vitaminic.co.uk/** Big European music download site, where you can get some MP3s for free and buy others.

< 305 >

COMEDY

Brunching Shuttlecocks **http://www.brunching.com** This has all the usual gags, plus some amusing toys – Alanis Morrisette lyric generators and the like.

Comedy Central **http://www.comedycentral.com/** The online presence of the US comedy channel – home to 'South Park' and John Stewart amongst others.

Gigawit **http://www.gigawit.com/** Billing itself as a grown-up net comedy site, which seems to mean parodies of net slang.

The Onion **http://www.theonion.com** Still the funniest site online – even though everyone else is now ripping off its spoof news approach.

TV Go Home **http://www.tvgohome.com/** Very funny, slightly foul-mouthed site that uses a Radio Times parody as the starting point for inspired media satire.

GAMES

Barry's World **http://www.barrysworld.com** Nice name, nice site – one of the better online gaming locations.

Battlemail **http://www.battlemail.com** Play games with your friends via email. Sounds like fun and it is, sort of.

Classic Gaming **http://www.classicgaming.com** One of the better sites devoted to old video games – lots of reviews and games to download.

Fun Planet **http://www.funplanet.co.uk** Games, quizzes, contests and various other ways of wasting time at work (or at home).

Gamespot **http://www.gamespot.co.uk** Excellent computer/video games site, with news, reviews, demo downloads and tips.

Netbabyworld **http://www.netbabyworld.com** Online gaming network built around simple retro games and a deliberately kitschy aesthetic – lots of fun.

< 306 >

The Sims **http://www.thesims.com** The web site for one of the best recent computer games has extras for the game and lets you network with other Sim heads.

SissyFight 2000 **http://www.word.com/sissyfight** Online game built around becoming the most popular person in the playground. Meaner than it sounds.

Soda Play **http://www.sodaplay.com** Construct wireframe models then watch them move – then look at other models in the SodaZoo. Hugely diverting.

Yahoo Games **http://play.yahoo.com** Play traditional games (poker, backgammon, chess) with punters from around the world.

Zap Spot **http://www.zapspot.com** Sign up and get little games via email. If you like them, they're easy to email to friends.

NEWS AND WEATHER

Ananova **http://www.ananova.com/** Formerly the Press Association site – great for news, plus some good entertainment listings too.

BBC News Online **http://news.bbc.co.uk** One part of the Beeb's online operation. An excellent news site.

Institute of War and Peace Reporting **http://www.iwpr.net/** An powerful site that showcases independent reporting in areas of conflict, for example the Balkans.

Met Office **http://www.meto.govt.uk/** Weather forecasts from the people who are supposed to know.

Moreover.com **http://www.moreover.com** The world's largest collection of web feeds, apparently – in others words, news from everywhere on just about anything.

NewsMaps.com **http://www.newsmaps.com** An attempt to represent news

< 307 >

and information in a visual map. More interesting than illuminating, but still fascinating.

Oneworld.net **http://www.oneworld.net** Global news, with an ecological spin and a campaigning edge.

Out There News **http://www.megastories.com** Interesting award-winning site that tries to provide the background to global news headlines.

COMPUTERS AND TECHNOLOGY

C Net **http://www.cnet.com** A huge site that tells you just about everything you need to know about techno-culture.

Clay Shirky **http://www.shirky.com** Home page set up by one of the most thoughtful writers on technology – lots of interesting stuff about Napster, WAP and more.

Eric Raymond **http://www.tuxedo.org/~esr/** Essays, FAQs and more from one of the prime movers in the Open Source movement.

Need To Know **http://www.ntk.net** Sarcastic British digest of the week's technology/net news, plus updates on geek culture.

PC Webopedia **http://www.pcwebopedia.com** Find out what the jargonauts are going on about at this useful computer dictionary.

Red Rock Eater **http://dlis.gseis.ucla.edu/people/pagre/rre.html** Phil Agre's mailing list delivers informed discussion of the social and political side of technology – catch up with it here.

The Register **http://www.theregister.co.uk** Attitude-heavy British technology news site that's always worth a visit.

Slashdot **http://www.slashdot.org** Slightly overwhelming site in which geeks from around the world thrash out the issues of the day.

Tasty Bits from the Technology Front **http://www.tbtf.com** Highly digestible alternative to big tech/net news sites.

< 308 >

What Is **http://whatis.com** Another site that helps you cuts through the techno-jargon.

Wired News **http://www.wired.com** An excellent technology news site, featuring sections on culture, technology, business and politics.

ZD Net UK **http://www.zdnet.co.uk** Get the latest net news, with a British spin, along with general features about computer culture.

WEBZINES

Artbyte **http://www.artbyte.com** A 'magazine of digital culture', which means lots of critical essays about speed culture and the new economy.

The Drudge Report **http://www.drudgereport.com** Washington gossip, planted 'scoops' and newsak from right-wing info-junkie Matt Drudge.

The Drudge Retort **http://www.drudge.com** Left-leaning answer site to Matt Drudge's rants with parodies of his reports and lots of links.

Feed **http://www.feedmag.com** Yet another excellent American webzine, covering techno-culture with intelligence and wit.

McSweeneys **http://www.mcsweeneys.net** The super smart, deliberately low tech online presence of the offbeat satirical zine.

Mr Showbiz **http://www.mrshowbiz.com** Celebrity gossip. All the usual tabloid fare. Lots of fun.

The Obscure Store **http://www.obscurestore.com** Jim Romanesko's 'daily news zine' offers links to offbeat stories from the US media.

Pop Bitch **http://www.popbitch.com** Sign up here to get the funniest British net pop gossip mag – you can read sample issues too.

Salon **http://www.salon.com** Updated daily, this has great news and media coverage and an excellent technology section.

< 309 >

Schnews **http://www.schnews.org.uk** More alternative news from the anti-corporate massive.

Stay Free **http://www.stayfreemagazine.org/index.html** Carrie McLaren's excellent anti-capitalist zine delivers lots of adbusting critique. Worth it.

Suck **http://www.suck.com** A daily blast of wordy spleen aimed at the big, soft target that is the net. Still funny.

The Obvious **http://www.theobvious.com** Michael Sippey's zine delivers occasional thoughts on digital tech. Worth waiting for.

Urban 75 **http://www.urban75.com** British webzine covering all strands of alternative culture, from direct action to outdoor raves.

Wallpaper **http://www.wallpaper.com** The web site for the flashy design mag, this looks appropriately wonderful.

SPORT

Cric Info **http://www-uk.cricket.org** News, scores and opinion from all round the world.

Explore **http://www.explore.com** Slick site that celebrates adventure – which means everything from snowboarding to hiking.

Football365 **http://www.football365.com** This now has video and audio, but it's the fannish feedback that makes it stand out.

Formula 1 **http://www.formula1.com** Unofficial site, but still a good place for news about those fast cars covered with ads.

Golf Today **http://www.golftoday.co.uk** It's the new rock and roll, apparently. Find out how to swing with the best here.

Scrum.com **http://www.scrum.com** The place to come for all your rugby news online.

Sneaker Nation **http://www.sneaker-nation.com** Catch up with the latest on sneaker, trainers and the rest, plus some good shopping links.

< 310 >

TRAVEL/GOING OUT

AA – Where to Stay, Where to Eat **http://www.theaa.co.uk/hotels/index.asp** Search the AA's reviews database for hotels and restaurants in the region you're travelling to.

A2B Travel **http://www.a2btravel.com** Useful UK-slanted travel resource with details on cheap flights and holidays, airport guides, ferry times, currency converters and much else.

Aloud **http://www.aloud.com** Buy tickets for all sorts of live events. A good place for gig/tour news too.

Expedia **http://www.expedia.co.uk** Excellent place to come to research and book journeys and holidays.

Knowhere **http://www.knowhere.co.uk** An offbeat directory of places to go in the UK, with reviews contributed by ordinary punters.

Multimap.com **http://uk2.multimap.com/** Enter the name of the British town you're going to, or the street, and get a map of the area you can print out.

Railtrack **http://www.railtrack.co.uk** Access the train information you need in a fraction of the time it takes to use the telephone timetable.

Rough Guides **http://travel.roughguides.com/** Very useful set of guides to countries and cities. Surprisingly detailed.

Time Out **http://www.timeout.com** This has London listings, as you'd expect, plus guides to an increasing number of cities around the world.

The Train Line **http://www.thetrainline.com** Book your train tickets online.

Wcities **http://www.wcities.com/** Detailed guide to over 200 cities around the world.

What's On When **http://www.whatsonwhen.com** A global listings site with surprisingly detailed coverage of the UK.

< 311 >

SHOPPING

Alt-Gifts **http://www.alt-gifts.com** Gently offbeat gift shop that might just help you out of a present crisis.

Amazon **http://www.amazon.co.uk** A predictable choice, perhaps, but still the best online shop – get books, music, videos and DVDs, gadgets, software, kid's stuff and much more.

Archie McPhee **http://www.mcphee.com** A sort of online joke shop – get your potato guns and Pez dispensers here.

Bull Electrical **http://www.bull-electrical.com** Online heaven for those who like to build their own radios/computers or fancy their own solar panels or a tank laser.

Ebay **http://www.ebay.com** The open access online auction/global car boot sale where you can buy everything and anything.

Eyestorm **http://www.eyestorm.com** Buy yourself some contemporary art here – fun to browse.

The MoMA Store **http://www.moma.org** New York's Museum of Modern Art online shop – get furniture, lighting, kids toys much else here, all done by big name designers.

ShopSmart **http://www.shopsmart.com** Probably the best UK online shopping directory, this has reviews, links and price comparison tools.

Last Minute **http://www.lastminute.com** Suffered a backlash earlier this year, but the idea – buy stuff at the last minute, give yourself a break etc – is still strong, as is the site.

Let's Buy It **http://www.letsbuyit.com** Club together with others to drive down prices. Fun to browse, though it makes buying rather drawn out.

The Teddington Cheese **http://www.teddingtoncheese.co.uk** A strangely wonderful online cheese shop. Get your Camembert and Cheddar here, along with crackers and chutneys.

< 312 >

NET CULTURE

Am I Hot Or Not? **http://www.amihotornot.com** The web fad of the moment – come here to rate the 'babes' and 'hunks' on view, and possibly put yourself up for review. Dubious fun.

The Bot Spot **http://www.botspot.com** This site delves into the world of bots, automated programs that do all sorts of things for us on the net.

Carl Steadman **http://www.freedonia.com** The co-founder of the webzine Suck puts his online diary here, along with links to his multiple online projects.

The Darwin Awards **http://www.darwinawards.com/** Award site for those who have managed to end their lives in the stupidest way possible.

DiaryLand **http://diaryland.com** A home to all sorts of net diaries, kept by people who want the world to feel their pain. You can add your own journal too.

Dialectizer **http://rinkworks.com/dialect** Silly web toy that turns text or web page into different comedy dialects – jive, cockney, hacker, etc.

Disinformation **http://www.disinfo.com/** Come here for the 'hidden information' that 'falls through the cracks of the corporate-owned media conglomerates'.

Inconspicuous Consumption **http://www.core77.com/inconspicuous/** Charming site that celebrates and dissects long forgotten consumer junk.

JenniCam **http://www.jennicam.org** The original show-all web cam – net voyeurism or online happening/ performance art?

Memepool **http://www.memepool.com** A regularly updated page of links to interesting sites, complete with little reviews.

Mirrorshades Archive **http://www.well.com/conf/mirrorshades** Online archive of a discussion group devoted to cyberpunk science fiction, the net and more – look out for the links to work by Bruce Sterling.

< 313 >

Obsessive Fan Sites **http://www.ggower.com/fans** Singgering at bad sites is default behaviour online – this gives it a bit of a spin, highlighting dodgy shrines to David Cassidy, Gillian Anderson and the rest.

Online Caroline **http://www.onlinecaroline.com** Clever web fiction that uses web cams, personalisation and email to spice up the usual romantic comedy.

OpenLetters **http://www.openletters.net** Letters from ordinary people pondering everything from the news to their own lives.

Philip Greenspun **http://philip.greenspun.com** Home page for writer/ programmer/teacher Greenspun, who supplies stories, software and more. Very worthwhile.

The Smoking Gun **http://www.thesmokinggun.com** View actual documents relating to celebrity crimes and cover-ups – sad and voyeuristic, but fun.

Seven Questions **http://www.sevenquestions.com** Journalist Tom Mangan interviews regular people rather than celebs. Often very interesting.

Urban Legends Archive **http://www.urbanlegends.com** The web archive of the newsgroup devoted to logging and debunking urban legends.

WOMEN

Beme **http://www.beme.com** One of the better UK women's portals, thanks in part to the design.

GURL **http://www.gurl.com** Attitude-heavy US site aimed at younger women.

iVillage **http://www.ivillage.co.uk** Vast portal site aimed at thirtysomething women online – advice on everything from parenting to finance and working from home.

WWWomen **http://www.wwwomen.com/** Useful search site that specialises in women's resources online.

< 314 >

KIDS/FAMILY/EDUCATION

Babyworld **http://www.babyworld.co.uk** Useful site packed with information on pregnancy and babies and lots product reviews and buying guides.

BBC Schools Online **http://www.bbc.co.uk/education/schools/index.shtml** Learning resources for primary/secondary school kids, plus a section for parents who want to help out with homework.

Bonus **http://www.bonus.com** Enjoyable site packed with kids' games, some educational, some just for fun. Very bright and very American.

Disney.com **http://disney.go.com** If you're a parent, you know that resistance if futile. Typically bright site packed with activities built around the films and TV shows.

GCSE Answers **http://www.gcse.com** A good place for revision tips and tutorials for English, Maths and Science GCSEs.

Homework High **http://www.homeworkhigh.com/** Stuck with your homework? Log on here and ask a teacher for some tips.

Kids Events **http://www.kidsevents.co.uk** Lots of useful ideas and information if you're looking to take the kids out and about.

UK Parents **http://www.ukparents.co.uk** All sorts of parental advice, plus reviews, features and discussion boards. Useful.

Yahooligans **http://www.yahooligans.com** Lots of links to kid-centred sites, along with advice and the usual community-building extras.

POLITICS/NET POLITICS

Consumer Project on Technology **http://www.cptech.org** Information on anti-trust actions against Microsoft, biotechnology and intellectual property, amongst other things.

Corporate Watch **http://www.corpwatch.org** Come here to keep track on multinational misdemeanors around the world.

< 315 >

Cyber Rights and Cyber Liberties **http://www.cyber-rights.org** Ignore the clunky design and check out the info on privacy and censorship on the net in the UK.

Electronic Privacy Information Centre **http://epic.org** Check in here for news about privacy online, plus lots of related research papers.

Foundation for Information Policy Research **http://www.fipr.org** Useful British site showcasing research into technology and society – come here for information about net surveillance in the UK.

The Hunger Site **http://www.thehungersite.org** Just by visiting here and clicking on the ads, you donate money to feed people in the Third World.

Independent Media Centre **http://www.indymedia.org** Grassroots, non-corporate coverage of the news, albeit with an American focus.

Lawrence Lessig **http://cyber.law.harvard.edu/lessig.html** Lessig's a lawyer who has taken a special interest in the net. Find his journalism and essays on privacy, spam and censorship here.

McSpotlight **http://www.mcspotlight.org** Set up during the McLibel trial and still arguing the case against McDonald's and multinationals in general.

No Logo **http://www.nologo.org** Online companion to Naomi Klein's book about anti-capitalist protest.

You Gov **http://www.yougov.com** Site that sets out to use the net to get people more involved in the UK political process.

LIFE/HEALTH/FOOD

BBC Health **http://www.bbc.co.uk/health** Typically strong site covering all sorts of health-related matters.

Curry Pages **http://www.currypages.com** Fancy a jalfrezi. Check this directory of UK curry houses.

< 316 >

Embarassing Problems **http://www.embarrassingproblems.co.uk** Slightly tacky design but excellent content for people suffering from touchy medical problems.

Flametree **http://www.flametree.co.uk** Interesting site devoted to finding balance in life and juggling work, kids, relationships and more.

NHS Direct **http://www.nhsdirect.nhs.uk** Simply designed site with lots of useful medical information and links to services.

The Recipe Centre **http://www.recipecenter.com** American site (so make sure you spell the address right), with lots of nice sounding recipes.

Simply Food **http://www.simplyfood.co.uk** Carlton's food site has everything from restaurant finders to recipes and wine guides.

Think Natural **http://www.thinknatural.com** Interesting mix of content and shopping at this site devoted to healthy organic living.

WORK/MONEY

Buy.co.uk **http://www.buy.co.uk** Come here to find out if you're being overcharged for your gas, electric, water and more.

Guru **http://www.guru.com** Lots of advice on how to manage your own career here, from making the most of your time to hacking the media.

The UK Home Repossession Page **http://www.home-repo.org** Advice and help on how to cope if you have problems with your mortgage repayments.

Money Extra **http://www.moneyextra.com** Slick site which helps you search for the best rates on mortgages, credit cards, personal loans and more.

Net Slaves **http://www.disobey.com/netslaves/** Frontline reports on the problems of working in the net business.

Word's Work Archive **http://www.word.com/work** Word proper is worth a look, but their section on work, with ordinary people talking about their jobs, is consistently excellent.

< 317 >

SCIENCE

BBC Science **http://www.bbc.co.uk/science** Anotehr good BBC site, this has news, special features and links to the corporation's various science shows.

Edge **http://www.edge.org** Techno-gurus and celebrity scientists ponder big questions. Always interesting.

Golem Project **http://golem03.cs-i.brandeis.edu/** Fascinating site devoted to research into self-evolving robots. You can get involved too, by loaning them the unused processor power on your desktop.

NASA **http://www.nasa.gov** The US space agency site has a vast amount of material on various missions and projects, along with some fun toys.

New Scientist **http://www.newscientist.co.uk** Online companion to the well known science magazine, with useful sections that organise archive material around themes like artificial intelligence and biotechnology.

< 318 >

6 LOOKING AFTER YOURSELF ON THE NET

Despite the claims of self-appointed moral guardians, the net is not an alien, hostile space. But you do need to take care. Like the real world, there are people online who do not have your best interests at heart. And, unlike the real world, the net is such a new space that sometimes you might not realise you're getting into trouble. So here are a few . . . no, not survival tips, just bits of advice on how to make your time online as painless as it is enjoyable.

Pornography, free speech and protecting your kids online

Yes, there is a lot of porn online. But it doesn't generally jump out at you when you log on. That said, junk email advertising porn sites can be a problem. And in the past, on some search sites, a search on 'little women' might have found links that were a long way from Louisa May Alcott. Worse, the various programs running the site might have thought you were after porn, and so would have loaded ads for X-rated pages. However, most search sites now have filters you can turn on to block adult content.

< 319 >

Some porn sites have web addresses that are very close to the addresses of popular sites. Some porn sites use familiar addresses but change the top level domain. The url of the Whitehouse is **http://www.whitehouse.gov**, but there's a big porn site at **http://www.whitehouse.com**.

So, it is possible for unwanted porn to find its way onto your computer screen. But usually you have to look for it. If you're a consenting adult who likes that sort of thing, there's plenty online for you. If you don't, don't go looking for it. Of course, adults aren't the problem here. The problem is hormonal teens and curious children. However, most porn sites are commercial operations. To get in, you have to enter credit-card details and sign up with a service to verify that you are an adult. That said, all sites offer free samples as a come-on. And there are plenty of completely free porn sites online. The more responsible use some sort of adult check. But plenty don't. Porn is also available in some Usenet newsgroups – usually the alt.binaries groups.

In addition, there are newsgroups covering the more bizarre sexual practices. There are some groups devoted to circulating child porn. Your ISP should already block access to these. There are plenty of other things for parents to worry about – racist web sites, pages denying that the Holocaust took place, sites that feature accident scene photographs or bomb making information. There's also plenty of uncontroversial, non-visual material that just isn't suitable for young children – discussion about recovering from sexual abuse, for example. Chat rooms are a source of concern as well. Some paedophiles do hang out in chat rooms frequented by children. Online, visual cues that might alert you to potential problems (i.e. the fact that the person claiming to be a fifteen year old boy is a forty four year old man) are absent. So it's harder to spot dodgy characters.

< 320 >

So there's material and people online you want to keep away from your children. But the net is not packed with pornography and perverts. It's mostly used by ordinary people like you. So don't believe the moral panic-mongers. The presence of pornography and dodgy characters online is no reason to keep your kids offline. Most children use the net happily without ever coming into harm's way. Your kids will enjoy the net and learn from it. Don't deprive them out of ill-informed fear.

I once heard a net user point out that, although certain city streets are used at night by prostitutes, it doesn't stop families using the road system in general. The analogy doesn't really work. Red-light districts in cyberspace run 24 hours a day. Plus, your children aren't likely to wander into a real red-light district in the middle of the night. But it's easy for them to find their way to porn sites on the net. The barriers we find in the real world – physical, legal, social – aren't there yet in cyberspace. In the real world there's a top shelf. Bomb-making information is kept under the counter at independent bookshops or in the less accessible parts of a library. Eventually a set of similar barriers will develop in cyberspace.

For example, some suggest a top-level domain for pornography – X-rated sites would end in .porn for example – would make it easier to keep children out. It might work, though it wouldn't be without problems. But

---

Read about it online - Child-friendly Sites

For links to kid-friendly material online, try Yahooligans **http://www. yahooligans.com**. Chat can be a risky area for kids, but some parts of the IRC network are specifically for kids. Try KidLink (an IRC net for kids) **http://www.kidlink.org/rti/irc/**. ▲

< 321 >

many pornographers would be happy to go along with it. Most don't want children on their sites. They just want to make money. Hence they generally want to avoid anything that might lead the police to stop them making money. Some people think governments should set up legal barriers online to protect children. But this remains problematic. There are areas where everyone seems to be in agreement (banning child porn, for example). But the laws concerning things like hard-core porn and hate speech is different, country to country. So far, attempts by individual countries at drafting legislation have been so vague that, if put into practice, they would cover more than pornographic material, would treat adults as children and ruin much that's good about the net.

Some free-speech activists claim that, aside from being undesirable, censorship on the net is also impossible, that 'the net interprets censorship as damage and routes around it'. There is something glib about the way free-speech fundamentalists repeat this as if it closed the argument, as if the technology was going to decide things for us. But without taking draconian measures, national governments have found it difficult to block access to a site in another country that contains political or pornographic material they don't like. There always seems to be a way for smart people to get to the forbidden information. And the job of would-be censors is made harder by activists who delight in putting up mirror sites of banned web pages. Hence the rather bizarre spectacle of right-on activists hosting pages put up by scumbag Holocaust revisionists.

In the UK, the police have argued that existing laws do apply online and have put pressure on UK ISPs to block access to newsgroups that carry illegal material or face prosecution themselves. Critics argue that the police are setting themselves up as censors and are disregarding a complex set of legal issues. Put simply, the police claim the ISPs are 'publishers' of this

< 322 >

material and are legally responsible. ISPs argue that they are merely carriers of this stuff and hence are not responsible. You don't prosecute the telephone companies if people use their lines to conspire to commit crimes, they suggest. The whole thing's more complex than this, but you get the gist. Even though the arguments aren't resolved, you'd be hard pressed to find a UK ISP that doesn't block access to paedophile newsgroups.

The UK net industry argues that it can regulate itself, via things like the Internet Watch Foundation **http://www.iwf.org.uk**, which collects reports about child porn online and alerts ISPs. The net industry in general is anti-legislation. It would prefer a system in which sites are rated and parents then use special software to block access to pages defined as adult. Many techno-gurus still think this is the perfect solution, because it gives individuals control without affecting the net as a whole. Unfortunately, it's not that simple. The various ratings systems, in particular PICS, aka Platform for Internet Content Selection – allow ISPs and even countries to block access to certain sites. And once a site is rated and filtered, it will disappear completely. You won't know it exists. Worried by this, some net users now think carefully framed legislation might be the best way to protect children online and preserve adult freedoms. Unfortunately, the net has become caught up in the larger, ongoing moral panic about children. So it's unlikely that people will take the time to develop sensible laws. But you can do your bit, simply by taking a realistic attitude to the net and your children.

Setting guidelines and boundaries for children online

The net is not a risk-free environment. Parents should not let children use it without guidance, boundaries and some form of supervision, any more

< 323 >

than they would let them play out in the street without the same. So here's a few tips.

If you have a family computer, don't set it up in your child's bedroom. Put it in a communal space where they will at least feel you're keeping an eye on them. Don't let them password-protect areas of the computer. Use the computer yourself and check any new programs or files that appear on it. You may want to give older children their own computer (and net connection) but recognise the implications of that decision. It means that you will (a) have to talk to them more about what they do online (not something teenagers will relish) and (b) have to trust them more. You can make the choice not to let your kids use the net on their own. Certainly with younger children this is the best bet. With children approaching their teens, it's probably not going to work.

So set some basic guidelines. Put time limits on their net use. Be clear about where they can and cannot go. Tell them they can talk to you if they find material that makes them uncomfortable. Tell them to never give out personal information online (everything from name, address, telephone number and the location of their school to personal photographs). Incidentally, they may be at risk here not from dodgy individuals but from

Read about it online - Resources For Parents

Larry Magid has established himself as an authority on child and teen safety online. Check his sites **http://www.safekids.com** and **http://www.safeteens.com** for advice, tips and some good links to kids/teens sites. For some more general advice that takes in computers and CD ROMs, try the Parents Information Network **http://www.pin.org.uk**. ▲

< 324 >

ecommerce and netmarketing companies trying to get information about parents. Check the privacy policy on sites your kids use a lot. Finally, make sure your kids know that they must never meet online friends without checking with you first. If you do agree they can meet someone, go with your children and make sure the meeting is in a public place.

If you don't trust your children to resist temptation, you can set up some technological barriers. AOL and a few 'family' ISPs provide ways for you to block access to 'unacceptable' material. If you want uncensored access to the net for yourself but not for your kids, try installing a filterware program, for example, Cyber Sitter **http://www.cybersitter.com**, Cyber Patrol **http://www.cyberpatrol.com**, Net Nanny **http://www.netnanny.com** or Surf Control **http://www.surfcontrol.com**. These do the same sorts of things but all work in slightly different ways, so get more information from their sites. Filterware blocks access to prohibited sites and lets you set times during which the net can (or cannot) be used. They all use a list of unsuitable sites. Some let you take sites off the list if you think they're fine for your kids. Some let you add more to the list. Most record attempts to access restricted web sites. Some let you restrict access to certain areas of your computer as well.

These programs are fine if you want to let younger children use the net unsupervised. If you've got teenage children, they may find a way round them. Filterware also needs maintenance. The list of banned sites is constantly changing. New sites appear. Old ones disappear. So you'll need to download a new list of censored sites fairly frequently. More importantly, many of these programs come with a built-in right wing agenda and block access to non-pornographic sites promoting gay/feminist politics. Often, you won't know if that's happening. Some of the companies behind these programs keep their banned list secret.

< 325 >

Read about it online - Filterware Critics

One of the most determined filterware critics is Bennett Haselton. His Peacefire site **http://www.peacefire.org** has extensive reviews of different filterware programs, plus the latest news. ▲

They work hard on it and see it as their crucial piece of intellectual property.

It's obviously up to individuals whether they use these programs. However, the increasing use of filterware programs by public libraries is more contentious, especially since some seem unaware of their hidden agendas. In general, if I were going to use one of these programs, I'd want to know what they blocked. I'd also want to be able to add sites to the blocked list and to remove others I thought were fine.

You don't necessarily need to install software to begin blocking sites. Both browsers allow some web filtering. If you want to try it out:

▶ In **Internet Explorer** select the **Tools** menu, then **Internet Options**, then click the **Content** tab. Click the **Enable** button in the **Content Advisor** section. You'll go to a **Content Advisor** dialog box. Once you set a password, you can use a little slider control to set acceptable levels as far as Language, Nudity, Sex and Violence are concerned. You can also set up a list of approved sites and create passwords that allow access to restricted material.

▶ In the **Mac** version of **Internet Explorer**, select the **Edit** menu, then **Preferences**, then in the **Web Browser** section, click on **Ratings**.

< 326 >

▶ In **Navigator**, get online, then select the **Help** menu, then **NetWatch**. Then click the **NetWatch Set Up** link, then click the **New User** button. You then have to specify the levels of nudity and language that you'll tolerate and choose a password.

Both browsers use the RSACi ratings and the Safe Surf ratings. Both are PICs-compliant ratings systems. You can either pick one or use both at the same time. For more information on how each system works, go the Internet Content Rating Association **http://www.icra.org** or try the Safe Surf page **http://www.safesurf.com**. Both pages have more information on how to set up content filters in the two big browsers.

Blocking access isn't the only option. You can also snoop on your children's use of the net. Filterware programs allow a measure of this. But there are now surveillance programs that will tell you everything your child gets up to online, home versions of the software now used in many offices. Using this kind of thing does seem rather drastic – if you don't tell your kids you've installed it, you might find out more than you bargained for. Are you ready for outing by software, for example? Actually, your browser is already a surveillance tool. It records where you've been (in the History file), stores pages you've visited in the cache, retains addresses entered in its location bar and has a file filled with cookies – special identifying files placed by some sites on your hard disk (more about these later). So if you do want to check what Junior has been up to, look in these.

▶ In **Internet Explorer**, your cookies will be in a **Cookies** folder in the general **Windows** directory.

▶ In **Navigator**, the cookies will be in cookies.txt in the **Users** folder. You'll find it under **Netscape** in your computer's general file directory

< 327 >

Smart kids will know about all this. Be suspicious if you find a completely clear History file and an empty cache after a couple of hours' surfing. Messenger and Outlook Express also save details of newsgroups that have been subscribed to, then unsubscribed. Just spend some time looking around in the files and folders. If you're really obsessive, a good utilities program will also enable you to recover deleted files. So you can tell if your child has downloaded images, transferred them to a floppy disc, then deleted them. Of course, if you're that obsessive, especially without grounds for suspicion, it may be you that needs help, not your kids.

Finally, when people talk about protecting kids online, they always seem to go on about porn. Plain vanilla chat can also end up being harmful. Some children find it incredibly compelling. Even if all they're doing is nattering about Robbie Williams, it can be a problem if done to excess. So keep a tactful eye on them and make sure that chat (and the net in general) doesn't stop them from enjoying other things. You could use software that tots up the time spent online (also useful when it comes to controlling your own net use). Try Net Meter **http://www.cracker.u-net.com/**.

Tips – Clearing Your Machine

If you check out online porn using the same software as your kids, it's your business. However, your browser can make it your kids' business. The URLs will be in the History file and there will be cookies in your browser identifying whoever is using the browser as a porn consumer. Some sites may then target X-rated advertising at that browser. So, if you want to protect your kids, clear History and get rid of any offending cookies. ▲

< 328 >

Read about it online – EPIC

For information on privacy online, try the Electronic Privacy Information Centre at **http://epic.org**. For more general information on privacy, try Privacy International **http://www.privacy.org/pi/**. For a British perspective, try Cyber Rights and Cyber Liberties site **http://www.cyber-rights.org**. ▲

Privacy on the net

The fact that the net allows ordinary people to communicate anonymously has been much discussed. The net may allow a superficial kind of anonymity – one that lets people mess around in chat rooms pretending to be someone else. But at a more fundamental level, much of what you do online is accessible to all sorts of people who know how to look. As activists have pointed out, the net is redefining the nature of privacy, allowing governments and corporations greater access to ordinary people's lives. Be aware of this. Don't assume that anything you do or say online is private. Take precautions and get involved in the ongoing debate about privacy online.

Over the last year, that debate in Britain has been focused on the Regulation of Investigatory Powers (RIP) Act, a misconceived piece of legislation that became law just as this book was going to press. The government say RIP will give the police the power they need to track terrorists, drug dealers and other criminals on the net. According to critics, there are two big problems with the act. First, it compels ISPs to install 'black boxes' that can track their users' clickstreams i.e. the addresses of the web sites and chat rooms they visit and the emails they send and receive. Unlike telephone tapping, all this will happen without

< 329 >

a warrant being issued. These black boxes will automatically relay that data to MI5's monitoring centre. Installing them will also be costly for ISPs. Costs may be passed on to customers. All this may also drive UK net businesses out of the country. It has other ramifications. A while ago, the renegade MI5 office David Shayler sent email to The Guardian and The Observer. The police tried to compel the papers to hand over the emails. They refused, things went to court and The Guardian and The Observer won the appeal. If RIP had been around, things would never have gone to court. The police would just have demanded the mail.

Second, if you attempt to keep your email and activities online secret via encryption (more on this shortly), the act forces you to give up your encryption keys, if the police decide they want access to your data. If you refuse, you could go to jail for up to two years. If you tell someone you've been asked to hand over a key, the sentence could be even higher. The government says that keys will only be required in very special circumstances. Critics point out that this reverses the burden of proof and that people could in theory be jailed for innocently forgetting their keys.

No other country in the West has this kind of legislation on its statute books. Ireland, France and Germany all seem relatively relaxed about ordinary people using encryption. American privacy activists say that, for all its problems in this area, the US government would never attempt something like RIP. If you want to find out how it all happened, the Foundation for Information Policy Research led the fight against the RIP act and has an archive of material relating to it **http://www.fipr.org/rip**. Guardian Unlimited has a page laying out the basics of the act, which you'll find in the special report on Net Privacy **http://www.guardian. co.uk/netprivacy/**.

< 330 >

Privacy online at work

RIP gave employers powers to snoop on their employee's email and online activities. But in a way, it only formalised what was becoming standard practice. So, put simply, there is no online privacy at work. Assume that your boss is using software to track your use of the net. Assume that he or she owns whatever you say online. Don't use the net at work for serious personal communications. Don't use email for anything that might get you into trouble. It will be impossible to delete it easily, since it will be stored in all sorts of places. Don't use the web at work for non-work related activities. It's likely the boss will know exactly what you're doing. Download porn on company time and you may be fired. You can keep personal communications at work private by using web mail but your boss will still know if you spend a lot of time at a web mail site. The only thing you can really do at work is find out what your employer's privacy policy is and act accordingly.

Internet Service Providers and privacy

The RIP Act compels ISPs to take measures that allow for the tracking of their users online. In the run-up to RIP becoming law, some ISPs said they were looking into transferring their operations offshore, to avoid surveillance and keep their big corporate clients happy, many of whom expressed reservations about the act. So before you sign up with an ISP, why not ask them what they're doing about RIP. Check their general privacy policy too. Make sure they're not going to sell your personal details to junk mailers, on or offline. Check whether they include any personal/sensitive information in their member directories. Be careful with the password to your net account. Obviously, if someone gets your password, they will be able to read your mail and use your account to

< 331 >

cause mischief in your name. So don't ever give it out to anyone online, even if they identify themselves as working for your ISP. Your ISP will never ask for your password online. Never email your net account password to anyone. Change it frequently and choose a random combination of letters and numbers.

Email and privacy

Standard email is not private. On its way to and from your computer it sits around unprotected on various computers. Even after you read it and delete it, someone with a good utilities program can still get at it. Just ask Monica Lewinsky. The only way to completely remove it is with a file-wiping program. And the only way to ensure email privacy is to use encryption. An encryption program scrambles your messages so that they look like gobbledegook. The most popular form of encryption online is public key cryptography. The idea here is that a net user has two 'keys', one public, one private. The public one is distributed to friends and colleagues. Often people tack it on the end of their emails. The private key is kept secret and secure. If you want to encrypt a message to someone, you use their public key. When they get your message, they need their private key to decrypt it. Without access to the private key, communications encrypted in this way are very difficult to unscramble. Encryption software also allows you to create digital signatures so that you know for certain who sent a particular piece of email.

Worried that criminals will use encryption to frustrate law enforcement, the US government has tried in the past to introduce encryption programs which allowed back door access to the powers that be. The net community campaigned vigorously against this kind of thing, with some resorting to direct action. In 1991, a programmer called Phil Zimmerman

< 332 >

Read about it online – UK Crypto Links

For more general information about cryptography, try UK crypto activist Ross Anderson's home page **http://www.cl.cam.ac.uk/~rja14/** or Sam Simpson's page **http://www.scramdisk.clara.net/**, where you'll find some interesting links and software. ▲

---

finished a public key encryption program called Pretty Good Privacy. He sent it to friends who made it freely available on the net. Zimmerman was then taken to court by the US government on a charge of illegally exporting munitions. The case collapsed a few years back and Zimmerman has since gone into the encryption business proper, selling commercial versions of PGP **http://www.pgp.com**. It remains the most popular encryption program online, thanks to its rebel history. You can find download the program at the PGP International site **http://www.pgpi.com**. If you do use it, remember that, thanks to the RIP act, the government will be able to compel you to give up your private key, if they decide they want to have a look at your mail, though they would argue that this is unlikely to happen unless you give them reason to be suspicious.

Email privacy isn't just about stopping nosey people from reading what you say. Sometimes you want people to read what you say. You just don't want them to know it was you that said it. You might want to post to a public mailing list about depression or alcoholism. You might want to send anonymous email exposing malpractice where you work. You can, if you use an anonymous remailer. You send your mail to one of these, it strips away identifying details, then sends it on.

< 333 >

Read about it online – Anonymity

For more information about anonymity online, with links to software, academic research and other resources, try the site put up by the American Association for the Advancement of Science at **http://www.aaas.org/spp/anon**. ▲

Remailers remain controversial (and hard to find), thanks to claims in the past that they were primarily used to circulate child porn. The most famous anonymous remailer – anon.penet.fi – closed after coming under fire from hysterical hacks and the Church of Scientology. There are still a few anonymous remailers up and running. Try The Global Internet Liberty Campaign **http://www.gilc.org/speech/anonymous/remailer.html** or the links at The Electronic Privacy Information Centre **http://www.epic. org/privacy/tools.html**. You can achieve a superficial anonymity by entering a false name and address when you configure your email software. It means people won't be able to reply to your mail. You could

Tips – Encrypted Web Mail

There are now several companies offering encrypted web mail. Best known is Hush Mail, **http://www.hushmail.com**, though you could also try ZipLip **http://www.ziplip.com**. Other secure mail services worth a look include Safe Message **http://www.safemessage.com**, which lets you 'shred' email you're finished with and Mail2Web **http://mail2web.com/**, which lets you check your normal POP3 mailbox securely via the web. ▲

< 334 >

Tips – Avoiding Spam

When you put a return email address on your newsgroup postings, create an address that will confuse the programs used by spammers but will be easily decoded by human readers. Try **yourname@ stripthisbitouttoreply.yourisp.net** or something similar. ▲

also a non-gender specific nickname rather than your real name in your email address.

Newsgroups, mailing lists and privacy

In theory, you should put your email address in your newsgroup postings. That way, people can respond privately if they wish. In practice, if you do reveal your email address, it may be collected by the programs used by spammers and you may then find yourself deluged with junk email. So when you configure your newsreader, you may want to enter a bogus name and email address. Many sites now archive newsgroups and mailing lists (for example, Deja.com **http://www.deja.com/usenet**). There have been claims that some employers run searches on potential employees to see what they've said in these groups. Changing your name and keeping your email address might help avoid any potential problems. Some archive sites allow you to add details to your postings which prevent them from being archived and searched. Check in their help files.

The web and privacy

Your browser collects all sorts of information about what you do on the web. The information stored in the cache and the History files is only the

< 335 >

half of it. The real problem is cookies, little identifying text files which some sites place on your computer when you visit them. When you go back to a particular site, it looks at the cookie to find out what you did there before. It also adds more information. Many sites use cookies to log your personal preferences. Shopping sites use cookies so that they can remember what you bought before and direct you to other things you might like. Whilst this sounds fine, you might feel less comfortable about companies surreptitiously snooping around your cookies, building a database on you and then sharing it with others who then use the information to target advertising at you.

As mentioned before, you can check on which sites have put cookies on your computer.

▶ If you use **Internet Explorer**, look for the **Cookies** folder in the general **Windows** directory.
▶ In **Navigator**, look in the **User** folder.

You can instruct your browser to refuse cookies.

▶ In **Internet Explorer**, select the **Tools** menu then **Internet Options**, then click the **Advanced** tab, then scroll down to the section on **Cookies**. Disable both options.
▶ In the **Mac** version of **Internet Explorer**, select the **Edit** menu, then **Preferences**, then in the **Receiving Files** section, click on **Cookies**, then select **Never Accept** via the drop down menu.
▶ In **Navigator**, select the **Edit** menu, then **Preferences**, then **Advanced**. In the **Cookies** section you can choose to block all cookies or **Accept only cookies that get sent back to the**

< 336 >

originating server, which in theory ought to offer more privacy, if you trust the originating server.

Cookie Central **http://www.cookiecentral.com** has more information on cookies, plus links to programs you can use to control them, for example Cookie Cutter, Cookie Crusher and Cookie Pal. You can also find some links to these on EPIC's privacy tools page **http://www.epic.org/privacy/tools.html**. Many let you specify which cookies you want to accept, so you can benefit from personalisation at some sites.

Cookies aren't the only threat to privacy on the web. As you surf, your browser reveals all sorts of other bits of information about you. To find out what exactly, visit Privacy.net at **http://privacy.net/anonymizer/**. Some sites use JavaScript to copy your email address while you're browsing. You can stop this by not entering your email address into the relevant sections of your browser. That means you won't be able to use it for email. Alternatively, change the settings on your browser to block Java and JavaScript.

▶ In *Internet Explorer*, select the *Tools* menu, then *Internet Options*, then click the *Advanced* tab, then scroll down to the *Java* section.
▶ In the *Mac* version of *Internet Explorer*, select the *Edit* menu, then *Preferences*, then in the *Web Browser* section, click on *Java*, then make the changes you want in the *Java Options* box.
▶ In *Navigator*, select the *Edit* menu, then *Preferences*, then *Advanced* and look for the *Java* section.

You can achieve complete anonymity on the web via an anonymiser, which sets up a protective barrier between you and the sites you surf. Try

< 337 >

Anonymiser.com **http://www.anonymiser.com**, Zero Knowledge's Freedom **http://www.freedom.net/** and Safe Web **http://www.safeweb.com**.

Giving away personal data without realising is one thing. What about information you hand over when you register with a site or buy something? Always check a site's privacy/security policy if you are revealing personal details. The net industry hasn't always shown it can be trusted on consumer privacy. In the UK and Europe, we have some legal protection, when it comes to keeping our personal information private. Things are looser in the States, something it's as well to consider when you use American web sites (especially online shops). In an attempt to show willing, some web sites now sign up with TRUSTe **http://www.truste.org**, which is attempting to set certain industry standards regarding privacy and commercial web sites. If a site has signed up, you should see a little TRUSTe logo somewhere. Their site has lots of useful information about online privacy.

Harassment on the net

Some people do use the net to make mischief and cause problems. This can encompass everything from sabotaging discussion groups with wind-ups to making someone's life a misery with abusive, unwanted email. The press calls the latter cyberstalking, which may sound a little melodramatic. However, a continual unwanted presence in your mailbox does feel like an invasion of your personal space. This obviously isn't a problem that only afflicts women but clearly women in particular need to take precautions. Problems often start in chat rooms. So configure your software so it doesn't reveal anything important or real about you. Pick a non-gender-specific nickname. If someone gets on your nerves, use the *Ignore* function on your chat software to make them disappear.

< 338 >

If problems persist, report them to the people running the chat room. If someone gets hold of your email address and sends you abusive mail, use mail filters to block it. But not before saving some of it and sending it to your tormentor's ISP to complain (try mailing **postmaster@ispname.com**). If their mail gives a false name and address, look at the header for more information about them and their messages. Get help from your ISP. Ultimately, if you're worried, save the mail and get the police involved. You can get more information about tackling online harassment a Women Halting Online Abuse **http://www.haltabuse.org/**.

Spam

Spam, as in unwanted junk email, generally comes ahead of governments and clueless journalists when net users are putting together their top ten lists of hate objects. It's pretty obvious why. Spam costs time and money. Deleting it can be a lengthy process. And in contrast to real world junk mail, the recipient actually pays for the privilege of getting spam. Spam has also destroyed certain online communities. If you actually read the stuff, you'll find that much of it consists of fraudulent get-rich-quick offers, fake charity appeals, pyramid schemes and other cons, all designed to trick the gullible into handing over money. So the first piece of advice for net newcomers concerning spam is: don't read it. Don't open the mail when it turns up in your mailbox. If you do read it, don't believe it. Sick kiddies collecting email addresses for charity? A chance to get in early on the next hot stock? A killer scheme in which if you send money and addresses of friends now you will, in just a few weeks, receive thousands of pounds? All rubbish. The second tip is: get angry by all means, but don't let it take over your life. Spam has become a fact of life online. You can do certain things to minimise the problems it causes. But

< 339 >

Read about it online - Spam

The web is packed with sites about spam and how to deal with it. For legal angles and links, try the Coalition Against Unsolicited Commercial Email **http://www.euro.cauce.org**. Alternatively, try Fight Spam on the Internet **http://spam.abuse.net/** for links to some useful tools. ▲

you can't make it go away completely. So do what you can and then get on with your online life.

Many spammers assemble their mailing lists with addresses they get from newsgroups and web pages. So you could avoid contributing to the newsgroups and avoid putting up a web page. That seems a bit drastic. A better bet might be to set up several email accounts and keep one for dealings in the newsgroups. You can also use filters either to automatically send anything that looks like spam into the trash folder or to stop your mail program from downloading the stuff in the first place. None of these will block everything but they're still worth trying.

There's some good advice on how to set up spam filters in Eudora at Pat Beim's Eudora page **http://wso.williams.edu/~eudora/eudora-3-0-spam-filter.html**, along with some good anti-spam links. Even if you use Outlook Express or Messenger, it's worth checking this out, since it will help you attempt something similar with your software. You can get extra bits of software to deal with spam. Try Spam Killer **http://www.spamkiller.com** or Email Chomper **http://www.sarum.com/echomp.html**. The best of these programs let you identify spam before you download it. They also provide safeguards so you can avoid deleting mail you actually want. Cyber-Info's Email Notify and Webmail Notify **http://www.cyber-info.com** let you check

< 340 >

multiple mailboxes and web mail accounts for new mail and delete spam at the same time. POP3 Scan Mailbox **http://www.netcomuk.co.uk/ ~kempston/smb/index.html** will also scan for spam on your ISP's mail server. Your ISP should also be taking anti-spam action. If you are having problems, call them and find out what they're doing.

At the end of spam, you'll usually see a return address you're invited to use if you want to stop receiving mail. Don't reply. If you do, you'll get even more spam. Spammers often do this to find out if a particular account is still live. Most spammers don't supply a working email address. In that case, complain to their ISP (for example, send email to **postmaster@ispname.com**). If all the addresses on the spam are faked, you can find the real address from the mail header – Junkbusters **http://www.junkbusters.com** has some tips on this. Get That Spammer **http://kryten.eng.monash.edu.au/gspam.html** has more information on tracking down spammers. There are also programs that decode headers, track down spammers and draft legal threats – try Spamcop **http://spamcop.net** or Spam Hater **http://www.cix.co.uk/~net-services/ spam/spam_hater.htm**.

Trust and security

It's pretty easy to fool people if all they've got is words (and their willingness to believe). That's why the net has been prey in the past to all sorts of hoaxes. It seems to happen less now, perhaps because people are now more cynical about what they read online. But never forget – though there's plenty of useful and reliable information on the net, there's also tons of rubbish. And there's lots of information that is tricked up to look official and reliable, but isn't. Some people are similarly tricked up. Playing around with identities online can be fun. But as the net has

< 341 >

become more commercial, there's more at stake. Put simply, there are conmen and women online looking to part you from your money. They might do this with email offers to 'make money fast'. They might do it with official-sounding email that seems to have come from your ISP and requests you send in your personal information and credit card details again. ISPs never ask you to do this kind of thing. If you get mail like this, at the very least ring your ISP up to check it out.

Faking mail which seems to have come from someone else, aka mail spoofing, is easy to do and much used by net pranksters. So if you get mail from **tony.blair@newlabour.org**, don't start planning the outfit you'll wear to Number 10. Instead work out which of your friends might play that kind of trick. If you get mail from a friend that seems out of character, don't immediately assume they sent it. Similarly, on discussion groups, if postings don't fit someone's previous profile, it's likely they're spoofs. If you want email that you and your friends can definitely trust, try creating digital signatures using the encryption software mentioned above. In general, be sceptical when you're on the web. It doesn't cost that much to make a web site look good or official. Always think about who put the site up and why they're telling you what they're telling you. Always look for a real-world address/contact number before you hand over information. Be sceptical about 'guaranteed money-making offers' and the like. For more information on net cons, try Internet Fraud Watch **http://www. fraud.org/internet/intset.htm**, Scambusters **http://www.scambusters.org** or Net Watch **http://www.internetfraudwatch.com**.

Viruses

One common net scam you'll undoubtedly encounter is the fake virus alert – mail warning of an email virus that will infect your computer if

< 342 >

you download and read it. These messages are viruses of a sort: mental viruses that cause you to waste valuable time wondering whether they're true. Ignore them. Don't pass them on. However, do take precautions about viruses. Get a good anti-virus program and always virus-check programs before you install them. (There are three big anti-virus programs: Doctor Solomon's Home Guard – **http://www.drsolomon.com/**; Norton AntiVirus – **http://www.symantec.com**; and McAfee's VirusScan – **http://www.nai.com**).

Similarly, be wary of email attachments created using Word. These may contain macro viruses and should be checked before you open them. This was how much-talked about viruses like Melissa and the Lovebug spread. In general, be cautious with attachments. If they arrive from someone you don't know, dump them in the bin. If they come unexpectedly from people you know, there still may be a problem. Viruses like the Lovebug work by sending themselves on, in the form of an attachment, to all the addresses in the email address book they find on a computer they've infected. So if a message turns up unexpectedly, with a slightly stilted subject lines or messages, contact the friend who sent it to

---

Read about it online – Virus Myths

For a very useful guide to online hoaxes, try the About.com Urban Legends page **http://urbanlegends.about.com** and look for the Net Hoaxes and Virus Hoaxes links. Alternatively, try Vmyths.com **http://www.vmyths.com/**. For news about real viruses (and lots of stuff about information war in general), try The Crypt **http://sun.soci.niu.edu/~crypt/**. ▲

< 343 >

find out if it's bona fide, before you open the attachment. Microsoft critics say that you can minimise the risk of infection from viruses like the Lovebug by not using Outlook Express. So far, these viruses have tended to be targeted at Microsoft programs. It might help, but it's no guarantee. Incidentally, if you're running a network, either at the office or at home, there are now programs you can get to try to stop email-borne viruses entering your system – try MyCIO.com's Virus Screen ASaP **http://www. mycio.com/content/virusscreen_asap/default.asp**.

Hackers

Some people seem convinced that once you get online, hordes of malicious hackers will seek you out and make your life a misery. The truth is, most hackers spend their time either trying to make other hackers' lives a misery (and hence prove how hardcore they are) or trying to break into government/military computers (and hence prove how hardcore they are). Generally, they won't bug you if you don't bug them. That said, take care in certain online locations, especially IRC chat rooms. If you're in a chat room and someone tells you to type a particular command, don't do it. It may let them take over your computer. Be careful about the software you download from sites that seem less than reputable. There have been reports in the past of programs designed to let hackers charge telephone bills to users who installed them.

Broadband connections to the net are 'always on' and so are visible on the network to anyone poking around in the right places. As a result, they are theoretically more vulnerable to intruders than the standard dial-up connections. So if you get one, you should probably take certain security precautions. First, get some advice from your ISP. Whilst installing your broadband connection, they can configure your computer

< 344 >

to make it more secure. They may also suggest you disable the file- and print-sharing option.

▶ If you've got a **Windows PC**, select the **Start** menu, then **Settings**, then **Control Panel**. Then click on the **Network** icon, then the **File and Print Sharing** button. You'll find two boxes referring to sharing files and allowing others to print files. Make sure both are unticked.

▶ If you've got a **Mac**, select the **Apple** menu, then **Automated Tasks**, then turn off the file sharing option.

To block potential intruders, you can also install home firewall software. Try Zone Alarm **http://www.zonealarm.com**, Norton Internet Security **http://www.symantec.com/region/uk/product/nis/nis2000.html**, Personal Firewall or Internet Guard Dog **http://software.mcafee.com** and Black Ice Defender **http://www.networkice.com**. Mac Users should try Net Barrier **http://www.intego.com**. Some of these programs also offer general security features – they filter content, track cookies and encrypt personal data.

Copyright and libel on the net

Digital technology makes it easy to make copies of things. The net makes it easy to share those copies with other people. As a result, some theorists think that old intellectual property laws don't work any more online and that we need to work out a new way of compensating people for the content they create. Against this, there have been signs that, under cover of responding to the net and digital technology, various corporations are trying to extend intellectual property laws in a way that would drastically curtail free public discussion. Certainly, over the last few years, both individual

< 345 >

Read about it online – Intellectual Property

For news on currently copyright legislation, try the Intellectual Property section on the Consumer Project on Technology **http://www.cptech.org**. For some utopian musing on intellectual property, try John Perry Barlow's 'The Economy of the Mind on the Global Net' **http://www.eff.org/pub/Intellectual_property/idea_economy.article**. ▲

artists and the creative industries as a whole have tried to take action against web sites they claim are illegally using copyrighted material.

There's the Record Industry Association of America's action against the file-sharing network Napster (see page 229). And everyone from Oasis to Rag Doll (the people behind the Teletubbies) has tried to stop fan sites from 'abusing' their material. There are obvious problems with this. The RIAA action against Napster pits them against some of their own best customers (the music-mad students who share MP3s via the network). Similarly, the web is what it is today thanks to fan sites. They're often brilliant adverts for the objects of their devotion. So hard line crackdowns seem somewhat perverse.

The net makes possible all sorts of novel abuses of copyright. Take domain squatting, in which people buy up desirable online addresses in the hope of selling them in the future. There's something dubious about big companies and celebrities assuming they have the rights to certain names. For example, if you happen to be called Chris Evans and you've registered chrisevans.com, why should you have to give it to the ginger haired guy with specs just because he's more famous than you. However, if you've only registered a name because it is already in the public eye in

< 346 >

some way – because it belongs to a company, famous author or prime ministerial child, you're on shakier ground. You'll find more details about domain squatting back on page 26.

In the past, some businesses have tried to argue that links made by another site to stories on their site were an attempt to benefit illegally from their intellectual property. In another 'only on the net case', Playboy attempted to take action against a former Playmate whose site used the word 'Playboy' as one of its meta-tags – the things web designers use to indicate what's on the site to roaming search engines. They claimed the meta-tag constituted copyright infringement and was an attempt to steal their traffic. In a related area, Amazon came under fire this year for patenting 'one click shopping' (buying something online using just one click of one button). Various online activists attempted to organise boycotts of the site, arguing that trying to patent something so general would hold up the development of e commerce and ran counter to the spirit of the net. You can read a discussion between Amazon founder Jeff Bezos and publisher Tim O'Reilly about this at **http://www.oreilly.com/ ask_tim/bezos_0300.html**. The science writer James Gleick wrote an interesting piece in the New York Times about the patent system in general **http://www.nytimes.com/library/magazine/home/20000312mag-patents.html**.

It will be interesting watching all these problems get sorted out over the next few years. In the meantime, how do you avoid getting a letter from a lawyer about something you've done online? First, think about the copyright status of material you use online. If you use pictures you've scanned from magazines on your site, it's likely that, legally, they belong to someone else. So get permission or give credits and indicate who owns the copyright. If you re-post material to a newsgroup – an interesting newspaper story, say – make sure you give the appropriate credits. Check

< 347 >

with the authors before you send one newsgroup posting on to a new discussion group. It will probably be fine, but since they will own the copyright, you should check anyway.

Incidentally, you own the copyright on any original material that you put online. So you might want to put a little copyright sign on it. That way, if someone decides to put it in a print collection of the wit and wisdom of the net, you have a chance of getting some sort of credit. If the material you put online is any good, it will be passed around. Be flattered. Don't immediately call a lawyer. (A few features I've written have appeared without my permission on various web sites. So long as my name is still on the copy, it's fine by me. It means more people get to read my work.) Finally, with regard to your own creations, written or otherwise, remember that the libel laws do seem to apply on the net. People have been successful in suing for libel over things that were said online, though, truth be told, things are still a little unclear. If you want to avoid hassle, think before you sound off on the web, in a newsgroup, in mailing lists or in chat rooms. People are reading and taking notes. Make sure you cover yourself.

Next step

You should now know how the net works. It's up to you what you do with it. Have fun. Here's one last tip to be going on with. There's a lot of rubbish talked about net addiction. However, there's so much information online, it's easy to get into a 'wood for the trees' situation, visit loads of web sites without actually paying any real attention to any of them and confuse a vast amount of apparently relevant information with knowledge and wisdom. So take it easy: more information isn't always better. And remember – there is a real world out there. Sometimes the best thing you can do with the net is log off. ▲

< 348 >

< 349 >

INTERNET SERVICE PROVIDERS

• •

You used to know exactly where you were with ISPs. In the mid-nineties, you could choose between two basic kinds – online services like AOL where you paid for net access by the minute, on top of your phone bills and subscription ISPs like Demon, where you paid a flat monthly rate for net access as well as your phone bills. Then Freeserve started up and changed everything. Then your choice was between free ISPs, where you only pay for your telephone calls and subscription ISPs where you pay for net access and telephone time.

However, in the last year, things have become a tad more confusing, thanks to the rise of unmetered access deals, in which you pay a flat monthly rate that covers net access and unlimited telephone calls. Many of the free ISPs now offer unmetered deals as well. Similarly, many subscription ISPs do unmetered access alongside their standard deals. Consequently, it's hard to divide the numerous ISPs currently trading in the UK into hard and fast categories. The lists that follow do try, however, splitting companies up into consumer-focused ISPs and those that are aimed primarily at business users. The ISPs in the 'consumer' list

< 350 >

offer a variety of deals – 'free', unmetered and standard subscription. With the 'business' ISPs, you tend to pay more, but you do get more services for your money. Incidentally, some of the ISPs in the business list do offer consumer deals, and vice-versa. Perhaps the best thing to do is ring them up, or check out their web sites and see what's on offer.

These lists only feature a fraction of the hundreds of UK ISPs. If you want something more comprehensive, try Internet Magazine **http://www.internet-magazine.com/resource/isp**. The paper version of the magazine, which runs regular monthly ISPs is definitely worth a look too, especially the table which rates the ISPs' performances over the last six months. If you want an online guide to the various free ISPs, and there are still loads, try Daily E Deals **http://www.dailyedeals.com/free_internet/access_uk.htm** or Free ISPs **http://www.ukfreeisps.abelgratis.co.uk/**. Alternatively, have a look at ISP Review **http://www.ispreview.co.uk/**.

CONSUMER ISPS

AOL **http://www.aol.co.uk**
℃ 0800 3765432

Breathe Online **http://www.breathe.com**
℃ 0800 2983030

BT Internet **http://www.btinternet.com**
℃ 0800 800001

Bun.com **http://www.bun.com**
℃ 0845 3063636

< 351 >

Cable and Wireless Internet **http://home.cwcom.net/**
☎ 0800 0923013

Cix **http://www.cix.co.uk**
☎ 0845 355 5050

ClaraNet **http://www.clara.net**
☎ 0800 3582828

Compuserve **http://www.compuserve.co.uk**
☎ 0800 289378

Demon **http://www.demon.net**
☎ 0845 2722999

Direct Connection **http://www.dircon.net**
☎ 0800 072 0000

EasyDial **http://www.easydial.co.uk**
☎ 0845 333 4000

Freebeeb **http://www.freebeeb.net/**
☎ 0808 1004950

Freedom to Surf **http://www.f2s.net/**
☎ 0172 7811530

< 352 >

Free Online   **http://www.free-online.net/**
℡ 0870 7060504

Freeserve   **http://www.freeserve.net**
℡ 0870 872 0099

Free UK   **http://www.freeuk.com/**
℡ 0845 3555555

Gateway.net   **http://www.gateway2000.co.uk**
℡ 0800 973132

IC24   **http://www.ic24.net**
℡ 0870 9090925

LibertySurf   **http://www.libertysurf.co.uk**
℡ 0800 988 8888

Line One   **http://www.lineone.net**
℡ 0800 111210

Madasafish   **http://www.madasafish.com**
℡ 0800 027 3373

MSN UK   **http://www.uk.msn.com/**
℡ 0345 002000

< 353 >

Netscape Online **http://www.netscapeonline.co.uk**
✆ 0800 9230009

Poptel **http://www.poptel.net/**
✆ 0800 781 3344

Prestel **http://www.prestel.co.uk/**
✆ 0990 223300

RedHotAnt **http://www.redhotant.com/**
✆ 0870 011 4040

TescoNet **http://www.tesco.net/**

UK Online **http://www.ukonline.co.uk/**
✆ 0845 333 4567

UUNet (Pipex) **http://www.pipex.net/**
✆ 0500474 739

Virgin.net **http://www.virgin.net/**
✆ 0845 6500000

Which? Online **http://www.which.net/**
✆ 0845 9830240

WH Smith Online **http://www.whsmith.co.uk/**

< 354 >

World Online   **http://www.worldonline.co.uk/**
✆ 0800 376 5262

Yahoo Online   **http://uk.docs.yahoo.com/yahooclick/yahooclick.html**

BUSINESS-FOCUSED ISPS

Altohiway   **http://www.hiway.co.uk**
✆ 01635 573300

Global Internet   **http://www.global.net.uk**
✆ 0870 9098041

I-Way   **http://www.i-way.co.uk**
✆ 020 7734 5734

Mistral   **http://www.mistral-uk.net/**
✆ 0800 328 7253

Netkonect   **http://www.netkonect.net**
✆ 0808 163 0000

Nildram   **http://www.nildram.net**
✆ 0800 496 2903

Onyx   **http://www.uk.onyx.net/**
✆ 01642 216216

< 355 >

Pinnacle Internet   **http://www.pinnacle.net/**
℡ 0845 200 1213

Portland Communications   **http://www.portland.co.uk/**
℡ 0870 741 0994

Primex   **http://www.primex.co.uk**
℡ 01908 279900

REDNET   **http://www.red.net/**
℡ 01494 513333

Skynet   **http://www.skynet.co.uk/**
℡ 01604 670717

Sonnet Internet   **http://www.sonnet.co.uk/**
℡ 020 7891 2000

U-Net   **http://www.u-net.net/**
℡ 0845 330 8000

< 356 >

INDEX

< 357 >

< 358 >

< 359 >

< 360 >

< 361 >

www.dell.co.uk/home

THE INTELLIGENT WAY
TO BUY YOUR PC.

Design your ideal system and enjoy the latest, greatest value for money deals on Dell PCs and notebooks. It's easy to get exactly what you want at our secure online store.

stop searching
start finding

QVC is the UK's first and most successful shopping channel, with over a million satisified customers in 2000, and winner of the prestigious Jewellery Retailer of the Year award for 2000. QVCUK.com is its online presence – a whole department store on the internet.

Quality QVCUK.com isn't just the TV channel repackaged for the internet – it's an original, totally secure, fully searchable site that hits the highest standards of ease of use. Viewing, choosing and buying products are simple, smooth and straightforward.

'An excellent store from the Home Shopping Channel'

Shopsmart.com

QVCUK.com

Choice
Browse through over 8,000 products spread across six major departments: Jewellery, Health and Beauty, Electrical, Home and Garden, Fashion, Collectables and Gifts.

Security
We belong to the 'Which?' Webtrader code of practice. Every purchase you make is backed by our 30-day money back guarantee.

Bargains
Offers and bargains are regularly updated, like Today's Special Value, Last Clicks, Click of the Week.

Brands
Leading brands, and plenty of them. Beauty products from Molton Brown, Decleor, SmashBox, Liz Earle. Electrical products from Sony, Aiwa, Philips, JVC, Ricoh, and more...

Information
Clear, detailed product descriptions. Expert advice in areas like Technology and Health and Beauty. Features, including our Essential Beauty magazine.